Turkey and the Balkan

This book delves into Turkey's increasing ethno-religious, pragmatic, and complicated involvement and activism in the Balkans since 2002, under the Justice and Development Party (Adalet ve Kalkınma Partisi – AKP). It primarily focusses on the intersectionality between domestic and foreign policy that has played an important role in Turkey's recent relations with the Balkan countries as well as exploring how the Europeanisation process influences this relationality.

Broadly, the chapters in this volume posit that religion, ethnicity and kin politics are indispensable components of identity politics and have the capacity to transform Turkey's foreign policy attitudes as well as the orientations of the Balkan countries. The book also asserts that the impact of the processes of Europeanisation and de-Europeanisation on the relationship between Turkey and the Balkans needs to be included into the analysis.

This book will be useful to students, researchers and academics interested in Politics, International Relations and Southeast European Studies. The chapters in this book were originally published as a special issue of *Southeast European and Black Sea Studies*.

Başak Z. Alpan is Associate Professor and Lecturer in European Politics and Political Sociology at the Department of Political Science and Public Administration and Centre for European Studies at the Middle East Technical University, Ankara, Turkey. She is also the coordinator of the LEAP ('Linking to Europe at the Periphery') Network, funded by the Jean Monnet Networks Scheme under Erasmus Plus Programme, and the executive board member of the Centre for European Studies of the Middle East Technical University.

Ahmet Erdi Öztürk is Associate Professor of Politics and International Relations at London Metropolitan University, UK. He also works as Marie Sklodowska-Curie fellow at Coventry University in the UK and GIGA in Germany; an associate researcher at Institut Français d'Études Anatoliennes; and Non-Residence Scholar at ELIAMEP's Turkey Programme. He has authored and edited five books, around 30 journal articles, numerous policy reports, opinion pieces, and he is the co-editor of four special issues on Turkish politics.

Turkey and the Balkans

Between Europeanisation and De-Europeanization

Edited by
Başak Z. Alpan and Ahmet Erdi Öztürk

LONDON AND NEW YORK

First published 2023
by Routledge
4 Park Square, Milton Park, Abingdon, Oxon OX14 4RN

and by Routledge
605 Third Avenue, New York, NY 10158

Routledge is an imprint of the Taylor & Francis Group, an informa business

Introduction, Chapters 1–9 © 2023 Taylor & Francis

All rights reserved. No part of this book may be reprinted or reproduced or utilised in any form
or by any electronic, mechanical, or other means, now known or hereafter invented, including
photocopying and recording, or in any information storage or retrieval system, without permission in
writing from the publishers.

Trademark notice: Product or corporate names may be trademarks or registered trademarks and are
used only for identification and explanation without intent to infringe.

British Library Cataloguing in Publication Data
A catalogue record for this book is available from the British Library

ISBN13: 978-1-032-38936-3 (hbk)
ISBN13: 978-1-032-38937-0 (pbk)
ISBN13: 978-1-003-34755-2 (ebk)

DOI: 10.4324/9781003347552

Typeset in Minion Pro
by Newgen Publishing UK

Publisher's Note
The publisher accepts responsibility for any inconsistencies that may have arisen during the
conversion of this book from journal articles to book chapters, namely the inclusion of journal
terminology.

Disclaimer
Every effort has been made to contact copyright holders for their permission to reprint material
in this book. The publishers would be grateful to hear from any copyright holder who is not here
acknowledged and will undertake to rectify any errors or omissions in future editions of this book.

Contents

Citation Information	vii
Notes on Contributors	ix

Introduction: Turkey and the Balkans: bringing the Europeanisation/
De-Europeanisation nexus into question   1
Başak Alpan and Ahmet Erdi Öztürk

1 A rival or an awkward partner? Turkey's relationship with the West in the
  Balkan   11
  Dimitar Bechev

2 Reconstruction of the 'regional power' role during the pandemic: Turkey's
  COVID-19 diplomacy towards the Balkans   25
  Birgül Demirtaş

3 Turkish foreign policy in the Balkans amidst 'soft power' and
  'de-Europeanisation'   44
  Başak Alpan and Ahmet Erdi Öztürk

4 A delicate balancing act: Turkish-Bulgarian relations within the context of
  foreign and domestic politics   63
  Emilia Zankina

5 Securitizing the Aegean: de-Europeanizing Greek–Turkish relations   80
  Nikos Christofis

6 Foreign direct investment (FDI) as indicator of regime type: contemporary
  Serbian–Turkish relations   98
  Sabina Pacariz

7 Measuring Turkey's contemporary influence in Bosnia and Herzegovina:
  myth and reality   118
  Adnan Huskić and Hamdi Firat Büyük

8   Relations between Turkey and Kosovo: factors and dynamics   142
    Afrim Hoti, Bardhok Bashota and Bekim Sejdiu

9   Assessing a decade of Romania-Turkey strategic partnership in an era of
    ambivalence and 'De-Europeanisation'   161
    Aurel Lazăr and Miruna Butnaru-Troncotă

    Index   182

Citation Information

The chapters in this book were originally published in the journal *Southeast European and Black Sea Studies*, volume 22, issue 1 (2022). When citing this material, please use the original page numbering for each article, as follows:

Introduction

Turkey and the Balkans: bringing the Europeanisation/De-Europeanisation nexus into question
Başak Alpan and Ahmet Erdi Öztürk
Southeast European and Black Sea Studies, volume 22, issue 1 (2022), pp. 1–10

Chapter 1

A rival or an awkward partner? Turkey's relationship with the West in the Balkan
Dimitar Bechev
Southeast European and Black Sea Studies, volume 22, issue 1 (2022), pp. 11–24

Chapter 2

Reconstruction of the 'regional power' role during the pandemic: Turkey's COVID-19 diplomacy towards the Balkans
Birgül Demirtaş
Southeast European and Black Sea Studies, volume 22, issue 1 (2022), pp. 25–43

Chapter 3

Turkish foreign policy in the Balkans amidst 'soft power' and 'de-Europeanisation'
Başak Alpan and Ahmet Erdi Öztürk
Southeast European and Black Sea Studies, volume 22, issue 1 (2022), pp. 45–63

Chapter 4

A delicate balancing act: Turkish-Bulgarian relations within the context of foreign and domestic politics
Emilia Zankina
Southeast European and Black Sea Studies, volume 22, issue 1 (2022), pp. 65–81

Chapter 5

Securitizing the Aegean: de-Europeanizing Greek–Turkish relations
Nikos Christofis
Southeast European and Black Sea Studies, volume 22, issue 1 (2022), pp. 83–100

Chapter 6

Foreign direct investment (FDI) as indicator of regime type: contemporary Serbian – Turkish relations
Sabina Pacariz
Southeast European and Black Sea Studies, volume 22, issue 1 (2022), pp. 101–120

Chapter 7

Measuring Turkey's contemporary influence in Bosnia and Herzegovina: myth and reality
Adnan Huskić and Hamdi Firat Büyük
Southeast European and Black Sea Studies, volume 22, issue 1 (2022), pp. 121–144

Chapter 8

Relations between Turkey and Kosovo: factors and dynamics
Afrim Hoti, Bardhok Bashota and Bekim Sejdiu
Southeast European and Black Sea Studies, volume 22, issue 1 (2022), pp. 145–163

Chapter 9

Assessing a decade of Romania-Turkey strategic partnership in an era of ambivalence and 'De-Europeanisation'
Aurel Lazăr and Miruna Butnaru-Troncotă
Southeast European and Black Sea Studies, volume 22, issue 1 (2022), pp. 165–185

For any permission-related enquiries please visit: www.tandfonline.com/page/help/permissions

Notes on Contributors

Başak Alpan is Associate Professor and Lecturer in European Politics and Political Sociology at the Department of Political Science and Public Administration and Centre for European Studies at the Middle East Technical University, Ankara, Turkey. She is also the coordinator of the LEAP ('Linking to Europe at the Periphery') Network, funded by the Jean Monnet Networks Scheme under Erasmus Plus Programme, and the executive board member of the Centre for European Studies of the Middle East Technical University.

Bardhok Bashota is Professor of Political Science at the Faculty of Philosophy of the University of Prishtina. In 2014 he earned a PhD in International Relations at the University of Tirana. He is serving as researcher at LEAP (Linking to Europe at the Periphery) project, in frame of Jean Monnet Network under Erasmus+ programme. His interest research area is state building, theories of international relations and European studies.

Dimitar Bechev is Lecturer at the Oxford School of Global and Area Studies (OSGA), University of Oxford, and Visiting Scholar at Carnegie Europe. He is the author of *Turkey under Erdogan: How a Country Turned from Democracy and the West* (2022) and has written extensively about the Balkans, Turkey, and Russian foreign policy.

Miruna Butnaru-Troncotă is Associate Professor at the Department of International Relations and European Integration and coordinator of the Center for European Studies at the National University of Political Studies and Public Administration (SNSPA), Bucharest, Romania. She has a direct research interest in EU studies, Europeanization, Black Sea geopolitics and the post conflict reconstruction of the Western Balkans.

Hamdi Firat Büyük is a PhD candidate in political science at the University of Sarajevo and in international relations at the University of Ankara, Turkey. He is a political analyst and a journalist at Balkan Investigative Reporting Network's (BIRN) flagship publication Balkan Insight. Buyuk holds an MSc degree in international relations from the University of Essex.

Nikos Christofis is Associate Professor at the Centre for Turkish Studies and School of History and Civilizations, Shaanxi Normal University in Xi'an, China. He is also an adjunct lecturer at the Hellenic Open University, Greece, and affiliate researcher at the Netherlands Institute at Athens (NIA), Greece.

Birgül Demirtaş is Professor of International Relations at the Department of Political Science and International Relations of Turkish-German University in İstanbul, Turkey.

Her studies concentrate on Turkish foreign policy, Balkan Politics, German foreign policy, Turkish political parties and migration, city diplomacy and gender. She was the managing editor of the academic peer-review Journal of *Uluslararası İlişkiler* (*International Relations, indexed in SSCI*) between 2019–2021 and worked as the assistant editor of the journal between 2004–2018. She was also the assistant editor of the *Perceptions* journal between 2014–2018.

Afrim Hoti is Professor at the Department of Political Sciences of the Faculty of Philosophy at the University of Prishtina, Kosovo. He served at different institutions in Kosovo like Prime Minister's Office, Special Chamber of the Kosovo Supreme Court, Kosovo Assembly and international organizations like USAID, UNDP, GIZ to name a few. He has published a book, a monography, and many articles in various international academic journals.

Adnan Huskić is Christian Schwarz-Schilling Chair at Sarajevo School of Science and Technology's Department of Political Science and International Relations. He is also a political analyst, president of Centre for Election Studies and Project Manager of Friedrich Naumann Foundation for Freedom in Bosnia and Herzegovina. Huskic holds a PhD degree from the University of Graz, Austria.

Aurel Lazăr is PhD Candidate at the National University of Political Studies and Public Administration (SNSPA), Bucharest, Romania. In his work, he studies the security dynamics in the Wider Black Sea Region and their implications for the European Union and NATO.

Ahmet Erdi Öztürk is Associate Professor of Politics and International Relations at London Metropolitan University, UK. He also works as Marie Sklodowska-Curie fellow at Coventry University in the UK and GIGA in Germany; an associate researcher at Institut Français d'Études Anatoliennes; and Non-Residence Scholar at ELIAMEP's Turkey Programme. He has authored and edited five books, around 30 journal articles, numerous policy reports, opinion pieces, and he is the co-editor of four special issues on Turkish politics.

Sabina Pacariz is Lecturer in Politics at the Department of Political Economy at King`s College London. Her research interests focus on democratisation and authoritarianism, particularly at the intersection of foreign and domestic politics.

Bekim Sejdiu is Professor at the Department of International Law of the Faculty of Law of the University of Prishtina, Kosovo. He served as Ambassador of the Republic of Kosovo to the Republic of Turkey (2008–2012) and Consul General of the Republic of Kosovo in New York (2012–2014). From 2015 to 2021, Bekim Sejdiu served as a Judge of the Constitutional Court of the Republic of Kosovo. He has published 159 articles in various academic journals and has been awarded with decorations and medals for his public service.

Emilia Zankina is Associate Professor in Political Science and Dean of Temple University Rome campus. She holds a Ph.D. in International Affairs and Certificate in Advanced East European Studies from the University of Pittsburgh. Her research examines Eastern European and Bulgarian politics, populism, civil service reform, and gender political representation.

Introduction: Turkey and the Balkans: bringing the Europeanisation/De-Europeanisation nexus into question

Başak Alpan and Ahmet Erdi Öztürk

ABSTRACT
This article is about the main framework and the rationale of the special issue, which deals with Turkey's increasing ethno-religious, pragmatic and complicated involvement and activism in the Balkans since 2002, under the Justice and Development Party (Adalet ve Kalkınma Partisi – AKP). The main focus of the Issue is how the intersectionality between domestic and foreign policy has played an important role in Turkey's recent relations with the Balkan countries and how the Europeanization process influences this relationality. The overall claim is that religion, ethnicity and kin politics as indispensable components of identity politics, have the capacity to transform Turkey's foreign policy attitudes as well as the orientations of the Balkan countries and the impact of the processes of Europeanization and de-Europeanization on the relationship between Turkey and the Balkans needs to be included into the analysis.

Since the early 2000s, the motto, 'Turkey is back in the Balkans' (Bechev 2012), has found resonance in academic scholarship as well as in Turkish public opinion, which underlined contemporary Turkey's increasing influence in the Balkans and the social, cultural, economic and political repercussions of this influence (Anastasakis 2020; Noutcheva and Aydın-Düzgit 2012; Tanasković 2012). In this vein, it has been claimed that the AKP (Justice and Development Party-*Adalet ve Kalkınma Partisi*) governments' policies and President Recep Tayyip Erdoğan's political strategies regarding the Balkans have long been energized by Turkey's desire to re-establish political, economic, religious and cultural hegemony in the region, through various neo-imperialist and neo-colonial projects and to foresee the revitalization of the Ottoman multi-sided legacy (Somun 2011; Yavuz 2020). On the other hand, it is also argued, Turkey and the Balkans have reached the peak point of their mutually beneficial relations, economic enlargement and pro-active utilization of the transnational state apparatus on the part of Turkey (Ekinci 2014; Mitrovic 2014).

Beyond these general issues, the literature on Turkey-Balkan relations is rich and multi-dimensional. In this regard, while some argue that overdoes use of religion, identity, and common past has been creating some limits in Turkey's activism in the Balkans (Targański 2017), others argue that the broader shift in Turkish domestic and foreign policy under the AKP from a realist-secular orientation to an ambiguous coercive Sunni Islamic one has made Turkey and ambivalent actor in the Balkans (Öztürk 2021a). This means that the component of Turkey's 'ethno-nationalist religion-oriented foreign policy' (Öztürk and Sözeri 2018) deserves extra attention not only because it is a central factor that has been under-researched, but also because Turkey getting involved in other Balkans countries' public spheres via religious institutions is a sensitive issue and consistently garners a variety of reactions in the independent Balkan countries. The picture gets even more complicated when the problematic Europeanization process of the Balkan countries, as well as Turkey's tumultuous EU accession process and the debates on 'de-Europeanisation' trends within Turkish politics, are added to the analysis (Öztürk and Gözaydın 2018). In this respect, it has been claimed that against the background of deteriorating EU–Turkey relations and EU's multiple crises, Turkey has been attempting to use its soft power to consolidate its influence in the Western Balkans and fill a power vacuum left by the EU in the region (Dursun-Özkanca 2019). On the contrary, the EU dimension has been claimed by some to complement Turkey's activism in the Balkans (Demirtaş 2015). Similarly, the prospect of EU-Turkey engagement in the Western Balkans in terms of foreign policy had also been scrutinized in an attempt to uncover the cooperation and conflict potential between the two (Saatçioğlu 2019). Nevertheless, these analyses focus on either the EU's or Turkey's foreign policy perspectives and need to be complemented by insights from the countries in the region.

In this respect, the main claim of this special issue is that Turkey's activism in the Western Balkans does not emerge as an alternative to or as a complementary of the Europeanization process in the region but needs to be analysed independently and through a multidimensional lens. Moreover, it is obligatory to understand how these processes unfold at the domestic level in the Balkans. This article aims to introduce the general contours of the processes of Turkey's activism and the Europeanization trends in the Western Balkans and set the ground for understanding how these processes speak to the foreign policy and domestic politics prospects in Bosnia and Herzegovina, Bulgaria, Kosovo, Serbia, Greece and Romania as well as addressing how bilateral relations between Turkey and these countries are shaped by the Europeanization/de-Europeanization processes in the region.

Turkey's impact in the Balkans

It is evident that under the AKP rule, Turkey's rapid political transformation has thus been formative in multiple dimensions. After AKP came to power in 2002, scholars have noted Turkey's more active, culturally and ideologically driven foreign policy, primarily in its immediate region, but also at a global scale (Aydın-Düzgit and Kaliber 2016: Alpan 2016: Baser and Erdi Ozturk 2017). Particularly after the first decade of the new

Millennium, the instrumentalization of the very subjective understanding of Turkish history, culture and Sunni Islam under the influence of former Prime Minister and Foreign Secretary Ahmet Davutoğlu and his foreign-policy doctrine of strategic depth (Özkan 2014) has been the motivating force behind this shift. The novelty of Davutoğlu's perspective is its definition of Turkey as a state neither at the periphery of Europe nor at the periphery of the Middle East. Rather, Turkey sits (as it did in Ottoman times) prominently at the crossroads of the two continents and is thus a pivotal country due to its unique geographical, historical and cultural links with both regions. Furthermore, he focuses on the ontological difference between Islam and all other civilizations, particularly the West, and asserts that the differences between Western and Muslim paradigms cause an obstacle for the study of contemporary Islam as a subject in social sciences, especially in international politics. With such a mindset, the AKP has shifted Turkey's foreign policy by defining itself as the inheritor of the longstanding Ottoman cultural tradition, alongside its Sunni priorities and attempts to influence the former Ottoman territories more assertively.

As a result of the mostly domestic policy-oriented transformation of Turkey, the country has been experiencing a series of new foreign policy practices which rests on four inter-related parameters that pertain to the distinct priorities of the elements of the ruling power: militarization, Islam, civilization and power, and these manifest itself as de-Europeanization (Öztürk 2021b; Bulut and Hacıoğlu 2021; Adar and Toygür 2020). In other words, Turkey has been resorting to military force to an unprecedented degree, reflecting Sunni Islam in its foreign affairs in a multi-faceted manner, expressing itself in power terms and, moreover, viewing itself as superior and unique in terms of civilization. Indeed, all of these transformations have been affecting Turkey and the Balkan relations, which this special issue also aims to scrutinize.

Europeanization/de-Europeanization nexus in the Balkans

The process of Europeanization has been experienced and internalized at different degrees and paces in the Balkans.[1] Greece has been an EU member in 1981 and has been one of the first countries where European integration became an anchor for democratization (Cavallaro and Kornetis 2019). The EU integration also became the primary source of democratic consolidation and domestic reforms in Romania and Bulgaria (though at a slow pace and with a quality highly criticized by the EU) ever since their turbulent transition to democracy in the early 1990s (Papadimitriou and Gateva 2009). The EU has also been an important game-changer in the Western Balkans, at least since the early 2000s. The Balkan enlargement, announced at the 2003 EU Thessaloniki Summit, gave the concrete EU membership perspective to Albania, Bosnia-Herzegovina, Croatia, Macedonia and then Yugoslavia.[2] Currently, in terms of the EU terminology, Western Balkans consist of four candidate states (Serbia, Montenegro, North Macedonia and Albania) and two potential candidates (Kosovo and Bosnia-Herzegovina).

Against the background of the economic and financial turbulence of the last decade and the recent crises of the European Union (EU), such as migration crisis, Brexit, the limited effectiveness of the EU enlargement and the rising tide of populism, the notion of so-called, 'de-Europeanisation' has entered the agendas of the EU studies for the last ten years or so as an *explanan* for the 'deterioration of the quality of integration or more simply as "it is worse than it was"' (Domaradzki 2019, 221) for the candidate states as well as the member states. 'De-Europeanisation' is broadly defined as 'the loss or weakening of the EU/Europe as a normative/political context and as a reference point in domestic settings and national public debates' (Aydın-Düzgit and Kaliber 2016, 6). Although the growing scepticism and indifference towards Europe, and even a turning away from European project in many spheres of politics and society, would not necessarily indicate a fully-fledged de-Europeanization (Alpan 2016, 16), the prospect of the European project in the Balkans in its broader sense needs to be examined carefully.

Despite having a rather unproblematic relationship with the European integration, Greece inhibits a lot of prejudices that consider Europeanization as a sign of alienation and moving away from traditional Greek and Orthodox values. Some still equate the concept of 'Europeanisation' with the old concept of 'foreign protection' and even 'capitulation' and, for this reason, reject it (Tsardanidis 2015, 63–64). These considerations have been strengthened even more after the economic crisis and the increase of the recession and unemployment. The 2008 Eurozone crisis added further fuel to the 'how Europe hits home' debate by focusing in particular on a possible reverse trend in that process, through delegitimizing any progress achieved in terms of the Europeanization process and affecting in negative terms the way Greeks feel about the EU (Stavridis et al. 2015, 24–33). The entry into government in January 2015 of an anti-austerity coalition of SYRIZA and ANEL opened a new period in the Greek crisis. Greece's antagonistic negotiation with the Eurozone culminated in a referendum in June 2015, where more than 60% of Greeks rejected austerity despite the explicit threat of eviction from the Eurozone. All in all, scrutiny of the EU impact and Greece's dependence on Europe had been fiercely criticized during this period (Chryssogelos 2019, 614). During this period, amelioration of relations with Russia and shifting energy policy (Greece's participation in the Turkish stream pipeline project rather than South Stream) has even been shown to indicate the de-Europeanization trend (Chryssogelos 2019, 615).

Bulgaria and Romania are rather late-comers to the European integration, where Europeanization became the main engine of post-communist transition starting from the 1990s, culminating in full EU membership of these two countries in 2007. A large part of EU studies dealing with Bulgaria and Romania's EU accession process have pointed out the weakness of anti-corruption policies, deficiencies in the use of the rule of law or backsliding in democratic practices in these two EU member states (Buzogány 2021; Ganev 2013; Gateva 2013; Gherghina and Soare 2016; Spendzharova and Anna Vachudova 2012). Indeed, the EC progress reports 'repeatedly criticized Bulgaria and Romania's endemic corruption, the weak judiciary, the incompetent administrations, the widespread criminal networks, and the trafficking' (Dempsey 2012). For instance, in Romania, one of the latest European Commission progress reports on the 'Cooperation Verification Mechanism'[3] noted that 'the entry into force of the amended justice laws, the pressure on judicial independence in general and on the National Anti-Corruption Directorate in particular, and other steps undermining the fight against corruption have reversed or called into question the irreversibility of progress' (European Commission 2018a). Starting from the late 1990s, EU officials, as well as political actors in Europe, have voiced many doubts about the sustainability of the conditionality-induced impact of the EU on the South Eastern European states, arguing that EU transformative leverage will evaporate once membership is granted (Buzogány 2021, 185).

The return of identity politics in these two countries also influenced the prospects of Europeanization. The single-issue politics that defined the accession phase have returned under the guise of identity politics in the post-accession phase, allowing voters to easily ascertain their preferences in an uncertain political landscape. Issues that once were recipes for political success – fighting corruption, guaranteeing welfare, addressing environmental concerns, catering for the regional or ethnic cleavages, and tackling immigration – eased the arrival of parties mobilizing around markers of identity (Agarin, 2020, 155).

The course of Europeanization in the Western Balkans, which went hand-in-hand with the process of state-building, has also been complex and uneasy from the start. Consolidated statehood has emerged as the fundamental prerequisite for Europeanization, which most states of the region still lack (Denti 2014). For Börzel, 'limited statehood is the main impediment for the Western Balkans on their road to Brussels' since it 'affects both the capacity and the willingness of countries to conform to the EU's expectations for domestic change' (Börzel 2013, 174).

The pace of Europeanization in the region is not very coherent and expeditious either. No significant momentum in the EU accession has emerged after the Thessaloniki Summit for a long time. The renewed attention on the region came in February 2018 when *the European Commission* published the Commission's new enlargement strategy offering a 'credible enlargement perspective' to the Western Balkan countries, stating that Western Balkans' entry into the EU is in the Union's very own interest, from a political, economic and security perspective, as it would lead to a united Europe based on common values (European Commission 2018b). The announcement of the strategy has been followed by the May 2018 EU-Western Balkans Summit where the European Commission president Juncker declared that Serbia and Montenegro could be ready to join the EU as early as 2025 (European Council 2018). June 2018 European Council meeting signalled that the negotiations with North Macedonia and Albania were not to be launched, despite positive advice by the Commission and a preliminary agreement to resolve the Macedonia name dispute (Council of the EU 2018). In the 2020 'Work Programme', the Commission committed itself to 'putting forward ways to enhance the accession process' (European Commission 2020a) and set out the obligations which need to be undertaken by both sides if accession is going to be a viable proposition (European Commission 2020b). Despite this seeming re-engagement with enlargement, the EU is far too concerned with internal crises and convulsions which bring into question the very future of the 'European project' itself – or at least the existing version – for it to envisage early acceptance of new members to the club (Economides 2020, 1).

Another important point regarding the Western Balkan states' Europeanization process has been the EU's intense reliance on the elites. Since the early 2000s, the EU actively influenced the domestic politics of the Western Balkan states, putting pressure on local elites to comply with certain designated criteria as a part of the EU conditionality (Anastasakis 2008, 365). This sometimes meant the EU's support for the region's authoritarian leaders to maintain regional stability against the legacy of the wars of Yugoslavia's dissolution (Economides 2020, 7; Bieber and Kmezić 2017).

Against this background, it would be fair to argue that in the Western Balkan countries, a Europeanization fatigue has emerged, and experts question the EU's real objectives, asking whether the European Commission and the EU Member States really strive for reform or, given other challenges at hand, have for the time being settled for the status quo (Zweers 2019, 3; Kmezić 2019, 90). The creeping nationalization of the EU enlargement where EU member states instrumentalize enlargement for domestic political gains, and national agendas hold the process hostage also raises questions about the credibility of the EU commitments towards aspirant states. The politicization of the EU enlargement is also a new dimension added to the picture (Zweers 2019, 5).

One problem also emerges in terms of the elites. Starting from the 2000s, the strength of reformist elites emerged as the most crucial factor determining the success of EU conditionality strategy in the Western Balkans (Elbasani 2013). Nevertheless, the current situation shows us that the Europeanization process in the region may have vested too much attention on elites rather than paying attention to bottom-up and grassroots movements (Dzihic and Schmidt 2021).

With this background in mind, this special issue mainly focuses on the key power relations of the Turkish Republic and its impact on the relations between different Balkan countries against the background of the EU accession process. This special issue also aims to offer a forum for academics, think-tankers, experts and journalists from the Balkans to assess various aspects of Turkey's influence in the region from a critical perspective and the country's particular relationship with individual individuals Balkan countries. In this regard, it scrutinizes four main questions; 1) What factors determine Turkey's scope of activity in the case of each country? 2) How do local actors and public opinion respond to Turkey's newly-emerging activism in the Balkan region? 3) What is the role of Turkey in the region, and how has it shifted since the beginning of the 2000s? 4) How does the Europeanization/de-Europeanization nexus work at the domestic level in each country?

The contributions to this issue

Against this background, the contributions in this Special Issue tackle various country cases in the Balkans in terms of their relation to Turkey against the backdrop of the ascent of the process of de-Europeanization of Turkey and the Western Balkans. Departing from the argument that Turkey is rather an internal player in the Balkans rather than an external player like China and Russia, the paper by Bechev contends that Turkish foreign policy is not posing a frontal challenge to the EU and NATO. Instead, it benefits from its close relationship and membership in the two institutions and the West in general. The paper also argues that the de-Europeanization trends in Turkey and the Balkans are parallel processes due to the EU having lost its leverage over domestic politics and institutions compared to the 2000s.

Also focusing on Turkey's regional power in the Balkans, Demirtaş elaborates on the use of health diplomacy by the country during the CoViD-19 pandemic. Employing a constructivist perspective, the core aim is to assess how Turkish decision-makers have reconstructed a 'regional power' identity for the country during this period. The paper shows that pandemics provide an opportunity for regional powers to exert their influence in competition with other actors, displaying a 'great country' image, just like the AKP did during the Covid-19 pandemic.

Similarly, Alpan and Öztürk's article focuses on Turkish foreign policy with respect to its impact in the Balkans. The article argues that Turkey's 'soft power' foreign policy perspective that had been prevalent in the 2000s within the context of the incumbent AKP's 'zero problems with neighbours' policy and the EU accession process has remained intact in the Balkans in the 2010s although it had been replaced by the de-Europeanization process and been intensely securitized in the 2010s at a general scale. Against this background, the article examines the normative, material and personalized aspects of Turkey's soft power in the Balkans through interviews conducted with political and social elites in Turkey and the Balkans.

On a different note, Zankina's article elaborates on Turkish-Bulgarian relations and the way in which they influence domestic politics in both countries, as well as at the EU level. In this respect, Zankina's central argument is that to understand current dynamics in bilateral relations, we need to focus on Turkey-EU relations and Bulgaria's impact on this relation and domestic politics in Turkey and Bulgaria. The article also presents a thorough discussion on how we need to adopt a long-term perspective to understand the role that Turkey takes on in the region as well as the relations between Turkey and Bulgaria rather than solely focusing on recent political dynamics and political actors.

The focus of the study by Christofis, on the other hand, is the relations between Turkey and Greece and the rising tensions between the two since 2016 due to the developments revolving around the Aegean Sea, Cyprus and the refugee crisis. Underlining that Greece presents a 'deviation' to the rest of the Balkan countries in the sense that it is already an EU and NATO member with a more stable economy and democracy than some of the other countries in the Balkan region, the article explores the factors that determine recently Turkey's scope of activity towards Greece against the background of the EU accession in the Balkans and Turkey. By locating the relations into a historical perspective, the article argues that Greek–Turkish relations would run smoothly within an EU framework that will mediate and provide a basic list of principles and conditions.

Serbia and the country's relations with Turkey is the focus of Pacariz's paper. Her paper investigates the relationship between regime type and foreign policy by focusing on the Serbian-Turkish relationship between 2009 and 2018. By engaging with a conceptual debate on the sources of authoritarian power concerning the convergence between domestic and foreign policy and the impact of foreign direct investment (FDI) in hybrid regimes on the consolidation of incumbent power, the paper argues that while Turkish FDI are of smaller financial worth than investments of EU actors, they are highly valuable in qualitatively portraying the complexity of political power. This, according to Pacariz, shows the embeddedness of informal mechanisms throughout formal institutions, the fusion of economic and political authorities, and the personalization of political power in Serbia.

The article by Huskić and Büyük aims to assess Turkey's influence in Bosnia and Herzegovina through expert interviews, which show that the de-Europeanization process characterizes Turkish domestic and foreign policies at the moment is affecting the bilateral relations between Turkey and BiH negatively. By the same token, according to the authors, Turkey could become a reliable partner if it were to return to democratic values and its support for BiH and the Balkan countries in the field of Euro-Atlantic cooperation.

On a different note, the Kosovar case is at the focus of Hoti, Bashota and Sejdiu. After providing a historical account of Turkey's approach towards the dissolution of Yugoslavia during the 1990s, with a particular focus on Kosovo. The study explores the shift of the Turkish foreign policy in Erdoğan's era and Ankara's relations with Kosovo. The analysis by the authors provides a general overview of the factors and dynamics that underlie the relations between Kosovo and Turkey against the background of the EU accession, paying particular attention to Turkey's growing activism in Kosovo and its perception in the latter. The main argument here is similar to the previous country case studies: Kosovo considers Turkey as a strategic partner, but whose relevance is associated with its Euro-Atlantic orientation and political and economic potential.

Last but not least, the article by Lazăr and Butnaru-Troncotă assesses the bilateral relations between Turkey and Romania between 2008 and 2020 by elaborating on the main diplomatic interactions between the two governments in line with the context of significant regional events and Turkey's new foreign policy identity. Turkey, according to the authors, is still relevant as an economic partner and NATO ally for Romania at the Black Sea, whilst displaying de-Europeanization in its foreign policy and assuming a regional role.

Notes

1. In terms of EU's enlargement process, we could even talk about three different groups of countries within the Balkans: Southern Europe (Greece), South East Europe (Bulgaria and Romania) and Western Balkans.
2. At the time, Yugoslavia consisted of Serbia (including Kosovo) and Montenegro.
3. When they joined the EU in 2007, Romania and Bulgaria still had progress to make in the fields of judicial reform, corruption and (for Bulgaria) organized crime. The Commission set up the Cooperation and Verification Mechanism (CVM) as a transitional measure to assist the two countries to remedy these shortcomings (*European Commission*, 2021).

Disclosure statement

No potential conflict of interest was reported by the author(s).

References

Adar, S., and İ. Toygür. 2020. Turkey, the EU and the Eastern Mediterranean crisis: Militarization of foreign policy and power rivalry. *SWP Comment* 62: 4.

Agarin, T. 2020. The (not so) surprising longevity of identity politics: Contemporary challenges of the state-society compact in Central Eastern Europe. *East European Politics* 36, no. 2: 147–66. doi:10.1080/21599165.2020.1714598.

Alpan, B. 2016. From AKP's 'conservative democracy' to 'advanced democracy': Shifts and challenges in the debate on 'Europe'. *South European Society & Politics* 21, no. 1: 15–28. doi:10.1080/13608746.2016.1155283.

Anastasakis, O. 2008. The EU's political conditionality in the Western Balkans: Towards a more pragmatic approach?'. *Southeast European and Black Sea Studies* 8, no. 4: 365–77. doi:10.1080/14683850802556384.

Anastasakis, O. 2020. Greece and Turkey in the Balkans: Cooperation or rivalry? In *Greek-Turkish relations in an era of Détente*, ed. A. Çarkoğlu and B. Rubin, 45–60. London: Routledge.

Aydın-Düzgit, S., and A. Kaliber. 2016. Encounters with Europe in an era of domestic and international turmoil: Is Turkey a de-Europeanising candidate country? *South European Society & Politics* 21: 1–14. doi:10.1080/13608746.2016.1155282.

Baser, B., and A. Erdi Ozturk. 2017. *Authoritarian politics in Turkey: Elections, resistance and the AKP*. London: Bloomsbury Publishing.

Bechev, D. 2012. Turkey in the Balkans: Taking a broader view. *Insight Turkey* 14, no. 1: 131.

Bieber, F., and M. Kmezić. 2017. The crisis of democracy in the Western Balkans: Authoritarianism and EU stabilitocracy. *Policy Brief*. Balkans in European Policy Advisory Group.

Börzel, T. 2013. When Europeanization hits limited statehood: The Western Balkans as a test case for the transformative power of Europe. In *European integration and transformation of the Western Balkans: Europeanization or business as usual?* ed. A. Elbasani, 174. London: Routledge.

Bulut, A., and N. Hacıoğlu. 2021. Religion, foreign policy and populism in Turkish politics: Introducing a new framework. *Democratization* 28, no. 4: 1–20. doi:10.1080/13510347.2020.1865318.

Buzogány, A. 2021. Beyond Balkan exceptionalism. Assessing compliance with EU law in Bulgaria and Romania. *European Politics and Society* 22, no. 2: 185–202. doi:10.1080/23745118.2020.1729048.

Cavallaro, M.E., and K. Kornetis, eds. 2019. *Rethinking democratisation in Spain, Greece and Portugal*. Switzerland: Palgrave McMillan.

Chryssogelos, A. 2019. Europeanisation as de-politicisation, crisis as re-politicisation: The case of Greek foreign policy during the Eurozone crisis. *Journal of European Integration* 41, no. 5: 605–21. doi:10.1080/07036337.2018.1544249.

Council of the EU. 2018. *Enlargement and Stability and Accession Process-Council Conclusions*, June 26.

Demirtaş, B. 2015. Turkish foreign policy towards the Balkans: A Europeanized foreign policy in a de-Europeanized national context? *Journal of Balkan and near Eastern Studies* 17, no. 2: 123–40. doi:10.1080/19448953.2014.994283.

Dempsey, J., 2012. The EU's flawed enlargement strategy. *Carnegie Europe*, July 16.

Denti, D. 2014. The Europeanisation of candidate countries: The case for a shift to the concept of EU state-building. *Contemporary Southeastern Europe* 1, no. 1: 9–32.

Domaradzki, S. 2019. Opportunistic legitimisation and de-Europeanisation as a reverse effect of Europeanisation. *Global Discourse* 9, no. 1: 221–44. doi:10.1332/204378919X15470487645475.

Dursun-Özkanca, O. 2019. Turkish foreign relations in the Balkans. In *Turkey-west relations: The politics of intra-alliance opposition*, 38–62. Cambridge: Cambridge University Press.

Economides, S. 2020. From fatigue to resistance: EU enlargement and the Western Balkans. *Dahrendorf Forum IV Working Papers*, London.

Ekinci, M.U. 2014. A golden age of relations: Turkey and the Western Balkans during the AK party period. *Insight Turkey* 16, no. 1: 103–25.

Elbasani, A. (2013). *European integration and transformation in the Western Balkans: Europeanization or business as usual?*. Routledge.

European Commission. 2018a. Report from the commission to the European parliament and the council on progress in Romania under the cooperation and verification mechanism. *COM* 851: 17.

European Commission. 2018b. A credible enlargement perspective for and enhanced EU engagement with the Western Balkans. *Communication*, 6 February.

European Commission. 2020a. *Commission work programme 2020*. Brussels: European Commission.

European Commission. 2020b. *Enhancing the accession process: A credible EU perspective for the Western Balkans*. Brussels: European Commission.

European Council. 2018. *Sofia declaration of the EU-Balkans summit*. Press Release, May 17.

Ganev, V.I. 2013. Post-accession hooliganism democratic governance in Bulgaria and Romania after 2007. *East European Politics and Societies: And Cultures* 27, no. 1: 26–44. doi:10.1177/0888325412465086.

Gateva, E. 2013. Post-accession conditionality-Translating benchmarks into political pressure? *East European Politics* 29, no. 4: 420–42. doi:10.1080/21599165.2013.836491.

Gherghina, S., and S. Soare. 2016. A test of European Union post-accession influence: Comparing reactions to political instability in Romania. *Democratization* 23: 797–818. doi:10.1080/13510347.2015.1020792.

Kmezić, M. 2019. EU rule of law conditionality: Democracy or 'stabilitocracy' promotion in the Western Balkans? In *The Europeanisation of the Western Balkans – A failure of EU conditionality*, ed. J. Džankić, S. Keil, and M. Kmezić, 87–109. London: Palgrave Macmillan.

Mitrovic, M. 2014. *Turkish foreign policy towards the Balkans*. Berlin: Humboldt-Universität zu Berlin, Philosophische Fakultät III, Institut für Sozialwissenschaften.

Noutcheva, G., and S. Aydın-Düzgit. 2012. Lost in Europeanisation: The Western Balkans and Turkey. *West European Politics* 35, no. 1: 59–78. doi:10.1080/01402382.2012.631313.

Oran, B. 2010. *Turkish foreign policy 1919-2006*. Utah: University of Utah Press.

Özkan, B. 2014. Turkey, Davutoğlu and the idea of pan-Islamism. *Survival* 56, no. 4: 119–40. doi:10.1080/00396338.2014.941570.

Öztürk, A.E. 2021a. *Religion, identity and power: Turkey and the Balkans in the twenty-first century*. Edinburgh: Edinburgh University Press.

Öztürk, A.E. 2021b. Turkey's post-2016 foreign policy drivers. *Policy*: 3–10.

Öztürk, A.E., and İ. Gözaydın. 2018. A frame for Turkey's foreign policy via the diyanet in the Balkans. *Journal of Muslims in Europe* 7, no. 3: 331–50. doi:10.1163/22117954-12341370.

Öztürk, A.E., and S. Sözeri. 2018. Diyanet as a Turkish foreign policy tool: Evidence from the Netherlands and Bulgaria. *Politics and Religion* 11, no. 3: 624–48. doi:10.1017/S175504831700075X.

Papadimitriou, D., and E. Gateva. 2009. Between enlargement-led Europeanisation and Balkan exceptionalism: An appraisal of Bulgaria's and Romania's entry into the European Union. *Perspectives on European Politics and Society* 10, no. 2: 152–66. doi:10.1080/15705850902899172.

Saatçioğlu, B. 2019. Turkey and the EU: Partners or competitors in the Western Balkans? *Südosteuropa Mitteilungen* 05-06: 82–97.

Schmidt, Paul, and Vedran Dzihic. "Vaccine diplomacy and enlargement fatigue: why the EU must rethink its approach to the Western Balkans." LSE European Politics and Policy (EUROPP) blog, (2021).

Somun, H. 2011. Turkish foreign policy in the Balkans and 'neo-ottomanism': A personal account. *Insight Turkey* 13, no. 3: 33–41.

Spendzharova, A.B., and M. Anna Vachudova. 2012. Catching up? Consolidating liberal democracy in Bulgaria and Romania after EU accession'. *West European Politics* 35: 39–58. doi:10.1080/01402382.2012.631312.

Stavridis, S., C. Tsardanidis, and G. Christou. 2015. The impact of international financial and economic crisis on the de-Europeanisation of national foreign policies in the Mediterranean. *Hellenic Studies* 23, no. 1: 23–37.

Tanasković, D. 2012. Turkey and the Balkans: Old traditions, new aspirations. *Israel Journal of Foreign Affairs* 6, no. 2: 51–62. doi:10.1080/23739770.2012.11446502.

Targański, T. 2017. Neo-ottomanism. An empire being rebuilt? *New Eastern Europe* 27, no. 3-4: 78–83.

Tsardanidis, C. 2015. Greek foreign policy: The De-Europeanisation impact of the economic crisis. *Hellenic Studies* 23, no. 1: 59–81.

Yavuz, M.H. 2020. *Nostalgia for the empire: The politics of neo-ottomanism*. Oxford: Oxford University Press.

Zweers, W. 2019. Between effective engagement and damaging politicisation: Prospects for a credible EU enlargement policy to the Western Balkans. *Policy Brief*, Clingedael, May.

A rival or an awkward partner? Turkey's relationship with the West in the Balkans

Dimitar Bechev

ABSTRACT
In the 2000 and 2010s, Turkey embarked on an activist policy in Southeast Europe reliant on personal diplomacy, economic outreach, and the projection of soft power. Coupled with the drift away from the West, such overtures have prompted observers to qualify Turkey as a revisionist power similar to Russia, China and other non-Western actors making inroads into the region. This article seeks to correct this view. It argues that Turkey is not an external player but very much part of the Balkans. Secondly, the article contends that Turkish foreign policy is not posing a frontal challenge to the EU and NATO, the two anchors of regional order. Rather, it benefits from its close relationship and membership in the two institutions. Though it has shifted from multilateralism to unilateralism, Ankara pursues a parallel, as opposed to an adversarial, strategy to that of the West.

Under the rule of the Justice and Development Party (*Adalet ve Kalkınma Partisi* – the AKP), Turkey reinvented itself from a pillar of the Western alliance into an ambitious regional power. With 'zero-problems with neighbours' policy in the late 2000s and its response to the Arab Spring in the following decade, Ankara sought to project diplomatic, political and economic influence over a neighbourhood spanning the Middle East, the Southern Caucasus and, of course, Southeast Europe (Kadıoğlu et al. 2012; Kirişci 2012). The rhetoric of a 'Turkish model' of institutional development and market reform to be exported towards proximate countries gathered momentum (Tugal 2016). Although Turkey's economic performance since the mid-2010s has been lacklustre while the authoritarian turn also undermined its claim to inspire democratic change (Waldman and Çalışkan 2017; Akkoyunlu and Öktem 2019), the bid for regional leadership has remained unchanged. It transpires in President Tayyip Erdoğan's and other senior officials' discourse but also in the Ankara's activist posture: from the disbursement of financial assistance to neighbours all the way to the use of military force beyond borders as in Syria, Libya, Iraq and Nagorno-Karabakh (Çağaptay 2019).

The Balkans have always been central to this effort. Since the early 2000s, the area has seen a growth of diplomatic, economic and cultural exchanges with Turkey: be it FDI, high-profile political initiatives spearheaded by Ankara, the advent of popular Turkish TV series, the establishment of educational institutions, and most recently, assistance related to the COVID-19 pandemic (Demirtaş 2015; Aydıntaşbaş 2019; Dursun-Özkanca 2019; Öztürk 2021). Diplomacy has made inroads too. Thus, back in 2009–2010, then Foreign Minister Ahmet Davutoğlu took credit for mediating in local disputes, having orchestrated a series of three-way meetings with the foreign ministers of Bosnia and Herzegovina and Serbia, Sven Alkakaj and Vuk Jeremić. President Erdoğan has built a close relationship with local leaders such as Serbia's President Aleksandar Vučić, Edi Rama, prime minister of Albania, or Boyko Borisov, head of Bulgaria's cabinet between 2009 and 2021 (Büyük and Öztürk 2019). Turkey remains an influential player in Bosnia and Herzegovina and throughout the Western Balkans. It is also increasingly central to the region's energy security, having gradually moved from a major consumer to a country transiting natural gas.

Turkish foreign policy has been conditioned by the process of de-Europeanization, where the EU has progressively lost influence over the country's domestic affairs and institutions as well as over its external relations (see Balpan and Öztürk in this issue). But aspects of de-Europeanization are traceable in the Western Balkans as well. Firstly, there is no palpable trend towards democratic and rule-of-law consolidation driven by EU membership conditionality. Secondly, because the Union has effectively put enlargement on halt. The article argues that de-Europeanization in Turkey mirrors de-Europeanization in its Balkan neighbourhood.

For all those reasons, Turkey's involvement in Southeast Europe has caused frictions with the West. Officials, journalists and policy analysts on both sides of the Atlantic commonly perceive Erdoğan's agenda in the region as fundamentally antithetical to the European Union (EU) and the United States' values and interests (Vuksanović 2018; Hopkins and Pitel 2021). Indeed, Turkey is commonly bracketed alongside Russia and China, two major states which compete with the West, both at the global and the regional level (Bieber and Tzifakis 2019). Authoritarian rule, harnessing Islam as a foreign policy tool, Erdoğan's frequent use of abrasive anti-EU rhetoric, Turkey's partial alignment with Russia; all support such a view. The latter is also reinforced by the Turkish president's ties to local politicians who seem to embrace and propound the strongman model of governance.

This article takes issue with the above view. It argues that Turkey's strategy in the Balkans is not inherently revisionist or driven by a desire to roll back Western influence. On the contrary, Ankara benefits from its long-standing ties to the West. Though Turkish foreign policy has veered towards unilateralism, resilient economic and institutional ties continue to bind Turkey into the Western sphere. NATO membership and the EU-Turkey Customs Union continue to shape and influence Turkey's external behaviour, as illustrated by the Balkans. Rather than posing a frontal challenge, Ankara runs a *parallel* – as opposed to *adversarial* – policy to that of the West and occasionally joins in the EU and NATO initiatives.

The article is structured in the following way: Section 1 argues that Turkey does not qualify as 'external power' in Southeast Europe, in contrast to Russia and China, and as such, it is partly invested in the status quo. In Section 2, the article explores the ways in which in the AKP era Turkish foreign policy has come to be at odds with the Western priorities and objectives. The last section then looks at areas of convergence to contend that the Turkish partnership with the EU is not entirely a thing of the past as commonly believed, while NATO continues to be relevant to Turkey's policy in the region.

In the Balkans or *of* the Balkans?

There is a fundamental misconception when it comes to Turkey's position in the Balkans. Typically, foreign policy pundits relegate it to the category of 'external players', alongside its one-time imperial rival Russia, rising China, and even the Arab Gulf countries, which have provided significant volumes of FDI (Bieber and Tzifakis 2019; Rrustemi et al. 2019). In reality, Turkey is not an outsider to the Balkans, at least not in the same sense as the rest in the above list. Its geography, history and society are inextricable to the southeast corner of Europe. The 'Turkey returning to the Balkans' catchphrase, therefore, makes little sense.

It is true that, technically speaking, only a small fraction of Turkey's territory lies in the Balkans. The region of Eastern Thrace has an area of little over 23,700 sq. km, which is about 3% of the country's landmass. Thanks to the megalopolis that is Istanbul, it accounts for a much larger share of the population: about 14.3% or 12.05 million.[1] Put differently, if European Turkey were a separate state, it would be the second most populous one in Southeast Europe, following Romania and ahead of Greece.

One should also keep in mind that the sizable urban centres of Western Turkey, Istanbul but also including Izmir and Bursa, are in relative proximity to the Balkans. The Bulgarian capital Sofia lies some 551 km away from Istanbul and the second-largest city Plovdiv (or Filibe as it's known in Turkish), 421 km. The latter is closer than the distance between Ankara and Istanbul (448 km). The comparison could be extended further. Belgrade, for instance, is closer to Istanbul than Trabzon is, and Sarajevo – closer than Diyarbakır.

Population forms another bridge. About 20 million Turkish citizens (of 85 million in total)[2] have Balkan ancestry and, in most cases, have found themselves within the borders of the Turkish Republic as a result of migrations as the Ottoman state shrank over the 19th and the early 20th centuries. Migration from the Balkans continued throughout the republican period, the Cold War and the 1990s. These migratory waves give rise to connections, some immediate and some more distant. The imprint of Balkan Turks and other Muslim groups is visible not just in Thracian cities such as Edirne, Tekirdağ or Kırklareli (or Kırk Kilise, 'Forty Churches') but also in Bursa, Izmir, parts of Istanbul, Ankara and elsewhere in Anatolia. It is safe to assume that a fair share of the 10,000-strong multitude that welcomed Erdoğan in the Serbian town of Novi Pazar in October 2017 had relatives, friends and/or business partners in Turkey or had been to Turkey on more than one occasion (RFE/RL 2017). In addition, large populations in Balkan countries can trace their origins to Anatolia and Eastern Thrace in Greece, which harboured more than a million refugees Thrace under the exchange of populations in the 1920s, and in Bulgaria (Ladas 1932) Human connectivity relativizes socially constructed distinctions. Seen from the vantage point of sociology and history, the boundary between 'the Balkans' and 'Anatolia' is as diffuse as the one between the Balkans and Central Europe (Vezenkov 2017). Apparent certainties often do not stand to careful scrutiny.

Turkey and the Balkans are connected at a yet deeper level. They share an experience of modernization, Europeanization, nation- and state-building, which is ambiguous and ridden with trauma. Turks and other Muslims from the Balkans played a seminal role in the establishment of modern Turkey. The view of nationalism, state formation and state-driven transformation as a project foisted upon conservative Anatolian masses by the arrivals from the lands of Rumeli (or Turkey-in-Europe) is no doubt simplistic. Yet critical figures starting with the republic's founder Mustafa Kemal Atatürk did come from the Balkans, and in many ways, their ideas and general outlook at least in part reflected the conditions and circumstances they faced in their places of origin. Going further back in time, the Balkans was central to the late Ottoman Empire's interaction with the West and efforts at modernization. Ziraat Bank (Agricultural Bank), the second-biggest lender in Turkey, was started in 1863 by Mithad Pasha in the town of Pirot, in southeast Serbia (Ziraat Bankası 2021). Turn-of-the-century Macedonia gave a start to the Young Turk revolution of 1908. Talat Pasha, one of the three-men committee to lead the empire in its dying day and the architect of the extermination or genocide of Ottoman Armenians, came from Kardžali (Kırcaali) in present-day Bulgaria. The loss of the Balkans during the wars of 1912–3 bore heavily on the subsequent emergence of the Turkish Republic (Lewis 1961).

Even after the end of the Ottoman Empire, Turkey continued engaging in Balkan international politics. It was a founding member of multilateral initiatives such as the two Balkan Pacts of 1934 and 1953. The latter treaty was actually signed in Ankara, with Greece, Turkey and Tito's Yugoslavia as parties. Turkish officials attended all Balkan gatherings in the 1970s and 80s, including the foreign ministerial in Belgrade of 1988. Its disputes with neighbouring Greece and Bulgaria, on account of the forced assimilation and subsequent expulsion of local Turks, anchored it even tighter in the region. After the Cold War ended, Turkey, led by Prime Minister and later on President Turgut Özal, was quick to reach out to a number of Balkan neighbours (Hale 2013, 194–207).[3] It steered clear of unilateral intervention into the Yugoslav wars in the 1990s, preferring to work through NATO and other international institutions, but followed the conflict closely and opened its doors to refugees from Bosnia. Turkey joined the Peace Implementation Council (PIC) overseeing the Dayton Peace Accords. It also contributed to the relaunch of regional cooperation in the mid-1990s through bodies such as the Southeast European Cooperation Process (SEECP) and the Stability Pact (Bechev 2011).

Of course, Turkey is not *just* a Balkan country. It has a similar relationship to other areas. As Davutoğlu, amongst others, would point out, it is also a Middle Eastern and a Caucasus country as well as a neighbour of North Africa and Central Asia. Connections with Syria and Iraq, borders with whom were drawn only after the First World War, are at least as prominent. They have cut across communities and have recently become blurred as a result of forces ranging from war and forced migration to trade and investment. Politicians and personalities who began to dominate public life have no Balkan connections. Erdoğan's family roots, for instance, go back to the Black Sea village near Rize and, most likely, several generations back, Batumi in Georgia.[4] AKP's heartland is central and eastern Anatolia, while the Black Sea region has been overrepresented in Istanbul politics.[5] Turkey is both internally diverse and interwoven with its multiple neighbourhoods. It is also a crossroads but often, by virtue of its size and the lasting impact of nationalism in its various permutations, inward-looking. Having argued that Turkey is inextricably linked to the Balkans, the article will examine its role in regional politics and its relationship to the EU and, more specifically, the US.

A rival of the West?

Turkey's embeddedness in the Balkans still leaves open the question of whether its policy seeks to undermine Western primacy or not. The dominant geopolitical narrative, both in the West and to some degree in Turkey itself, suggests it does. It assumes that Ankara's overarching goal is regional hegemony, irrespective of its capabilities, the costs attached, or the actual opportunities the region offers to that end. The Balkans form part of 'Erdoğan's empire', to quote the title of Soner Cağaptay's book (2019).

This perspective also suggests that the EU's political and normative power is waning and giving way to great power competition. A return to the era of diplomatic rivalries and wars of the Ottoman and the Tsarist Empire coming back from the dead to contest Western domination and carve out their geopolitical spheres of influence. Looking at Turkey in particular, it has become standard to describe its presence and initiatives as a manifestation of 'neo-Ottomanism' – vaguely describable as nostalgia for imperial *grandeur* and aspiration to recuperate at least some of the influence lost with the end of the empire (Yavuz 2016, 2020; Tanasković 2013).

The reasons are manifold and have to do with the trajectory taken by both Turkey and its Balkan neighbours over the last decade or so. The underlying issue is that the political order centred on the EU and based on principles such as democratization, open borders, and multilateral cooperation is faltering. The Western Balkans, and more broadly Southeast Europe, is exposed to the repercussions. This happens at a time when Turkey and the West are drifting apart as well.

Democracy is coming under strain. In 2018, the international watchdog Freedom House downgraded Serbia, an EU candidate country, to 'partly free' (Freedom House 2018). It did the same with its neighboured Hungary, a member state. To be sure, democratic regimes in the Balkans have never fully moved to consolidation, even in the 2000s when the pull of EU conditionality was arguably at its strongest. But the 2010s have seen a resurgence of high-level corruption, pervasive clientelism, and the erosion of the rule of law. State capture is as entrenched as ever despite long-standing efforts by the EU and other Western actors to promote good governance, transparency and the rule of law. Nationalism is back, sadly not just in former Yugoslavia but also in the core EU too where nativist movements like Front National in France or the Alternative for Germany have carved a niche in domestic politics. The Balkan case shows some specificities, of course. Unlike the times Slobodan Milošević and Franjo Tudjman held power, nationalist mobilization is not coupled with state-promoted conflict as during the wars of the 1990s. Rather, today's battles take place on the front pages of the tabloids, beholden to the government of the day, on TV talk shows, and growingly in social media (Bieber 2019).

The region's EU integration is facing headwinds. The opposition to the start of membership negotiations by North Macedonia and Albania proves the point. In the North Macedonian case, France defied all other EU countries arguing that the Union needs internal consolidation before expansion, followed by a Bulgarian veto of North Macedonia.

Skopje has been unable to start accession talks for over three years, even though it settled its name dispute with Greece in 2018. There are also the cases of Serbia and Montenegro, whose ongoing membership negotiations proceed at a languid pace. Kosovo, in the meantime, has not been granted visa liberalization despite fulfiling the technical conditions. The EU's unwelcoming attitude vindicates the view that Europe is moving towards a differentiated model of integration where the Western Balkans, along with Romania and Bulgaria and other post-communist member states, find themselves in the outer circles of Europe.

The EU's weakening pull has a negative fall-out on domestic politics. European dignitaries' embrace of authoritarian-minded elites does even greater damage. Pro-EU constituencies in countries like Serbia and Montenegro are disheartened by Brussels and member state officials' reticence when it comes to ills such as state capture (Stratulat et al. 2020). At the same time, the apparent pro-EU consensus at the level of political parties does not translate into unqualified support for reforms to foster accountability and strengthen the rule of law. Put in simpler terms, Balkan politicians talk the EU talk but do not walk the walk. Sure enough, the status quo may not be as dire as the 1990s, but it is hardly a confirmation of Europe's 'transformative power' (Džankić et al. 2019). The real litmus test is not the number of negotiations chapters open or closed, or benchmarks fulfilled, but the strong desire of large groups in the region to emigrate, as evidenced in surveys.

All in all, the Western Balkans are stuck in the EU's waiting room, figuratively speaking, and exposed to de-Europeanization reminiscent of what Turkey has been going through over the past decade or so.

Turkey's trajectory has been even more problematic in comparison to that of the Balkan countries to the west of its borders. Its fragile democracy has morphed into what scholars term a competitive authoritarian regime. The transition to a presidential regime in 2017–8 has marked the endpoint in the dismantling of checks and balances on executive power (Esen and Gümüşçü 2016; Akkoyunlu and Öktem 2019). Despite gains by the opposition in the 2019 local elections, the country is both de facto and de jure in President Erdoğan's hands. Following a decade of EU-inspired reforms in the 2000s, the authoritarian turn in domestic politics has led to the sharp deterioration of relations with the West. Anti-American and anti-EU rhetoric, never absent from the Turkish public sphere, has now become the norm (Kirişci 2017; Ülgen 2021). Political and security ties have deteriorated dramatically. The standoff between Washington and Ankara over Syria and the occasional verbal duels between Erdoğan and Donald Trump have triggered concerns that a divorce is imminent. Though it is unlikely that Turkey would leave NATO or extricate itself from the Customs Union with the EU, it is fair to say that its relationship with Western partners has become largely transactional rather than rooted in long-term strategic interests, let alone values (Kirişci 2017).

Turkey's gradual decoupling from the West has stokes fears that it is on a mission to reclaim its former empire. It is not difficult to find evidence to that effect. Ottoman nostalgia has long been present in Turkish society and culture. Imperial past has served as inspiration for different political strands, from Islamist conservatives all the way to liberal proponents of minority rights and pluralism (Yavuz 2020). But under the AKP, it came to be associated with a pro-active foreign policy which strives to achieve regional hegemony, in contrast to the more restrained and Western-focused policy espoused of governments in power until the early 2000s (Mufti 2009; Kadıoğlu et al. 2012). AKP's alignment with the Nationalist Action Party (MHP) has furthermore brought to the fore a strand of pan-Turkist ultranationalism, which puts Ankara at odds with Western powers. While earlier versions of neo-Ottomanism, including Turgut Özal's and early AKP's, posited the EU and the US as natural partners, its latest reincarnation is deeply sceptical of the West.

In the Balkans, Turkish policy has been tapping into Ottoman memories and legacies too. In October 2009, for instance, Ahmet Davutoğlu delivered in Sarajevo what many took at the time as a programmatic speech in which he praised the Ottoman past as a source of guidance for the future in the Balkans. Only in the 16th century, the peak of the sultans' might, that region took centre stage in world history.[6] Having made peace with its past and harnessing its historical capital, the new Turkey was bringing the promise to remake the Balkans too. No more a stagnating and fragmented periphery of the West but a pivotal part of a new cluster in a multi-centric global environment. Needless to say, such messages have been ill-received by many of the locals. Politicians and commentators have accused Ankara of working to reclaim the empire, albeit with economic and soft power rather than military means, cultivating the fifth column amongst Balkan Muslims. Others have shown enthusiasm, however. 'Welcome Sultan' read one placard during Erdoğan's walk of fame in Novi Pazar in October 2017 (Vasović 2017).

In addition to Neo-Ottomanism, another complaint laid at Turkey's doorstep is that it is exporting authoritarian rule to its neighbours. It is a similar theme as the one about 'Putinization', that is, Russia promoting a governance alternative to Western liberal democracy. Critics point, for instance, at Erdoğan's cosy relationship with the new crop of Balkan strongmen such as Serbia's Aleksandar Vučić. Like his Turkish colleague, Vučić has built a presidential regime and amassed a great amount of power in his hands, though without going through the pains of overhauling the Serbian constitution (Bieber 2019). Another example would be the refugee deal concluded in March 2016 between Turkey and the EU, which has empowered, by default if not by design, Western Balkan countries to act as guardians of Europe's gates and therefore strengthen the hands of the governments and political leaders relative to parliaments or courts.

Last but not least, the Turkish government effort to root out the Gülenists (known now as the Fethullahist Terrorist Organization or FETÖ) has spread to the Western Balkans. There are examples of arrests and renditions of Turkish citizens without due process and the protections afforded by the law (Begisholli 2019). Balkan governments have come under pressure to close down educational institutions associated with the Gülen movement and transfer their assets to the likes of the conservative Maarif foundation, in cahoots with the AKP (Öztürk 2021). Put differently, Turkey has been interfering in the domestic affairs of a series of Balkan countries with its actions polarizing local societies and Muslim communities in particular. In the extreme, MIT has been responsible for abducting suspected members of 'FETÖ' residing in the Balkans. Such covert action has provoked considerable pushback in countries like Kosovo. It has also alerted Western governments, particularly in countries such as Germany, Austria or the Netherlands, where Ankara's influence, politicization and surveillance of local Turkish and other Muslim communities, as well as political exiles, is a hot issue (Deutsche Welle 2016).

Decoupling and de-Europeanization have put Turkey at odds with the West in the Balkans. However, as the next section argues, the divorce is far from complete. Indeed, overlapping interests still bring Turkey, on the one hand, and the EU and the US, on the other, together, on an issue-by-issue basis.

Turkey as an awkward partner

Despite the rift between Turkey and the West, Ankara's Balkan policy is neither disruptive nor entirely beholden to neo-imperialist fantasies. Rather it reflects a mixture of ideology and pragmatic calculations and is often a product of circumstances rather than grand designs.

To start with, there is no evidence that Erdogan or the AKP are systematically exporting authoritarian institutions and practices abroad, undermining the West. Authoritarianism in the Balkans is a home-grown phenomenon and not an import. In the 1990s, for instance, both Serbia and Croatia saw the emergence of strongman regimes led respectively by Slobodan Milošević and Franjo Tudjman. Such regimes combined democratic and authoritarian elements, e.g. competitive elections in tandem with state capture skewing the playing field, the propagation of illiberal ideology and the suppression of minorities. It would be far-fetched to fault Erdoğan, Putin, Viktor Orbán or anyone else about the rule of law and accountability deficits in a region with historical experience with competitive politics but is still a novice when it comes to democratic governance. External powers may take advantage of state capture and corruption, as they often do, but these are by and large local conditions liable to be exploited (Bechev 2017; Bieber and Tzifakis 2019). Foreign meddling could well exacerbate matters – e.g. Turkey's partnership with or outright patronage over certain politicians and factions in Bosnia and Herzegovina consolidates their grip on power and public resources – but is not the root cause of democratic dysfunctionality.

Secondly, Turkey is not always the lone wolf it appears to be. A 'neo-Ottoman' policy would imply that Turkey acts mostly unilaterally instead of through institutions or alliances such as NATO. To be sure, Turkish foreign policy has a strong unilateralist impulse, as many scholars and experts have pointed out. Self-reliance and distrust of foreigners are entrenched in the Turkish public's perceptions and attitudes (Aydın 2019). Ankara has made moves and asserted its interests in the Balkans, such as providing economic assistance through TİKA), supporting domestic political players aligned with the AKP, funding schools, trying to mediate in regional disputes etc. The same was very much true of the Middle East before the Arab Spring when Davutoğlu was touting the notion of Turkey as an order-setter (*düzen kurucu ülke*) (Davutoğlu 2001).

At the same time, even with President Erdoğan in complete control and nationalism rampant, foreign policy has played along and adapted to multilateral institutions. To give the obvious example, despite its strained relationship with NATO and the EU, Ankara continues to support their enlargement to the Balkans, as in the AKP's early years of power. Rather than pursue an obstructionist strategy, as does Russia, and try to wean countries into its diplomatic orbit, it ratified without delay Montenegro and North Macedonia's NATO accession treaty. There is no rhetorical or substantive opposition from Ankara vis-à-vis the EU's expansion (Daily Sabah 2020). That makes sense from a purely rational perspective. Bringing new members also means expanded market access for Turkey thanks to the Customs Union with the EU. Notably, Turkey is amongst the top five export markets for Romania, Bulgaria and Greece, all members of the Union.[7] In short, there still remains a multilateral dimension to Turkey's engagement with the Balkans, even if it gets overshadowed by Erdoğan's leader-to-leader diplomacy (Büyük and Öztürk 2019).

To sum up, despite the overarching trends towards de-Europeanization affecting both Turkey and the Balkans, there remains institutional ties and economic ties that bind them both in the Western sphere. This creates space for Turkey and Western actors to join forces in the region on an ad hoc basis.

It is also important to note that go-it-alone has not delivered that much for Turkey. Davutoğlu's shuttle diplomacy between Serbia and Bosnia and Herzegovina in 2010–11 looked excellent on paper but, beyond some initial concessions such as the Serbian parliament condemnation of the genocide in Srebrenica, it has failed to settle conflicts. Bosnia and Herzegovina is arguably more fragmented and dysfunctional now than it was a decade ago when Turkish embarked on its mission as a troubleshooter capable of replacing the EU or the US. The main achievement of that era turned out to be the opening with Serbia which, though initiated by Abdullah Gül and Davutoğlu in 2009–10, blossomed when Erdoğan and Vučić took charge. Though present in Bosnia, Turkey is not involved in the most significant security issue in the Balkans: the Kosovo issue. It is the EU presiding over the 'normalization talks' between Belgrade and Prishtina, with the US and occasionally Russia coming into the picture. All in all, Turkish ambitions have been scaled down. The Serbia-Bosnia-Turkey trilateral summits are now focused on more immediate issues, such as the highway connecting Belgrade and Sarajevo (BalkanInsight 2018).

Turkey's continued dependence on the West and the pitfalls of unilateralism do not mean that its presence and actions in the Balkans do not generate tensions and will not do so in the future. The reasons have to do with Turkey's domestic politics and AKP's ideological leanings.

Turkish politics appears to be driven increasingly by domestic political considerations. Thus, in May 2018, Erdoğan held a mass rally in Sarajevo ahead of the presidential and parliamentary elections in Turkey (Vuksanović 2018; Büyük and Öztürk 2019). The reason he chose the Bosnian capital was that he had been prevented from campaigning amongst Turkish communities in Western Europe. His partisans from Germany, the Netherlands, Austria and elsewhere had an opportunity to display their support by gathering in Sarajevo, halfway the distance to Turkey. In other words, Erdoğan's move targeted his voters first and only then Balkan audiences. Be that as it may, they added to tensions with key western European states, which were running high at the time.

With regard to ideology, Islam has become much more central to Turkish foreign policy with AKP at the helm, but that does not mean it was absent from the picture when secularists called the shots. The Directorate of Religious Affairs (*Diyanet İşleri Başkanlığı*, Diyanet) has a network across the Balkans, funding imams, mosques and other pious institutions (Öztürk 2021). Yet, its involvement dates back to the 1990s. Back then, one of its main concerns was counteracting Salafism coming from the Gulf. Nowadays, it is imperative to stamp out Gülenists who managed to expand their influence in the 2000s, when they were allied with the AKP. On the one hand, Turkey plays a hegemonic role in Balkan Islam. On the other, religious communities are the arena of struggles emanating from Turkish politics – which takes from the country's soft power. Once Gülen's *cemaat* was the vanguard of Turkey's influence in the Balkans. Now stands as the state's enemy number 1, as demonstrated by the actions of the Turkish government, MIT, and the Maarif Foundation described above.

At the same time, there is more to religious diplomacy than just Islam. Turkey has used faith to engage predominantly Christian countries. For instance, the Istanbul Municipality financed the renovation of the St. Stephen, the Bulgarian church in Fener. The opening ceremony in November 2017 saw Erdoğan and Prime Minister Boyko Borisov side by side. The meeting was a prequel to the EU-Turkey summit in March 2018 convened in Varna during Bulgaria's presidency of the Council of the European Union (EU Council 2018), where the implementation of the 2016 refugee deal, a matter of high priority for Ankara, was high on the agenda (Ibrahim 2018). Similarly, Alexis Tsipras became the first Greek prime minister to visit the seminary at the Island of Halki in February 2019 (Yackley and Hope 2019). Turkey touted the prospect of reopening the religious school forcibly closed in 1971.

Turkish activism in the Balkans has generated dividends but also costs. Perceptions of Turkey as well as of Erdoğan differ depending on one's ethnic affiliation and politics. He does have his admirers as the rally in Sarajevo or the impromptu gatherings in support in the aftermath of the coup attempt on 15 July 2016 show. Yet, there is no shortage of sceptics and detractors, including amongst Muslim populations. In Bosnia, for instance, Erdoğan tends to be popular amongst voters of the Party of Democratic Action (SDA), but many other strands are critical of Turkey's undemocratic turn, even if they retain the positive view of Turkey and Turks (Büyük 2018). In Bulgaria, the main political force representing the Turkish community and other Muslims, the Movement for Rights and Freedoms (DPS), has long been at odds with official Ankara and mended fences only recently. In North Macedonia, AKP is aligned with Besa competing with the Democratic Union for Integration (DUI), the dominant party amongst Macedonian Albanians. In Kosovo, Erdoğan aligned with President Hashim Thaçi but clashed with Ramush Haradinaj (prime minister between 2017 and 20) over the arrest and transfer of Gülenists. Turkey has no special links to the current Prime Minister Albin Kurti, a harsh critic of Thaçi and a left-wing populist.[8] In general, the combined effect of AKP's fusion with the Turkish state and alignment with local parties and politicians in the Balkans have had negative fallout in the region.

All in all, the balance sheet of Turkey's presence in the Balkans is mixed. There are certain synergies with the West but clearly points of friction too. Ankara has scored gains but also incurred costs.

Conclusion

What is Turkey's role in the Balkans? Is it a competitor of the West or simply a difficult partner? There is no conclusive answer to this question. At the level of discourse, Turkey poses as a rival. At the 2018 Sarajevo rally held in the Zetra Olympic Centre, Erdoğan accused 'certain European countries' of working against Turkey by driving a wedge amongst its citizens and exposing ethnic and sectarian divides (BBC 2018). So even without making a claim about the Balkans, he posited Europe as an adversary.

In addition, Turkey has been pursuing goals that are at odds with the transformative agenda espoused by the EU. Its policy is not geared towards promoting democratic values and the rule of law. On the contrary, the entrenchment of personalistic regimes characterized by a high degree of informality and state capture is a necessary condition for Ankara to seek influence. The reason is the highly personalized style of decision making and implementation in Turkey, which revolves around the persona of Erdoğan. His direct links to local leaders – Vučić, Izetbegović, Rama, Borisov, to name a few – has been the main transmission belt for Turkey to assert its interests to the west of its borders. In that sense, Ankara is adding to, albeit indirectly, a governance model in the Balkans, which is a hurdle to democratic consolidation.

This connection highlights the parallel processes of de-Europeanization that unfold in Turkey and its Balkan neighbourhood. In both cases, the EU has largely lost its leverage over domestic politics and institutions compared to the peak in the early and mid-2000s. De-Europeanization at the domestic level is reflected in the foreign policy domain too. Fewer references to shared European future on the rhetorical side, greater emphasis on bilateralism rather than multilateral initiatives, actions which are not compatible with EU- and US-promulgated norms (e.g. extraditions without due process, transparency and accountability in decision making and public policy).

Despite the considerable degree of divergence, Ankara acts in parallel but not necessarily *against* the EU and the United States. In the grand scheme of things, Turkey is tightly connected to the European economy, a fact highlighted by the ongoing recession, which puts at risk EU investors too. Turkish trade with EU members Romania, Greece and Bulgaria is by far more significant than with the Western Balkans, though Serbia is picking up too. On the security side, Turkey pursues a policy independently of NATO and has deepened ties to Russia. Yet, it remains part of the Alliance and contributes to its initiatives, including those aimed to deter Moscow. When it comes to the Balkans, Turkey has no alternative to offer to local countries to woo them away from Euro-Atlantic institutions. Its resources are limited, too, in comparison with the collective West. What is also important is that Balkan elites do not necessarily see a trade-off between ties to Western organizations and to Turkey. That is clearly visible in the policy of non-aligned Serbia, which has also been courting Russia, China and the Gulf while negotiating its membership in the EU. But it is also the case of Bulgaria which has emerged as a leading advocate of engagement with Turkey within the Union. The only country in Southeast Europe which has deep-seated concerns and fears about Turkish expansionism is Greece, which has long-standing territorial disputes with its neighbour only made worse by the looming conflict over offshore gas deposits in the proximity of Cyprus. But Greek policymakers have demonstrated the capacity to be flexible and deescalate tensions (Christofis in this issue).

Turkey is embedded in the politics, economies and societies of the Balkans. It is an autonomous player, and the cult of Erdoğan has become central to its presence in the region, often with divisive effects. However, there is no evidence that its actions or policies are geared at replacing the West as the lynchpin of regional order. Rather, Turkey is pursuing a *parallel* policy, which at times overlaps with that of the EU, US and NATO.

Notes

1. According to the 2020 Census the population of the 25 districts on Istanbul's European side stood at 10,221,936 while the population of Eastern Thrace was 1,831,151. Data from the Turkish Statistical Institute (TÜİK), https://data.tuik.gov.tr/.
2. Diaspora organizations estimate the figure at 20–22 million (Babaoğlu 2008).
3. Özal is credited with the establishment of the Turkish Cooperation and Coordination Agency (*Türk İşbirliği ve Koordinasyon İdaresi Başkanlığı*, TİKA) which is the main channel of development assistance to Turkey's neighbours, in the Balkans and elsewhere.
4. The president's wife Emine hails from Siirt in the southeast and is reportedly of Arab heritage.
5. Ekrem Imamoğlu, the opposition candidate who won the mayorship of Istanbul, is from Akçaabat, near Trabzon.
6. Davutoğlu's address at the Conference on 'Ottoman Legacy and Muslim Communities in the Balkans Today', Sarajevo, 16 October 2009. Quoted by Demirtaş (2015).
7. Turkey's major export markets in Southeast Europe in 2018 were as follows – Romania: $2.5 bn, Bulgaria: $1.7 bn, Greece: $1.4 bn, Slovenia: $1.06 bn, Serbia: $586 million, Albania: $308 million, Bosnia and Herzegovina: BiH: $294 million, Croatia: $272 million, North Macedonia: $253 million, Kosovo: $215 million, Montenegro: $80 million. Turkey's imports from the region – Romania: $1.557 bn, Bulgaria: Bulgaria: $1.527 bn, Greece: $918 million, Serbia: $233 million, Slovenia: $211 million, Croatia: $150 million, Bosnia and Herzegovina: $120 million, North Macedonia: $69 million, Albania: 13 m, Montenegro: $10 million, Kosovo: $3 million. Data from the Turkish Statistical Institute (www. turkstat.gov.tr).
8. Kurti shunned Erdoğan's request to reconsider opening an embassy in Jerusalem, a decision Kosovo took after obtaining Israel's recognition of its independence in September 2020.

Disclosure statement

No potential conflict of interest was reported by the author(s).

References

Akkoyunlu, K., and K. Öktem, eds. 2019. *Illiberal Governance in Turkey and Beyond*. Abingdon: Routledge. originally published as a special issue of the *Journal of Southeast European and Black Sea Studies* 16 (4), 2016.

Alpan, B., and A.E. Ozturk. forthcoming. Turkey and the Balkans: Bringing the europeanisation/ de-europeanisation nexus into question. *Southeast European and Black Sea Studies* 22(1).

Aydın, M. 2019. Foreign policy 1923-2018. In *The routledge handbook of Turkish politics*, A. Özerdem and M. Whiting ed., 367–78. Routledge.

Aydıntaşbaş, A. 2019. From myth to reality: How to understand Turkey's role in the Western Balkans. *Policy Brief, European Council on Foreign Relations.*

Babaoğlu, S. 2008 22 milyon Balkan Türkü Meclis'in neresinde? *Hürriyet*, February 15.

BalkanInsight. 2018. Erdoğan vows to help build Serbia-Bosnia highway. January 29.

BBC. 2018. Erdoğan Bosna Hersek'te: Avrupa'nın bize karşı tavrının sebebi oradaki Türklerin dağınıklığıdır. *BBC Türkçe*, May 20. https://www.bbc.com/turkce/haberler-turkiye-44189205.

Bechev, D. 2011. *Constructing South East Europe: The politics of Balkan regional cooperation.* Basingstoke: Palgrave Macmillan.

Bechev, D. 2017. *Rival power: Russia in Southeast Europe.* New Haven: Yale University Press.

Begisholli, B. 2019. Kosovo 'broke law' when deporting Turkish Gülenists. *Balkan Insight*, October 5. https://balkaninsight.com/2019/02/05/kosovo-broke-law-when-deporting-turkish-gulenists -02-05-2019/.

Bieber, F. 2019. *The rise of authoritarianism in the Western Balkans.* Abingdon: Routledge.

Büyük, H.F., and A.E. Öztürk. 2019. The role of leadership networks in Turkey-Balkan relations in the AKP era. *Turkish Policy Quarterly* 18(3): 119–27.

Büyük, H.F. 2018 Erdoğan's Sarajevo rally starts online war-of-words. *BalkanInsight*, May 8. https://balkaninsight.com/2018/05/08/erdogan-s-sarajevo-rally-starts-a-social-media-war-in-bosnia-05-08-2018/.

Bieber, F., and N. Tzifakis, eds. 2019. *The Western Balkans and the World. Linkages and relations with Non-Western countries.* London: Routledge.

Çağaptay, S. 2019. *Erdoğan's empire: Turkey and the politics of the Middle East.* London: Bloomsbury.

Daily Sabah. 2020. Turkey welcomes North Macedonia's NATO accession. March 18. https:// www.dailysabah.com/politics/diplomacy/turkey-welcomes-north-macedonias-nato-accession.

Davutoğlu, A. 2001. *Stratejik Derinlik: Türkiye'nin Uluslararası Konumu.* Istanbul: Küre Yayınları.

Demirtaş, B. . 2015. Turkish Foreign policy towards the Balkans: A Europeanised Foreign Policy in a de-Europeanised National Context? *Journal of Balkan and near Eastern Studies* 20(10): 1–17.

Deutsche Welle. 2016. Report: Turkey's MIT agency menacing "German Turks". *Report: Turkey's MIT agency menacing 'German Turks' | News | DW |.* August 21.

Dursun-Özkanca, O. 2019. 'Turkish foreign relations in the Balkans' in Turkey-West relations: The politics of intra-alliance opposition, 38–62. Cambridge: Cambridge University Press.

Džankić, J., S. Keil, and M. Kmezić, eds. 2019. *The europeanisation of the Western Balkans: Failure of EU conditionality?* Basingstoke: Palgrave Macmillan.

Esen, B., and Ş. Gümüşçü. 2016. Rising competitive authoritarianism in Turkey. *Third World Quarterly* 37(9): 1581–606. doi:10.1080/01436597.2015.1135732

EU Council. 2018. EU-Turkey leaders' meeting in Varna (Bulgaria). March 26. https://www. consilium.europa.eu/en/meetings/international-summit/2018/03/26/.

Freedom House. January 2018. Freedom in the world. *Democracy in Crisis.* https://freedomhouse. org/report/freedom-world/freedom-world-2018.

Hale, W. 2013. *Turkish foreign policy since 1774.* 3rd ed. Abingdon: Routledge.

Hopkins, V., and L. Pitel. January 14 2021. Erdogan's great game: Turkish intrigue in the Balkans. *Financial Times.*

Ibrahim, A. 2018. Varna summit unlikely to bring Turkey and the EU closer. *Al Jazeera*, March 26.

Kirişci, K. 2012. Turkey's engagement with its neighborhood: A 'Synthetic' and multidimensional look at Turkey's Foreign policy transformation. *Turkish Studies* 13(3): 1–23. doi:10.1080/ 14683849.2012.717444

Kirişci, K. 2017. *Turkey and the West: Faultlines in a troubled alliance.* Washington, D.C.: Brookings Institution.

Kadıoğlu, A., K. Öktem, and K. Mehmet, eds. 2012. *Another empire: A decade of Turkey's foreign policy under the justice and development party.* Istanbul: Bilgi Üniversitesi Yayınları.

Ladas, S. 1932. *The exchange of minorities: Bulgaria, Greece and Turkey.* New York: Macmillan.

Lewis, B. 1961. *The emergence of modern Turkey.* Oxford: Oxford University Press.

Mufti, M. 2009. *Daring and caution in Turkish strategic culture.* Basingstoke: Palgrave Macmillan.

Öztürk, A.E. 2001. *Religion, identity and power: Turkey and the Balkans in the twenty-first century.* Edinburgh: Edinburgh University Press.

Öztürk, Ahmet Erdi. 2021. Religion, Identity and Power: Turkey and the Balkans in the Twenty-First Century. Edinburgh: Edinburgh University Press.

RFE/RL. 2017. Turkey's Erdogan gets a warm welcome in Serbia's mostly Muslim Sandžak region. *Radio Free Europe/Radio Liberty,* October 11. https://www.rferl.org/a/turkey-serbia-/28785717.html.

Rrustemi, A. *et al,* et al. 2019. *Geopolitical influences of external powers in the Western Balkans.* The Hague: The Hague Center for Strategic Studies.

Stratulat, C., Kmezić, M., Bonomi, M., Tzifakis, N., Nechev, Z., et al. December 2020. Between a rock and a hard place: Public opinion and the EU integration in the Western Balkans. *Policy Brief. Balkans in Europe Advisory Group (BiEPAG).*

Tanasković, D. 2013. *Neo-ottomanism: A doctrine and foreign policy practice.* Belgrade: CIVIS.

Tugal, C. 2016. *The fall of the Turkish model: How the Arab uprisings brought down islamic liberalism.* London: Verso.

Ülgen, S. July 26 2021. Redefining the US-Turkey Relationship, Paper. *Carnegie Europe.* https://carnegieeurope.eu/2021/07/26/redefining-u.s.-turkey-relationship-pub-85016.

Vasović , A. 2017. Turkey's Erdogan gets warm welcome in mainly Muslim Serbian town. Reuters, October 11.

Vezenkov, A. 2017. Entangled geographies of the Balkans: The boundaries of the region and the limits of the discipline. In *Entangled histories of the Balkans Vol 4: Concepts, Approaches and (Self-)Representations* eds. , R. Daskalov, Mishkova, D., Marinov, T., and Vezenkov, A., et al., ed., 115–257. Leiden: Brill.

Vuksanović, V. 2018. Three lessons from Erdogan's rally in Sarajevo. *LSE Blog.* May 23.

Waldman, S., and E. Çalışkan. 2017. *The New Turkey and its discontents.* Oxford: Oxford University Press.

Yackley, A.J., and K. Hope. 2019. Tsipras seeks to mend Greece's fractious relations with Turkey. *Financial Times,* February 6.

Yavuz, H. 2016. Social and intellectual origins of neo-ottomanism: Searching for a post-national vision. *Die Welt des Islams* 56(3–4): 438–65. doi:10.1163/15700607-05634p08

Yavuz, H. 2020. *Nostalgia for the empire: The politics of neo-ottomanism.* Oxford: Oxford University Press.

Ziraat Bankası. Bankamız Tarihçesi. Accessed September 15, 2021. https://www.ziraatbank.com.tr/tr/bankamiz/hakkimizda/bankamiz-tarihcesi.

Reconstruction of the 'regional power' role during the pandemic: Turkey's COVID-19 diplomacy towards the Balkans

Birgül Demirtaş (iD)

ABSTRACT

The CoViD-19 pandemic has led to a resurgence of health diplomacy in international relations. Especially the great powers and middle powers have provided different kinds of assistance to countries in need and utilized health diplomacy as an opportunity to construct, reconstruct or consolidate their role in regional and global politics. Turkey was no exception with its assertive and ambitious health diplomacy, of which the Balkans were central. Crisis periods have proved critical junctures for Turkish decision-makers to assert their ambitions in the Balkans. This article examines Turkish diplomacy towards the Balkan countries during the CoViD-19 pandemic and examines how Turkish decision-makers reconstructed a 'regional power' identity. Informed by the constructivist theory, the paper critically investigates how Justice and Development Party tried to consolidate Turkey's identity as a regional power in the Balkans. It delves into the following questions: What are the main reasons for Turkey's coronavirus diplomacy towards the Balkans? How are Turkish decision-makers trying to reconstruct Turkey's role as a regional power during the pandemic? What does the Turkish case tell us about the coronavirus diplomacy of the middle powers in general?.

Introduction*

In the early months of the pandemic, Turkey's senior citizens above the age of 65 received a gift package from President Recep Tayyip Erdoğan, consisting of face masks and cologne, as well as a letter from him, in which he stated:

> "As the family of humanity, we are going through a difficult trial during this process of the pandemic. With thanks to God, our country, together with the state and nation, is becoming successful in this trial … During the pandemic, many countries were closed in, and they clung to the limited means at their disposal … We, as Turkey, have fulfilled our own needs, and furthermore, we have provided assistance to many people in many friendly and kin states. In a world in which global solidarity is mentioned a lot but not realised, we, as Turkey,

Turkey is one of the most prepared countries relative to the coronavirusvirus pandemic because of the change and transformation in fundamental service sectors in the last 18 years. Turkey has launched the most powerful general health insurance system in the world and has built the most modern hospitals, and therefore the country is taken as a model by the world . . . . Feel safe; no virus, no pandemic, is stronger than Turkey." (Letter of the President, 2020)

The letter was the central message of Turkey's leadership during the pandemic: praising the Turkish health system reconstructed during the reign of the Justice and Development Party (*Adalet ve Kalkınma Partisi* – AKP) and portraying it as one of the best in the world, giving the image of a self-sufficient Turkey, and creating a picture of a humanitarian Turkey helping other countries in need. During its two decades of government, the AKP has tried to build the image of a powerful and humanitarian Turkey in its foreign policy. CoViD-19 has provided an unprecedented opportunity for the AKP to reconstruct this image.

AKP leadership has used every kind of crisis to create an internal and external identity for Turkey based on the concepts of 'powerful state' and 'exemplary country' during its time in government, and the CoViD-19 crisis is no exception. It has tried to give the appearance that the government is coping with the pandemic so successfully that it does not only fulfil the healthcare needs of its own people but also provides every kind of assistance to many countries around the world, in addition to generously helping the Turkish diaspora abroad.

However, there has been a gap between reality and discourse from the beginning of the pandemic. Some 71,724 Turkish citizens had lost their lives as of 5 November 2021 (Website of Turkish Health Ministry). Turkey has the sixth-highest number of cases in the world (*Countries Where Coronavirus Has Spread*, n.d.). According to the Covid Performance Index of the Lowy Institute, Turkey ranks 72nd out of 102 countries in its performance (Covid Performance Index 2021). Its performance is thus below the median according to this evaluation. In October 2021, nearly every day, almost 30,000 Turkish people were infected with the virus, along with more than 200 people losing their lives. The official numbers are disputed by the Turkish Medical Association and opposition-led municipalities (Türk Tabipleri Birliği 2021; Euronews 2020). Despite the high number of cases and a high death toll, the government tried to show that Turkey successfully dealt with the pandemic.

Meanwhile, CoViD-19 came at a time when Turkey was vying to become a regional power in its neighbourhood, including the Balkans. From the early 1990s onwards, as the bipolar world order and the tight dependencies of the Cold War came to an end, Turkey has been trying to find a new manoeuvring space for itself in its regional policies to play a greater role in the neighbourhood. Turkey's policies during the wars of Yugoslav succession, its initiatives regarding the Black Sea, its policies in the Middle East, and its mediation attempts in different geographies exemplify these attempts. The pandemic has provided yet another opportunity for Turkey to build its agency in the Balkans.

In light of this, this article tries to answer the following research questions: What are the main reasons for Turkey's coronavirus diplomacy towards the Balkans? How are Turkish decision-makers trying to reconstruct Turkey's role as a regional power during the pandemic? What does the Turkish case tell us about the coronavirus diplomacy of regional actors?

The article is based on an analysis of primary sources, such as official websites of Turkish governmental institutions, newspaper sources, and secondary academic sources. It also draws on five interviews conducted with retired Turkish ambassadors and one interview with a former AKP parliamentarian in 2020.

There is an ongoing discussion on how Turkey is performing as a regional or middle power in its neighbouring regions (Öniş-Kutlay, 2017, 164–183; Parlar Dal 2016, 1425–1453, Parlar Dal 2018, 1–31). Under the guidance of the AKP, Turkey aimed to be a regional power as well as a central state. In his book *Strategic Depth*, Ahmet Davutoğlu, former prime minister and minister of foreign affairs, discusses how Turkey can benefit from its history and geography to become a powerful state (Davutoğlu 2001). Although Turkey's assertive regional policies started in the 1990s, the AKP has accelerated this process and tried to launch new initiatives and make Turkey an 'order setter country' in its neighbourhood. Regional powers can be defined as countries that try to play a leadership role in their neighbourhood, who have a claim to regional leadership and instruments to play that role (Parlar Dal 2016).

The Balkans have been one of the regions in which Turkey has tried to play this role through active diplomacy, and the crises proved crucial critical junctures for Turkish decision-makers to start new diplomatic initiatives. This article examines Turkish diplomacy towards the Balkan countries during the CoViD-19 pandemic and explores how Turkish decision-makers constructed a 'regional power' identity. From the lens of the constructivist theory of international relations, the paper critically investigates how the AKP tried to consolidate Turkey's identity as a regional power in the Balkans.

Identity is an inseparable aspect of Turkey's coronavirus diplomacy, as evidenced by the fact that the AKP's policy of providing different kinds of assistance to Balkan countries has been closely associated with discourses on Turkish identity, which the AKP leadership reiterated and reconstructed along with Turkey's place in regional and global politics with its coronavirus diplomacy. The Turkish government has recreated the discourse of 'us' versus 'them.' Because of the emphasis of Turkish leadership on identity when providing help to Balkan countries, this study uses constructivism as its theoretical framework.

The article consists of five parts. In the first part, the constructivist theory will be analysed with regard to the foreign policy-identity nexus. The second part examines the AKP's approach towards the Balkans. Turkey's own coronavirus policies is the topic of the third part, after which the fourth section will analyse the AKP's coronavirus diplomacy towards the Balkans. Lastly, the fifth section will summarize the main findings of the research.

Constructing identity through foreign policy: theoretical framework

Constructivism was the first international relations (IR) theory to focus on the importance of the interaction between identity and foreign policy. Introduced to the IR discipline by Nicholas Onuf in 1989, constructivism argues that not only material forces but also social forces determine the dynamics of world politics. Constructivists generally believe in the importance of norms, rules, identities and language in global politics, but with different ideas on the relative importance of these elements. Some constructivists argue that there is no reality in the world except as constituted by language, some argue for the relevance of norms, and others state the primacy of identity.[1]

The two fundamental characteristics of constructivism can be elaborated as follows: First, the international environment in which states are embedded is to a great extent made up of social factors, not material ones. Second, this social structure is determined by the identities and interests of states (Wendt 1999). As states interact, they gain an identity and attach an identity to others. Indeed, the international aspect of state identity is only one part of the whole picture; domestic factors also define what kind of entity a state would become. When one compares the relative weight of domestic and international factors in determining state identity, for Wendt, state identity is to a great extent established by the international system (Wendt 1999, 20–21). But the important thing at this point is the significance of the concept of 'state identity' for international politics. First, a definition of the concept is needed: state identity consists of 'a set of beliefs about nature and purpose of state expressed in public articulations of state actions and ideals' (Lynch 1998,1999, 349). It is about the definition of a state's rights, obligations and responsibilities, and the meaning attributed to other actors. In a way, it is about setting boundaries between oneself and others: Who are you relative to others? And who are the other actors relative to yourself? (Chafetz et al. 2007, 7)

States have, in fact, two kinds of identities: internal and external. While internal identity refers to a set of understandings within the boundaries of that state among its constituent parts, external identity stands for a state's place among others in international politics. The former can also be labelled as national identity. It is the latter concept that will be used in this paper.

There is an important relationship between state identity and foreign policy. One significant way for states to acquire a new identity or protect the current one is through foreign policy (Kowert 1998,1999, 4). Their interactions with other states are a way of getting themselves accepted as part of a certain international community. Especially during identity formulation or reformulation, foreign policy is a key instrument for decision-makers. Therefore, the constructivist approach is expected to have more explanatory power during periods of new identity creation (Checkel 1998, 346).[2] David Campbell's book *Writing Security: United States Foreign Policy and the Politics of Identity* (Campbell 1998) is an important work that elaborates on how the US identity has been constituted through foreign policy, both during the Cold War and afterwards. Campbell shows that US leadership used perceived dangers in global politics to conceptualize the American identity. The following section will focus on the interaction between Turkish foreign policy towards the Balkans and Ankara's search for identity in the post-Cold War era in light of the constructivist approach.

Turkish foreign policy towards the Balkans and the role of identity

This study attempts to understand how the AKP leadership is trying to construct the identity of the Turkish state in global politics via its active diplomacy towards the Balkan countries during the pandemic. This study hypothesizes that the AKP leadership is trying to create a new identity for Turkey as a strong state that is a guardian for states located in former Ottoman territories and other developing countries.

In the literature, Turkey is generally accepted as a middle power in global politics (Hale 2002; Oran 2001). Especially since the establishment of the BRICS in 2010, there has been an increasing number of works on the importance of emerging powers, rising states and middle powers in global politics, and the declining influence of the US in particular, and the West in general. In that context, it is argued that many regional actors on different continents are trying to play greater roles in international relations. Turkey is one of the MIKTA (Mexico, Indonesia, Republic of Korea, Turkey and Australia) countries that are assumed to pursue active foreign policy in regional and global politics. The Balkans is a key region where Turkish decision-makers are trying to launch new initiatives and play facilitation roles. For historical, geographical and cultural reasons, the Balkans has grown as an important region on the Turkish foreign policy agenda. This section will analyse the main parameters of Turkey's foreign policy towards the Balkan countries.

Turkey's relations with the Balkans have multidimensional characteristics compared to other actors, like the EU, Russia and China, all of which also try to play a role in the region. First of all, Turkey is not an external actor in the Balkans; on the contrary, it is an intrinsic part of the region that also played a historical role in the region's construction. Second, there are humanitarian ties between Turkey and the Balkans. The existence of Balkan-origin citizens of Turkey, as well as Muslim and Turkish populations in the Balkans, create transnational linkages between Ankara and regional countries, making the interaction more multidimensional. For these two reasons, decision-makers in Ankara perceive the Balkans as a region to which Turkey also belongs. Therefore, the AKP elite considers Turkey an actor *in* and *of* the Balkans, which is important in analysing Turkey-Balkan interactions. That is also the main reason why Turkey's Balkan policies include both state and non-state actors as well as political, economic and cultural elements. Municipalities, NGOs connected to the Balkan diaspora in Turkey as well as Turkish companies, who continue to establish close ties with the Balkans, are significant parts of Turkish foreign policy.

Whenever the Turkish minorities and Muslim peoples in the Balkan countries have faced difficulties, decision-makers in Ankara have been interested in helping them and coming up with solutions of their own. For instance, Turkey pursued an active foreign policy during the assimilation campaign in Bulgaria in the 1980s and during the conflicts in the former Yugoslavia in the 1990s. As the most organized group in foundations and associations, Turkey's Balkan-origin citizens have continuously influenced decision-makers to be receptive towards the people in the Balkans. Thus, Turkey is part of the region, and the Balkan identity is one of Turkey's regional identities. Since the end of the Cold War, Turkish decision-makers have emphasized that Turkey has multiple identities. Turkey is not just a European country, but also an Asian, Black Sea, Mediterranean as well as a Balkan country.

The end of the bipolar era has resulted in a radical change in Turkey's interactions with the Balkan countries. The Cold War had provided only limited opportunities for Ankara to establish ties with regional actors. However, after the Berlin Wall fell, there was an increasing interaction between Turkish people and citizens of Balkan countries, and the increasing flows of people across borders strengthened the ties. Indeed, Motherland Party (Anavatan Partisi-ANAP) governments led by Turgut Özal propelled the active Turkish foreign policy in the 1980s. Especially after the Yugoslav wars had spread to Bosnia Herzegovina, Turkey started pursuing a more assertive and vocal foreign policy.

Although the Ottoman past was remembered and glorified in the formulation of the Turkish reaction to the Yugoslavian wars, Ankara acted in harmony with its Western partners, though still launching its own initiatives from time to time.

After the AKP had won the elections of 2002, it promised to make Turkey more active in global politics.[3] The AKP's foreign policy can be divided into two periods: the first decade, between 2002–2012, and the second decade, after 2013. In the first period, the main characteristic of Turkish foreign policy was interdependence, and the foreign policy revolved around 'zero problems with neighbours,' a phrase coined by Davutoğlu. However, in the second period, the AKP has increasingly tried to achieve strategic autonomy by improving relations and aligning itself with non-Western powers (Kutlay and Öniş 2021, 1085–1104).

Basing its foreign policy on the instruments of soft power in the first period, AKP leadership tried to pursue an active foreign policy in the neighbourhood, including the Balkans. Basing its foreign policy on the Europeanization process and its economic credentials, it aimed to interact more with other actors in the Balkans on different levels. The military aspect of this cooperation has also been part of Turkey's regional policy. The Turkish military has extensively contributed to the peacekeeping missions of NATO and the EU in the Balkans, as seen in the cases of IFOR, SFOR, Althea, and EUFOR.

There has been a new impetus in Turkey's regional ties since the second half of the 2000s, as the AKP has tried to develop new initiatives in Southeastern Europe (For a review of AKP's Balkan policies, see Alpan and Ozturk 2022). The Yunus Emre Institute was established in 2007 and began its activities in 2009, contributing extensively to Turkey's cultural diplomacy. The Presidency for Turks Abroad and Related Communities was established in 2010, increasing Turkey's ties with Muslim and Turkish people abroad, including in the Balkan countries. The Turkish Cooperation and Coordination Agency (TİKA), established in 1992 to cultivate Turkey's ties with the Turkic Republics, has become a much more comprehensive institution under the AKP. TİKA's activities now cover almost the whole world. Although TİKA has been famous for its mosque restorations, its activities are much more comprehensive than classical IR literature would suggest. TİKA is providing equipment to schools and hospitals and drinking water supplies to people in the Balkans. In its Annual Report, TİKA stated that it provides help to consolidate Turkey to implement its responsibilities concerning international issues stemming from its historical character and virtuous position (TİKA 2012).

Another of Turkey's important initiatives in the Balkans under AKP reign is its trilateral initiative with regard to Bosnia and Herzegovina. From the perspective of the AKP, Bosnia is one of the key countries in the region; since Bosnia could achieve neither political stability nor economic recovery after the war ended in 1995. Believing that stability in Bosnia could only be possible with contributions from the neighbouring countries of Serbia and Croatia, the AKP initiated a trilateral dialogue with all three of these countries attended by their respective presidents and foreign ministers. Although sensitive problems in Bosnia remain, Turkey's diplomatic initiative has had some limited achievements. However, the politicians in Bosnia are still seeking Turkey's mediation to solve the country's political deadlock. The visits by Bakir Izetbegovic, the head of the Party of

Democratic Action and Milorad Dodik, the Serb member of the Bosnian Presidency, to Turkey in November 2021 to meet President Erdoğan and ask his help to solve the political crisis were important signs of Turkey's importance in regional politics.

The Presidency of Religious Affairs (Diyanet) is another institution that has become an integral component of Turkish foreign policy under AKP rule (Öztürk and Gözaydın 2018). Its budget, personnel and scope of activities have been considerably increased by the AKP leadership. The fact that the AKP has increased the role of Islam in domestic politics – witness the opening of the Imam Hatip Schools; the building of huge mosques in Taksim, Çamlıca and Beştepe; and the increase in the tax on alcohol – has repercussions on foreign policy as well (Uzer 2021, 5–22).

Diyanet has wide-ranging activities in its international relations and a special department dedicated to foreign relations (Dış İlişkiler Genel Müdürlüğü). The former State Minister Mehmet Aydın stated that ' . . . Diyanet's international responsibility is no less important (and difficult) than its responsibility in Turkey.' (Aydın 2008, 168) Diyanet holds annual meetings with heads of religious institutions of the countries in the Balkans. Meanwhile, it has been sending envoys to Turkey's diplomatic representations. It aims to spread the AKP's version of Islam to Balkan countries and increase the religious ties between Turkey and regional countries.[4]

Although Turkey now has wide-ranging institutions in its foreign policy towards the Balkans under AKP rule, this creates a new problem: the coordination of these different agencies. Some interviewees stated that coordinating the activities of these different institutions is a significant challenge and that Turkish decision-makers need to pay more attention (online communication with a former MP of AKP, Interviewee 6, 24 September 2020; online communication with a former Turkish ambassador, Interviewee 3, 19 October 2020; online communication with a former Turkish ambassador, Interviewee 4, 18 September 2020).

Concerning Turkey's economic ties with the Balkans, it can be noted that, although economic relations have increased since the 1990s, Turkey's importance to the Balkans in economic terms is limited compared to that of the European Union member states. Trade volume with Turkey constitutes less than 10% of regional countries' trade volume except Bulgaria, Albania and Kosovo (Hake 2019, 58). In addition, it should be noted that 65% of Turkey's trade relationship with the region consists of low-to-medium-technology goods (Türbedar 2018, 165). With regard to foreign direct investment, Turkish businesspeople have so far mainly invested in Kosovo, Albania and North Macedonia. Turkish investment has a share of 15% in Kosovo and 8% in Albania and North Macedonia (Hake 2019, 57). In other countries, Turkish FDI is quite limited. Statistical information shows that Turkey does not have economic hegemony in the region. Considering Turkey's financial difficulties at home in recent years, its economic role abroad might decline in the years to come.

Meanwhile, the Balkans have become an essential arena for gaining legitimacy in Turkey's tumultuous internal politics. Whatever happens in Turkey has immediate repercussions in the Balkans. Sometimes, these repercussions occur directly through the AKP; sometimes, pro-AKP groups take the upper hand to show their support for Turkey and the AKP. The presidential election campaign in 2018 exemplified the internal-external policy nexus. When several European countries did not allow

Erdoğan to hold rallies before the presidential elections in 2018, it was Sarajevo where he gave his campaign speech. Turks living in different European countries came to the capital of Bosnia to show their support for the AKP leader.

In addition, all the important events within or related to Turkey are directly felt in the neighbouring region. When the Hagia Sophia was turned from museum to mosque in July 2020, the Islamic Union of Montenegro decided to hold gratitude prostration (*şükür secdesi*) in the mosques. (Balkan Günlüğü, 20 Temmuz 2020) Similarly, the Deputy Head of the Islamic Union of North Macedonia has expressed his satisfaction with the decision to open the Hagia Sophia to Islamic prayers (Balkan Günlüğü, 31 Temmuz 2020).

Whenever the AKP faces difficulties in its domestic or foreign policy, it can find support from its supporters in the Balkans. During the Gezi protests in 2013, or after the coup attempt in 2016, various groups took to the streets in multiple countries to show their support for the AKP and Erdoğan. In addition, when Turkish soldiers were killed in Idlib, Syria, religious ceremonies were held in mosques from Sofia to Sarajevo. Similarly, when an earthquake hit Elazığ and Malatya on 24 January 2020 donations were collected after Friday prayer in accordance with the decision of the Islamic Union of Bosnia Herzegovina (Daily Sabah, 31 January 2020).

The same is true for Turkish responses to challenges in the Balkans. When an earthquake hit Albania on 26 November 2019 Turkey was among the first to send emergency aid and relief personnel to the region. In addition, the Ministry of Environment and Urbanism has decided to construct 522 houses in the earthquake-ridden area.

However, there are certain challenges in the AKP's policies towards the Balkans. Six online interviews were conducted in the framework of this study. Five were conducted with former Turkish ambassadors, and one with a former MP of the AKP, who have pointed out certain problems. First of all, Turkey's economic problems, becoming more visible in recent years, were mentioned as a significant limitation in Turkey's international relations. Second, institutional weaknesses and instabilities were cited as another problem (online communication with a retired ambassador, Interviewee 1, 2020).

It is striking that Turkey, as a moderately developed country, has been sending so much aid to its neighbouring countries even when it has been facing a ramping economic crisis. This analysis of the AKP's Balkan policies provides the background for understanding its CoViD-19 diplomacy towards the region. The pandemic started when the AKP had been trying to consolidate itself as a regional power in the Balkans. The following section examines the main dynamics of Turkey's pandemic policies.

Turkey's CoViD-19 experience: images vs realities

The first case of CoViD-19 was reported in Turkey on 11 March 2020. As of November 5th, 71,724 Turkish citizens have lost their lives in the last 20 months. When the pandemic spread to Turkey, the country was already going through a difficult period. While the Turkish lira was depreciating and a severe economic crisis was unfolding, the populist and de-Europeanizing tendencies of the government were becoming more visible. The local elections in 2019 have become an indicator of the

AKP's declining support as the coalition of opposition parties CHP and İyi Party, known as the Nation Alliance (*Millet İttifakı*), has won most of the largest municipalities all over the country (Aksoy 2020).

The declining level of democracy and the weakening of state institutions is evident. According to the Freedom House Index, Turkey is listed as 'Not Free' (Freedom House 2021). In addition, state capacity in Turkey has been declining considerably. According to the leading state capacity indicators, the country has been losing ground with regard to the rule of law, political stability and transparency (Kutlay and Öniş 2020, 22).

The coronavirus crisis has brought the realities of the Turkish health sector to the centre stage. The AKP leadership had carried out a transformation process in the health sector by building grand new city hospitals (*şehir hastaneleri*), which continually faced criticisms from many health authorities, one of them being their unsuitable locations. While these hospitals were built by the private sector with the 'build-operate-transfer' (*yap-işlet-devret*) model, the Turkish Medical Association elaborated corruption and performance problems involved in the construction and operation of these hospitals.

Both President Erdoğan as well as Health Minister Fahrettin Koca have claimed that Turkey is dealing with the pandemic very successfully because of its robust health system.

President Erdoğan, for example, stated:

"In a period in which the health systems of developed countries collapsed—people were dying in their houses, hospital corridors because of insufficient treatment—we should appreciate what we have … . We personally see the importance of being self-sufficient and, beyond that, being at a level to lend a helping hand to our friends. At a time when unions, global structures and international organizations founded with great ideals lost their meaning, Turkey showed its power by standing on its own feet. Of course, behind this success, especially the infrastructure we have established in 17-18 years, especially the steps we have taken during the period of our governments, the works that have been built have great importance." ("Cumhurbaşkanı Erdoğan: Türkiye sağlık hizmetlerinde destan yazdı" 2020)

Similarly, Health Minister Fahrettin Koca stated that the state is dealing with the pandemic successfully and that Turkey would see the end of the pandemic as one of the least affected countries. Arguing that Turkey's strength stemmed from the success of the health system, he claimed that Turkey showed a public-health-service success against the pandemic, something rare in the world.

The construction of the 'strong Turkey image' was the central message of a public relations campaign of the AKP. This has included the transportation of coronavirus-infected Turkish people from abroad via ambulance planes to Turkey with the claim that they were not being treated adequately in European countries. The case of Emrullah Gülüşken, who lives in Sweden, was noteworthy. After he was infected with the virus in Sweden, he was allegedly sent home without receiving proper treatment in the hospital. After his daughters called for help from Turkish authorities via social media, President Erdoğan ordered that an ambulance plane be sent to Malmö, Sweden, to take Gülüşken to Turkey. Reports of this particular transfer were broadcast extensively on pro-government television channels. After his treatment was completed, his following statement was an important sign of the new image the AKP was trying to construct:

"After a successful treatment, I became healthy again. I would like to thank President Recep Tayyip Erdoğan, Minister of Health Fahrettin Koca, Minister of Foreign Affairs Mevlüt Çavuşoğlu and other officials very much. I am proud of being a citizen of this country. There is no other country in the world that transports one of its citizens by private plane and gets him treated free of charge. The Turkish health system is unique in the world." (Kurt 2020)

Thanks to the extensive coverage of the pro-government television channels, the transnational help campaign aimed to address the domestic constituency. However, as this domestic show was going on, there were insufficient beds for Turkish people infected with CoViD-19 in many provinces (BBC News Türkçe 2020).

Turkey's populist and de-Europeanizing political system has been reflected in its struggle against the pandemic. President and AKP leader Erdoğan has frequently referred to 'local and national' (yerli ve milli) policies, a nationalist term AKP popularized. This discourse has had its reflection during the pandemic as well. AKP leadership has claimed that, although this is a global health problem, Turkey's struggle is national since it is trying to overcome this problem by its own means. ('Sorun Küresel Mücadelemiz Ulusal') The question of how a pandemic, an international crisis by its very nature, can be dealt with by means of national policies without the cooperation of other actors is not clear at all. The discourse and the PR campaigns are indispensable parts of AKP policies; thus, the slogan 'global problem, national struggle' reflect their strong nationalist outlook.

In addition, there are other problems with the pandemic policies of the AKP. The issue of face masks has been an important symbol of the lack of planning by the AKP leadership. The government has initially insisted that it would provide face masks to all citizens free of charge; however, the policy did not succeed since many citizens could not get the masks on time. However, at the time when Turkish people did not have access to face masks, Turkey was providing masks to different countries free of charge. After two months of insisting that masks not be sold, the government had to allow the sale of masks throughout the country beginning in May 2020.

The number of infections has become another controversial issue in Turkey. Both the Turkish Medical Association (TMA) and opposition-led municipalities have questioned the official numbers, stating that the actual number of people who died because of the pandemic is much higher than the official numbers. Although there are similar claims and question marks in other parts of the world, the fact that it is the Minister of Health, not an independent institution, who has announced the CoViD-19 infection statistics makes Turkey a 'special' case. Claims of the TMA and mayors of opposition-led municipalities about the actual number of deaths are rejected by the government. However, much official statistical information, such as the rate of inflation and the unemployment rate, is a point of contention in the country,

Turkey's *sui generis* new presidential governmental system has its reflections on its struggle against CoViD-19. After the Gezi Park protest movement in 2013, Turkish democracy took an illiberal turn, reflected in many democracy indexes. In that respect, the government has used the CoViD-19 emergency measures to ban new-year celebrations, prevent mass rallies, and put new limitations on the initiatives of opposition-led municipalities. In other words, the AKP has abused the CoViD-19 precautions to further its political aims and curb the political opposition.

After analysing Turkey's policies towards the coronavirus crisis and reviewing the impact of populist politics on the struggle against the pandemic, the next section will examine Turkey's coronavirus diplomacy towards the Balkans.

Regional powers and identity construction: the case of Turkish coronavirus diplomacy towards the Balkans

In a shifting global order, pandemics play a substantial role in the balance of power politics among great powers. Rivalry in the political and security realms has spread to competition in health diplomacy. During the very time in which states need to cooperate in dealing with the pandemic successfully, competition has predominated over collaboration in many parts of the world. In addition, not only has providing assistance for strategic reasons become the rule, but its advertisement for domestic constituencies and foreign public opinion has also gained importance.

In other words, health diplomacy during the CoViD-19 pandemic has become part of states' public diplomacy and national branding. From China to Russia, different actors are trying to reflect positive images of themselves through their domestic and external policies, as well as trying to upgrade their role in global politics (Kabutaulaka 2021, 254–261; Verma 2020, 248–258; Lee and Kim 2021, 382–396). Health diplomacy is thus not independent of global competition, even during a pandemic.

In this *Zeitgeist*, health diplomacy, mask diplomacy, pandemic diplomacy, CoViD-19 diplomacy and coronavirus diplomacy have become part of the terminology of the international relations literature (Lee and Kim 2021, 392). In her analysis of the pandemics of the 21st century (SARS, H1N1, MERS, Ebola and CoViD-19), Fazal (2020) found that, instead of trying to foster global cooperation, states preferred to make use of bilateral and regional diplomacy. This is an important indication of the weakness of international solidarity during these difficult times. Fazal (2020, E92) emphasizes the fact that there has been no global leadership during the CoViD-19 pandemic, a time in which no state or international organization has been able to play the role of global actor, resulting in a resurgence of geopolitical competition among great powers as well as among regional actors. Hence, as stated by Fazal (2020, E 78), ' ... pandemics also create opportunities for states to pursue foreign policy goals that primarily serve their national interest rather than serving global health.'

During this challenging time, the IR vocabulary has been enriched by health-related concepts from recent years. Fazal (2020, E78) defines 'health diplomacy' as 'international aid or cooperation meant to promote health or that uses health programming to promote non-health related foreign aims.' Meanwhile, 'pandemic public diplomacy' is described as 'state-initiated efforts involving non-state actors and networks aimed at communicating with foreign publics in a health pandemic context through sharing and transmission of material and immaterial resources to mitigate the health threat, foster a positive nation brand, and contribute to healthful global environment' (Lee and Kim 2021, 392). Cuban health diplomacy has been a pioneering example, showing how a country can use its health diplomacy to foster its image (Erman 2016, 77–94), and many others have followed this example. Russia and China are among the key actors in health diplomacy towards the Balkan countries during the CoViD-19 pandemic (Bastian 2020; Bechev 2020).

This study argues that Turkey is another example of a country trying to use the pandemic to improve its regional and global standing by recreating its identity through the discourse of a strong and humanitarian country, as opposed to other actors who were supposedly acting selfishly.[5] The AKP's CoViD-19 diplomacy has been a continuation of its efforts to focus on ex-Ottoman states to further Turkey's role. As the AKP leadership has been trying to construct a new identity for Turkey both in domestic and international politics as a strong, self-sufficient and influential country, the pandemic has provided an opportunity to prove these new role conceptualizations. In other words, Turkey's CoViD-19 diplomacy can be seen as a continuation of its attempts to be a 'great actor' in the Balkans (Öztürk 2020, 63). Throughout the CoViD-19 crisis, Turkey has been one of the most generous countries, providing medical help to 155 countries when, at home, Turkish people did not have access to basic medical equipment and infrastructure. During the early months of the pandemic, when the sale of face masks was forbidden and the complimentary packages sent by the Presidential office could not meet the need, when hospitals were overcrowded with CoViD-19 cases, and patients could not find a bed in intensive care units, the AKP leadership was providing generous help to many countries, including the USA as well as Balkan countries.

Then, how can we explain Turkey's health diplomacy in the case of the Balkans? What are the main motivations, dynamics and causes of the AKP's policies during the pandemic? This section will provide answers to these questions from the perspective of constructivism.

The Turkish Foreign Ministry has published a statement entitled 'Our Role and Mission during the Coronavirus Pandemic' (*Koronavirus Salginindaki Rol ve Vizyonumuz*, n.d.), in which Turkey's 'success' in the fight against the pandemic was emphasized with a clear focus on the role of the President, whose name was mentioned seven times in a one-page declaration. According to the Ministry's statement, the 'strong leadership' of the President, his instructions and his negotiations with other leaders had played an important role in Turkey's allegedly effective handling of the crisis. Praising Turkey's health infrastructure and its struggles, the Ministry claimed that other world leaders had asked the opinion of President Erdoğan concerning the pandemic. The Ministry tried to foster the image of strength in Turkey's health sector as follows:

> "At the national level, our institutions and society have realized the seriousness of the situation at an early stage under the shrewd leadership of our President, and thanks to the measures taken, the entry of the epidemic into our country has been delayed as much as possible. After the arrival of the epidemic, our country has successfully maintained its resistance against this serious disaster thanks to the opportunities offered by the health and physical infrastructure." (*Koronavirus Salginindaki Rol ve Vizyonumuz*, n.d.)

In April 2020, Turkey sent face masks, medical wares as well as test kits to five Western Balkan countries via a military cargo plane: Serbia, Bosnia Herzegovina, North Macedonia, Montenegro and Kosovo. Table 1 summarises Turkish aid during the pandemic towards the Balkans. On the aid packages appeared the following words of the famous Anatolian poet Mevlana Jalaluddin Rumi: 'There is hope after despair and many suns after darkness.' It is also important to note that the label of 'The Presidency of the Republic of Turkey' was put on all aid packages sent to the region, symbolizing that the

Table 1. Turkey's medical aid to the Balkans during the pandemic.

Date	Sending Institution	Receiving Country	Type of Aid
April 2020	Turkish state	Serbia, Bosnia Her., Kosovo, N. Macedonia and Montenegro	masks, medical wares and test kits
April 2020	Turkish state	Albania	six ambulances
April 2020	Turkish Embassy in Bucharest in coop. with Turkish Businessmen Association (TİAD)	Romania	medical aid
July 2020	Saruhanlı Municipality (Manisa)	Kırcaali (Bulgaria)	medical aid
July 2020	Mamak Municipality in cooperation with Yunus Emre Institute	Novi Pazar (Serbia)	medical aid
July 2020	Altındağ Municipality (Ankara)	Novi Pazar (Serbia)	medical aid
August 2020	Bursa Metropolitan Municipality (in coop. with businesspeople and NGO's)	Sancak (Serbia)	medical aid
October 2020	Turkish businesspeople and Prizrenliler Association	Prizren (Kosovo)	ambulance and respirator

Source: Compiled from the Turkish press by the author. This is not a complete list of Turkish medical aid but merely a sample of it.

aid was sent through the President. In the Turkish press, it was emphasized that President Erdoğan himself instructed to send the aid. (Balkanlar'a Türkiye'den korona ile savaş yardımı 2020; Gül 2020).

The pandemic has also provided an arena for Turkish leadership to consolidate the concept of 'the European other.' Ömer Çelik, the spokesman of the AKP, stated that Europe was not providing any help, but it was Turkey that was sending aid to Balkan countries during the pandemic. He stated that

"They would say, 'Turkey's growing influence in the Balkans must be prevented.' They spoke with a political ignorance that did not know of Turkey's historical ties to the Balkans. Now they have left the Balkans to their own devices. Turkey is there. The only goal of some European countries regarding the Balkans was to break the influence of Turkey. When the Balkans have needs in relation to the virus epidemic, none of them seems to be around. On the other hand, Turkey delivers aid to the Balkan countries at the most difficult time. What Turkey did alone, the EU could not do for Italy and Spain or for the Balkan countries. Turkey, as a deep-rooted and powerful European state, in addition to all its other dimensions, shows that it is the guarantor of European geography. Europe cannot be defined without Turkey." ('Koronavirüs', 2020)

Therefore, the new identity of Turkey, created step by step after the Gezi movement started in 2013, was brought to the forefront with the pandemic. However, it is also interesting to note that the same spokesman has labelled Turkey as a strong and rooted European country and the insurer of the European geography. Çelik also argued that Turkey represents the heart of the global conscience (Balkan Günlüğü, 2020). This is a reflection of the AKP's new and conflictual identity-creation process. Çelik's statement shows that Turkey perceives Europe as a rival, meanwhile referring to Turkey as a European country. This discourse provides a clear example of the AKP's complex relations with Europe: In Çelik's statement, Europe appears both as the other and an intrinsic part of Turkish identity. Hence, it can be noted that Turkey's CoViD-19 diplomacy has become another instrument to further Turkey's complex relationship with European identity and European actors.

During the coronavirus crisis, the Sandzak region of Serbia, in which Bosniaks constituted the majority, suffered a lot due to weak health institutions. The president of the national assembly of the Bosniaks in Sancak, Jasmina Curic, asked for help from Turkey's President in July 2020, as a result of which Erdoğan called his Serbian counterpart, Alexander Vucic, and asked him to provide support.

Turkey also provided help to Bosniaks in Sandzak through various channels, one of them being municipalities. It is noteworthy that mayors of the AKP reflected the discourse of the Party at the local level and tried to consolidate Turkey's identity as a regional power. Alinur Aktaş, Mayor of Bursa, stated that

"During the pandemic, the medical assistance provided by our country to different countries of the world is also appreciated. While we continue our struggle with the world at the same time, the aid we send to countries in need also shows the strength of our country. To combat CoViD-19, our brothers living in the Sancak region of Serbia sent a letter to our President, Recep Tayyip Erdoğan. With the instruction of our President, health supplies have started to be collected, to be sent to this region, from all over Turkey. We also send the materials supplied in Bursa." (" BBB BILGI 2020)

It is also interesting to note that Turkey's coronavirus diplomacy has been used for domestic purposes, and pro-government newspapers provided the main channel for that. One of the pro-government newspapers has published statements of Turkish ambassadors in some Balkan and European countries who praised Turkey's struggle against the virus and explained how Turkey had been followed and praised by Balkan countries. Turkish ambassadors' self-praise is an important indicator of how the government boosts its legitimacy. (Haykır 2020)

The list compiled above shows the multidimensionality of Turkish aid. During the pandemic, not only the Turkish state but also municipalities, NGOs, and businesspeople provided aid. This is an indication of the complexity of Turkish-Balkan ties.

This section found out that Turkey has been one of the countries that tried to use CoViD-19 as an opportunity to improve its regional and global actorness like Russia and China. Using its coronavirus aid policy in the Balkans as an instrument to increase its soft power in the region and internal support within the country, AKP leadership aimed to give the image of a 'powerful' country.

AKP's coronavirus diplomacy has a meaning in terms of Turkey's Europeanization process as well. Although the De-Europeanization process has speeded up, Europeanization has already impacted Turkey's Balkan policies (Demirtaş 2015). Turkey has been inspired by the EU foreign policy based on soft power. The increasing multidimensionality shows that the aid campaign is another niche area for Turkey to further its influence via soft power instruments.

In addition, Turkey's historical "love and hate relationship" with the EU is visible during the pandemic as well. AKP Spokesman Ömer Çelik's following statement is a sign of how Turkish leadership show Europe as the other of Turkey, however at the same time try to prove Turkey's European identity: 'What Turkey did alone, the EU could not do for Italy and Spain, or for the Balkan countries. Turkey, as a deep-rooted and powerful European state, in addition to all its other dimensions, shows that it is the guarantee of the European geography. Europe cannot be defined without Turkey' ('Koronavirüs', 2020). Hence, Turkey's complex relationship with the European identity can be perceived as Turkey otherwise and simultaneously glorifies Europe during the pandemic.

Conclusion

Pandemics present an important challenge for global actors. Although states need cooperation more than ever to minimize the impact of pandemics at the national and global levels, many actors perceive them as an opportunity to increase their standing in regional and international politics. CoViD-19 is no exception. Many great powers and regional actors use them as important opportunities to consolidate their identities and as a public diplomacy tool. Therefore, an important number of actors provided different kinds of assistance to countries worldwide, accompanied by a discourse addressed to local and international public opinion, of being a great actor.

Turkey's CoViD-19 diplomacy presents a critical case study to analyse how a regional actor tries to reconstruct its identity in a time of health crisis. This study examined Turkey's coronavirus diplomacy towards the Balkan countries from the perspective of constructivist theory. Believing in the central role of identity in international relations, one of the main arguments of constructivism is the nexus between foreign policy and identity. Constructivists argue that states construct their identities by pursuing a foreign policy. Turkey under the AKP government presents an interesting case for constructivism because the AKP leadership tries to build a new identity for Turkey in global politics as a regional power, strong state and model country, hence trying to achieve external legitimacy to consolidate its/a populist regime internally.

The study showed that Turkey had pursued active diplomacy towards the neighbouring Balkan region during the pandemic when the AKP decision-makers also tried to consolidate Turkey's regional-power role in the region. By making Turkey one of the first countries to send aid to regional countries, AKP leaders, ambassadors, and mayors used discourse to praise Turkey. That discourse did not always reflect reality. Therefore, the paper stated that the construction of a new identity has a direct connotation in domestic politics in the Turkish case. On the one hand, many Turkish people infected with the virus could not have timely access to quality health services, while on the other hand, Turkish leadership tried to convey the image that Turkey's health sector is one of the best in the world.

Turkey's de-Europeanization process has increased the AKP's discourse on being a great power. To achieve legitimacy in domestic politics, it has been resorting to the discourse of 'great country' that has been offering assistance to many countries in need. Therefore, the internal-politics dimension of AKP's pandemic diplomacy should be underlined. The AKP elite has to argue uninterruptedly that Turkey plays a vital role in different regions to win the support of the Turkish public.

It is also noteworthy that the pandemic occurred at a time when there were multiple problems in the accession process of the Western Balkan countries. As Alpan and Öztürk argued in the introduction of the special issue, 'The pace of Europeanisation in the region is not very coherent and expeditious either. No significant momentum in terms of the EU accession has emerged after the Thessaloniki Summit for a long time' (Alpan and Ozturk 2022). Therefore, we can argue that this suspended Europeanization provided an ample space for Turkey's coronavirus activism.

The article also provides a case study of a regional actor seeking to benefit from a global health crisis in order to consolidate its own power at the national and global levels. This article contributes to the literature in several ways. First, it analyzes how Turkey's diplomacy towards the Balkans has changed during the pandemic by showing that the AKP tried to recreate a 'great country' image. Second, the findings of the study also have repercussions for the literature on regional powers. The study shows that pandemics provide an opportunity for regional powers to exert their influence in competition with other actors. Hence, at the very time when bilateral, regional and global cooperation is needed at most to minimize the impact of the pandemic; reconstruction of 'powerful country' identity takes precedence.

Notes

1. For some studies comparing and contrasting different constructivist approaches, see Birgül Demirtaş-Coşkun, *Turkey, Germany and the Wars in Yugoslavia: A Search for Reconstruction of State Identities*, Berlin, Logos Verlag, 2006; Hans-Martin Jaeger, 'Konstruktionsfehler des Konstruktivismus in den internationalen Beziehungen,' *Zeitschrift für Internationale Beziehungen* 3, no. 2 (1996): pp. 313–340; Ronen Palan, 'A World of Their Making: An Evaluation of the Constructivist Critique in International Relations,' *Review of International Studies* 26, no. 4 (October 2000): pp. 575–598; Maja Zehfuß, 'Sprachlosigkeit schränkt ein Zur Bedeutung von Sprache in konstruktivistischen Theories,' *Zeitschrift für Internationale Beziehungen* 5, no. 1 (1998): pp. 109–137.
2. Checkel, 'The Constructivist Turn in International Relations Theory,' p. 346.
3. For an analysis of the changes during the AKP see Başak Alpan and Ahmet Erdi Öztürk, Turkey and the Balkans: Bringing the Europeanization/De-Europeanization Nexus into Question, *Southeast European and Black Sea Studies* Vol, 22, no: 1, 2022 (forthcoming).
4. A former Turkish ambassador states that Diyanet's activities in foreign policy are not in line with Turkey's secular characteristics. He argues that Diyanet's policies have negative impacts, even in countries like Bosnia Herzegovina, in which the majority of the population consists of Muslims. He argues that in the face of increasing radical Islam in the Balkans, Diyanet's policies are a burden for Turkey. Online communication with a retired Turkish ambassador 6, 22 September 2020.
5. AKP has been implementing health diplomacy as a soft power instrument for some time. For a review of health diplomacy in the world and in Turkey see Mehmet Fatih Aysan and M. Fehim Paluluoğlu, Sağlık Diplomasisi. In *Dönüşen Diplomasi ve Türkiye. Aktörler, Alanlar, Araçlar*, ed. Ali Resul Usul and İsmail Yaylacı. . 259–286. İstanbul: Küre, 2020.

Acknowledgement

I would like to dedicate this article to the lovely memories of my grandmother Vasfiye Avcı Kılıç, my aunt Kıymet Kılıç, as well as our dear relatives Kısmet Akyol and Sabahattin Avcı.

Disclosure statement

No potential conflict of interest was reported by the author(s).

ORCID

Birgül Demirtaş (iD) http://orcid.org/0000-0002-3214-1081

References

Aksoy, H. 2020. Turkey and the coronavirus crisis: The instrumentalization of the pandemic for domestic and foreign policy. *IEMED Mediterranean Yearbook*. 240–43.

Alpan, B., and A.E. Ozturk. 2022. Turkey and the Balkans: Bringing the Europeanisation/ De-Europeanisation Nexus into Question, *Southeast European and Black Sea Studies*,22,no: 1 (forthcoming).

Aydın, M. 2008. "Diyanet's Global Vision", *The Muslim World*. 2-3: 164–72. 2–3 10.1111/j.1478-1913.2008.00216.x

Aysan, M.F., and M.F. Paluluoğlu. 2020. Sağlık Diplomasisi. In *Dönüşen Diplomasi ve Türkiye. Aktörler, Alanlar, Araçlar*, ed. Ali Resul Usul and İ. Yaylacı. İstanbul: Küre, 259–86.

Bastian, J. 2020. The role of China in the Western Balkans during the CoViD-19 Pandemic. In *The CoViD-19 Pandemic in the Balkans: Consequences and Policy Approaches*, ed. V. Esch, and V. Palm., Aspen Institute Germany: Sprintout Digitaldruck GmbH: 50–56.

BBB BILGI. (2020, August 18). *Bursa'nın yardım eli Sırbistan'a uzandı*. Bursa Büyükşehir Belediyesi. https://www.bursa.bel.tr/haber/bursanin-yardim-eli-sirbistana-uzandi-29205

BBC News Türkçe. 2020. Koronavirüs: Doktorlar 'CoViD-19 yoğun bakım yatakları doldu, servislerde yer kalmadı' uyarısı yapıyor. November 13. https://www.bbc.com/turkce/haberler-turkiye-54935115

Bechev, D. 2020. CoViD-19 and Russian Influence in the Western Balkans. In *The CoViD-19 Pandemic in the Balkans: Consequences and Policy Approaches*, ed. V. Esch, and V. Palm, 57–62. Germany: Aspen Institute, Sprintout Digitaldruck GmbH.

"Balkanlar'a Türkiye'den korona ile savaş yardımı." 2020. *Balkan Günlügü, Weekly Newspaper*, 13 April.

Campbell, D. *Writing Security, United States Foreign Policy and the Politics of Identity*, Manchester, Manchester University Press, 1992

Chafetz, G., M. Spirtas, and B. Frankel. 2007. "Introduction: Tracing the Influence of Identity on Foreign Policy," *Security Studies* 8, no. 2–3, 7–22. 10.1080/09636419808429372

Checkel, J.T., 1998. "The constructivist turn in international relations theory", *World Politics* 50, no. 2. 324–48 10.1017/S0043887100008133

Covid Performance Index. 2021. Lowy Institute. https://interactives.lowyinstitute.org/features/covid-performance/#overview

Countries where Coronavirus has spread. (nd.). Retrieved 15 January 2022, from https://www.worldometers.info/coronavirusvirus/countries-where-coronavirusvirus-has-spread/

Daily Sabah, 2020. *Bosnians collect donations for quake victims in Turkey*. 31 January.

Davutoğlu, A., 2001. *Stratejik Derinlik, Türkiye'nin Uluslararası Konumu*, İstanbul, Küre.

Demirtaş, B., 2015. "Turkish Foreign Policy toward the balkan neighborhood: a europeanised foreign policy in a de-europeanised national context?", *Journal of Balkan and near Eastern Studies*, 17:123–40. 2 10.1080/19448953.2014.994283

Demirtaş-Coşkun, B., (2006). *Turkey, Germany and the Wars in Yugoslavia: A Search for Reconstruction of State Identities*, Berlin, Logos Verlag.

Erdoğan, Recep Tayyip *Letter of the President*. 2020 Ankara: Türkiye Cumhuriyeti Cumhurbaşkanlığı-Office of the President.

Erman, K., 2016. Sessiz ve Etkili: Küba'nın Tıp Diplomasisi. *Uluslararasi Iliskiler*, 48: 77–94. 10.33458/uidergisi.463048

Euronews, 2020. İmamoğlu: Türkiye için açıklanan günlük CoViD-19 ölümlerinin 50 kadar fazlası İstanbul'da. November 15. https://tr.euronews.com/2020/11/14/imamoglu-turkiye-icin-acklanan-gunluk-covid-19-olumlerinin-50-kadar-fazlas-istanbul-da

Faaliyet Raporu, T.İ.K.A., 2012, http://store.tika.gov.tr/yayinlar/faaliyet-raporlari/faaliyet-raporu-2012.pdf;www.tika.gov.tr

Fazal, T., 2020. Health diplomacy in pandemical times. *International Organization*. 74 Supplement: E78–E97. S1 10.1017/S0020818320000326

Freedom House. 2021. https://freedomhouse.org/country/turkey/freedom-world/2021

Gül, K., 2020. "Türkiye'nin gönderdiği tıbbi yardım 5 Balkan ülkesine ulaştı", *Anatolian News Agency*, 8 April. https://www.aa.com.tr/tr/dunya/turkiyenin-gonderdigi-tibbi-yardim-5-balkan-ulkesine-teslim-edildi/1797725

Hake, M., 2019. Economic Relations between Southeast Europe and Turkey. *Südosteuropa Mitteilungen*, 59: 46–63.

Hale, W., 2002,*Turkish Foreign Policy*, 1774–2000, London, Frank Cass. https://www.bbc.com/turkce/haberler-turkiye-52459231https://www.worldometers.info/coronavirusvirus/countries-where-coronavirusvirus-has-spread/

Haykır, F., *"Türkiye'nin Coronavirüs ile mücadelesi Avrupa ve Balkanlar'a örnek oldu"*, Sabah, 16 Mar 2020

Jaeger, H.-M., "Konstruktionsfehler des Konstruktivismus in den internationalen Beziehungen," *Zeitschrift für Internationale Beziehungen* 3, no. 2 (1996): pp. 313–40

Kabutaulaka, T., 2021. China's CoViD-19 Diplomacy and Geopolitics in Oceania. *Georgetown Journal of International Affairs*, 2: 254–61. 2 10.1353/gia.2021.0037

Kowert, P.A., (1998–1999). "National Identity: Inside and Out," *Security Studies* 8: 1–34. 2–3 10.1080/09636419808429373

Kurt, M., 2020. "İsveç'ten getirilen Türk hasta devlete minnettar", *Anatolian News Agency*, 16 July. https://www.aa.com.tr/tr/koronavirus/isvecten-getirilen-turk-hasta-devlete-minnettar/1912319

Koronavirüs: Türkiye hangi ülkeye ne kadar yardım gönderdi? (2020, April 28). *BBC News Türkçe*. https://www.bbc.com/turkce/haberler-turkiye-52459231

Koronavirus Salginindaki Rol ve Vizyonumuz. (nd.). T.C. Dışişleri Bakanlığı. Retrieved 15 January 2022, from https://www.mfa.gov.tr/koronavirus-salginindaki-rol-ve-vizyonumuz-6-11-2020.tr.mfa

Kutlay, M., and Z. Öniş. 2021. "Turkish foreign policy in a post-western order: Strategic autonomy or new forms of dependence". *International Affairs*. 97:1085–104. 4 10.1093/ia/iiab094

Lee, S.T., and H.S. Kim. 2021. Nation-branding in CoViD-19 era: South Korea's pandemic public diplomacy. *Place Branding and Public Diplomacy*. 17: 382–96. 4 10.1057/s41254-020-00189-w

Lynch, M., 1998–1999. "Abandoning Iraq: Jordan's Alliances and the Politics of State Identity", *Security Studies*, 8, no. 2–3. 347–88 10.1080/09636419808429382

Öniş, Z., and M. Kutlay. 2017. "The dynamics of emerging middle-power influence in regional and global governance: The paradoxical case of Turkey", *Australian Journal of International Affairs*, 71: 164–83. 2 10.1080/10357718.2016.1183586

Öniş, Z., and M. Kutlay. 2020. The anatomy of Turkey's new heterodox crisis: the interplay of domestic politics and global dynamics. *Turkish Studies*, Online version. doi:10.1080/14683849.2020.1833723

Onuf, N.G., 1989. *World of Our Making: Rules and Rule in Social Theory and International Relations*, Columbia: University of South Carolina Press.

Oran, B., (ed.), 2001, *Türk Dış Politikası*, Kurtuluş Savaşından Bugüne Olgular, Belgeler, Yorumlar, İstanbul, İletişim.

Öztürk, A.E., 2020. Turkey's activities in the Balkans during the CoViD-19 Crisis. In *The CoViD-19 Pandemic in the Balkans: Consequences and Policy Approaches*, ed. V. Esch, and V. Palm., Aspen Institute Germany: Sprintout Digitaldruck: 60–64.

Öztürk, A.E., and İ. Gözaydın. 2018. A Frame for Turkey's Foreign Policy via the Diyanet in the Balkans, *Journal of Muslims in Europe*, 7, 331–50. 3 10.1163/22117954-12341370

Online communication with a retired ambassador Interviewee 1, 2020. 21 September.

Palan, R., 2000. A World of Their Making: An Evaluation of the Constructivist Critique in International Relations. *Review of International Studies* 26: 575–98. 4 10.1017/S0260210500005751

Parlar Dal, E., 2016. Conceptualising and testing the 'emerging regional power' of Turkey in the shifting international order. *Third World Quarterly*, 37: 1425–53. 8 10.1080/01436597. 2016.1142367

Parlar Dal, E., 2018. Profiling Middle Powers in Global Governance and the Turkish Case: An Introduction, in E.P. Dal (ed.), *Middle Powers in Global Governance. The Rise of Turkey*, London: Palgrave.1–31.

Sağlık Bakanlığı, T.C., CoViD-19 Bilgilendirme Platformu, https://covid19.saglik.gov.tr/ (accessed on 29 October 2021).

Sözcü. 2020. İşte Türkiye'nin yardım etmediği tek ülke. April 9. https://www.sozcu.com.tr/2020/gundem/iste-turkiyenin-yardim-etmedigi-tek-ulke-5737404/

"Sorun Küresel Mücadelemiz Ulusal. Turkish Ministry of Health. https://www.saglik.gov.tr/TR,64342/sorun-kuresel-mucadelemiz-ulusal.html

Tabipleri Birliği, T., 2021. Sağlık Bakanlığı açıkladığı CoViD-19'a bağlı resmi ölüm rakamlarının gerçeği yansıtmadığını kabul etmiştir. June 25. https://www.ttb.org.tr/haber_goster.php?Guid=d74ff024-d5ba-11eb-891e-1ee00b95cb3b

TRT Haber, "Cumhurbaşkanı Erdoğan: Türkiye sağlık hizmetlerinde destan yazdı". 2020 *Habertürk*. 20 April. https://www.trthaber.com/haber/gundem/cumhurbaskani-erdogan-turkiye-saglik-hizmetlerinde-bir-destan-yazdi-477631.html

Türbedar, E., 2018. "*Balkanlar'ın Ekonomisi, Ticari ve Finansal Yapısı*", B.D. Şaban Çalış, and E. Balkanlar'da Siyaset, Eskişehir: Anadolu University Publication.

Uzer, U., 2021. "Making sense of Turkish foreign policy: What can international relations theory offer?". *The Review of International Affairs*. 72/1181, p. 5–22. 10.18485/iipe_ria. 2021.72.1181.1

Verma, R., 2020. China's Diplomacy and changing the CoViD-19 Narrative. *International Journal*. 2: 248–58. 2 10.1177/0020702020930054

Wendt, A., 1999. *Social Theory of International Politics*, Cambridge, Cambridge University Press.

Zehfuß, M., "Sprachlosigkeit schränkt ein Zur Bedeutung von Sprache in konstruktivistischen Theories," *Zeitschrift für Internationale Beziehungen*, 5: 109–37 1998.

Turkish foreign policy in the Balkans amidst 'soft power' and 'de-Europeanisation'

Başak Alpan and Ahmet Erdi Öztürk

ABSTRACT
Since the beginning of the 2000s, extensive academic research has echoed one popular opinion, 'Turkey is back to the Balkans'. These studies have been scrutinizing the complicated role of Turkey in the Balkans, usually drawing upon the use of soft power by the former. This impact in the region remained intact during the 2010s, although the overall Turkish foreign policy in the 2010s has been highly securitized and de-Europeanized, losing its soft power character that had been its trademark starting from the early 2000s. In this regard, this paper aims to decipher different dimensions of Turkey's foreign policy in the Balkans through a more general exploration of the de-Europeanization of Turkish foreign policy in the 2010s. Through more than 80 semi-structured interviews, which were conducted between 2016–2020, with political actors, diplomats, religious leaders, scholars and journalists in Turkey and the Balkans, we address the question of whether the divergence of Turkish foreign policy from a soft power perspective and its concomitant de-Europeanization tendency had been crystallized in its policy towards the Balkans within the context of the 2010s.

Introduction

'I would easily argue that Turkey is back in the Balkans during the AKP period.'

These are the words of Bulgarian Grand Mufti Dr Mustafa Hadzhi from our interview back in April 2017. Alongside Dr Hadzhi's clear argument, 'Turkey's back in the Balkans' had been the slogan used quite extensively to denote Turkey's increasing cultural, political and religious influence in the region, focusing on the soft power approach epitomized by excessive use of religion and nationalism and investments as well as through personal links between Turkish President Recep Tayyip Erdoğan and various Balkan leaders (Öztürk, 2021b). Indeed, Turkey has been associated with a thorough soft power approach in its foreign policy orientation starting from the early 2000s within the context of the 'zero problems with neighbours' policy of the ruling Justice and Development Party (*Adalet ve Kalkınma Partisi* – AKP) and Turkey's newly assumed leadership role in the East as a 'regional power and global force' (Davutoğlu 2011). This soft power approach had been substituted with a more securitized foreign policy perspective in the 2010s intertwined with a process what is called in the literature as *de-Europeanization*, which denotes a lesser and more limited Europeanization context. In this respect, the main argument of this paper is that Turkey's soft power foreign policy perspective remained intact in the Balkans in the 2010s. Nevertheless, due to Turkey's de-Europeanization in domestic governance, Turkey's soft power in the Balkans has taken a particular form in the 2010s, highly endowed with religious, nationalist, economic and neo-patrimonialist elements.

Turkey's foreign policy approach to the Balkans and the overall shifts and changes in Turkish foreign policy (TFP) had been thoroughly studied in the literature. Oft-debated topics in this respect include the authoritarian transformation that the incumbent AKP underwent (Başer and Erdi Öztürk 2017; Yılmaz and Bashirov 2018) as well as the institutional and normative distancing from the ideas of Europeanization (Aydın-Düzgit and Kaliber 2016; Alpan 2016; Kaliber and Kaliber 2019). The Balkan states' distancing from the ideals of liberal democracy due to populist right-wing leaders and institutional inadequacy has also been a common issue of debate (Bieber 2018; Lavrič and Bieber 2021). The way in which these transformations interacted, Turkey's aggressive and overdose use of religion and nationalism in foreign policy, and the positive and negative reactions to this development in the Balkans are among the key issues discussed in a multifaceted manner (Öztürk and Akgönül 2019; Szerencsés 2021; Noutcheva and Aydin-Düzgit 2012; Athanassopoulou 1994; Tanasković 2012; İçduygu and Sert 2015). Nevertheless, it is worth exploring in particular how Turkey's soft power approach in the Balkans could be located within the country's overall foreign policy trends and de-Europeanization claims, which forms the main crux of the article. In addition to this endeavour, the article will examine three dimensions of Turkey's soft power approach in the Balkans in the 2010s: a) *Normative soft power* (the use of religion, synthesized with nationalism), b) *material soft power* (Turkey's economic investments into various state and non-state-oriented apparatuses in the Balkans) and, finally, c) *personalized soft power* (use of neo-patrimonialism in light of the bilateral relations maintained by leaders and their inner circles).

Methodologically, this work relies on a rich ethnographic study conducted between 2016 and 2020. This ethnographic study utilized a series of interviews conducted with political and social elites in both Turkey and the Balkans between 2016 and 2020 and discussions held with experts over the internet after the first quarter of 2020. The primary reason why the study was not conducted directly in the region over the past year is mainly the restrictions on travel and face-to-face interviews due to the COVID-19 pandemic. A total of 83 face-to-face interviews were conducted in Turkey, Kosovo, North Macedonia, Albania, Bosnia-Herzegovina, Serbia and Bulgaria. These interviews featured clergymen, politicians, state officials and prominent members of the community. Additionally, interviews were held over the internet with 20 regional experts to better understand Turkey's changing role in the region during the era of COVID-19. This study also utilizes the official data from state sources, primarily on the economic relationship between Turkey and the Balkans.

The article will be divided into four main sections. The first section will examine the general contours of the TFP in the 2010s with a particular focus on the shift from the soft power perspective of the 2000s to the rather securitized hard power foreign policy orientation that had been prevalent in the 2010s. In the second part, we will pay particular attention to the Europeanization/de-Europeanization nexus within the context of TFP during the 2010s, which would lay ground to understand Balkan-Turkish relations in the same era. The third section will shed light on the historical background of Balkan-Turkish relations stretching from the Ottoman period until the AKP era and reveal how these relationships followed a degree of historical continuity. The fourth section will describe in detail the three dimensions of Turkey's soft power approach in the Balkans, as mentioned above. All these sections will predominantly benefit from the data of the ethnographic field study. Last but not least, the conclusion will discuss what the findings of the research tell us regarding both Balkan-Turkish relations and a more global context.

TFP in the 2010s: From a soft power approach to a security-oriented perspective

To start with, two diverse yet interlinked processes had been characterizing the TFP during the 2010s. As will be detailed in the forthcoming section, whereas Europeanization and European Union (EU from now on) accession had still been a significant agenda item of the TFP, it has been dramatically transformed into a security-oriented one that once more resorts to hard power and coercive diplomacy (Aknur and Durmuşlar 2019, 1356). Although such a security-centred approach dominated TFP throughout the 1990s, there was a dramatic shift in the 2000s towards more cooperative, liberal policies, which was termed as 'Europeanisation'. Throughout the 1990s, Turkey's relations with neighbouring states, including Iraq, Iran, Syria and Greece, significantly deteriorated due to their support for the PKK. This led Turkish governments to confront neighbouring states with military measures. However, starting from the mid-2000s, the AKP's 'zero problems with neighbours' policy and Turkey's newly assumed leadership role in the East as a 'regional power and global force' (Davutoğlu 2011) dovetailed with the EU's push for democratic reforms, which were still deemed as credible led to the 'Europeanisation and de-securitization of TFP' (Aknur and Durmuşlar 2019, 1356). Turkey's region-focused activism in the 2000s drew on the construction of a particular foreign policy identity that defined Turkey as a peace-promoting soft power bearing the capacity for 'instituting order' (Davutoğlu 2009) in its surrounding regions, namely the Middle East, the Balkans and the Caucasus. In this context, Turkey's policy towards its neighbourhood aligned with the EU's 'soft power' approach and employed resources such as 'cultural attraction, ideology, and international institutions' (Nye 1990, 167). Ankara attempted to establish peaceful and harmonious relations with its neighbours during this period. Yet, by the beginning of the 2010s, TFP had drastically shifted away from Europeanization and transformed its liberal policies back to security-oriented policies (Oğuzlu 2016).

The main turning point towards securitization was the transformation of the uprising in Syria into a civil war in the early 2010s. The shared 900-km border increased Turkey's security concerns related to revived PKK (The Kurdistan Workers' Party) terror and attacks by ISIS members entering the country alongside millions of Syrian citizens seeking refuge (Ayata 2014, 95–96). The nuclear deal that the five permanent members of the United Nations Security Council (UNSC) plus Germany (P5 + 1) signed with Iran in 2015 concerning Iran's nuclear program brought the possibility of Iran playing a much more decisive and assertive role in the region (Oğuzlu 2016, 63) plus the increased ISIS and PKK attacks leading to the death of many Turkish citizens. These all seem to demonstrate a realist readjustment process taking place in TFP. Things reached a whole new level when Turkey intervened in northern Syria after the attempted coup of 2016 and did so again early in 2018 (Tziarras 2018, 597). In August 2016 and January 2018, Turkey launched two military operations in northern Syria (Operation Euphrates Shield and Operation Olive Branch) with the objective of cleansing areas close to the border with Turkey of terrorists, including the PYD (Democratic Union Party)/ YPG (People's Protection Units International) and ISIS (Torun 2021, 334). The tremendous domestic turbulence that followed the coup attempt led to a 'belligerent foreign policy' with efforts made by authoritarian elites to divert popular attention from internal problems (Coşkun, Doğan and Demir 2017, 89). Concerning Operation Euphrates Shield, the then EU High Representative Javier Solana (2017) stated, 'the US and the EU are concerned about Turkey's attacks against the PYD, given its central role in pushing back the Islamic State' (cited in Torun 2021, 334). Similarly, regarding Operation Olive Branch, the then EU High Representative Federica Mogherini raised EU's concerns about Turkey's further operations in Syria, which might fuel up instability in the region (Aktan 2018). 'The bottom line is that TFP during the 2010s became increasingly revisionist and -as some could argue- expansionist' (Tziarras 2018, 597).

Europeanization/de-Europeanization of TFP in the 2010s

'It is better for us to host a pro-EU Turkey in our territories since it gives Turkey more credit in regional issues'

These words belong to one of the senior foreign ministry officers from Kosovo (dated back to October 2018), which have been echoed numerously by other interviewees in the region. Therefore, it is essential to scrutinize Turkey's EU journey to understand its role in the Balkans. Since the 1999 Helsinki decision, when Turkey was granted EU candidacy, Europeanization has been one of the leading conceptual approaches through which EU–Turkey relations have been examined. According to the seminal conception of the term by Radaelli, Europeanization is 'a process of construction, diffusion and institutionalization of formal and informal rules, procedures, policy paradigms, styles, ways of doing things, and shared beliefs and norms which are first defined and consolidated in the making of EU decisions and then incorporated in the logic of domestic discourses, identities, political structures and public policies' (Radaelli 2003, 320). As far as the EU–Turkey relations are concerned, Europeanization could be explained as the transformation of the way in which Turkish institutions, policies and 'way of doing things' are constructed and implemented to ensure Turkey's overall convergence towards EU standards (Alpan 2021, 108). Along this vein, Tonra explains the Europeanization of foreign policy as ' ... transformation in the way in which national foreign policies are constructed, in the way in which professional roles are defined and pursued and in the consequent internalisation of norms and expectations arising from a complex system of collective European policy-making' (Tonra 2013).

Therefore, Europeanization had also been the dominant trend in the post-Helsinki period as far as the TFP was concerned. This foreign policy approach had mainly been in the form of civilianization and initiatives taken for settlement of conflicts with Greece and Cyprus and aligning with the CFSP *acquis* (Aydın and Açıkmeşe 2007). Another essential point in the Europeanizing TFP is that Turkey has begun participating in the EU-led NATO operations. In time, Turkey has become the fifth-largest contributor to the EU force. Also, Müftüler-Baç and Gürsoy argued that 'Turkey's willingness to contribute to European security after 2003 shows that the Turkish military and government still support taking joint decisions with other European countries, at least for operations that draw upon NATO assets and provide for the security of the continent' (Müftüler-Baç and Gürsoy 2010). In other words, in the late 2000s, the security concerns of Turkey had close parallels with the EU's approach, especially in respect to the 'zero problems with neighbours' approach dominant in foreign policy.

Nevertheless, the post-2005 period has been characterized by a downturn in EU–Turkey relations and growing disenchantment on both sides. The notion of so-called *de-Europeanization* has entered the agendas of the EU studies for the last ten years or so to explain 'deterioration of the quality of integration or more simply as "it is worse than it was"' (Domaradski 2019, 221) for the candidate states as well as the member states. *De-Europeanization* is broadly defined as 'the loss or weakening of the EU/Europe as a normative/political context and a reference point in domestic settings and national public debates' (Aydın-Düzgit and Kaliber 2016, 6). This period of de-Europeanization in Turkish politics was mainly marked by 'the downturn in EU-Turkey relations and the growing disenchantment by both sides' (Aydın-Düzgit and Kaliber 2016, 1). Two important practical implications of the depreciation of the EU conditionality and the de-Europeanization process at the Turkish domestic scene had been the reduction of EU-Turkey relations on issue-based cooperation in various fields such as migration and energy and the concomitant selective Europeanization where policy reforms continued more as a continuation of the government's political agenda rather than as an attempt of harmonization with EU legislation (Alpan 2021, 126). Although the growing scepticism and indifference towards Europe, and even a turning away from European project in many spheres of politics and society, would not necessarily indicate a fully-fledged de-Europeanization (Alpan 2016, 16), the prospect of revisiting the European project emerged.

The conceptual framework of de-Europeanization with regard to Turkey had been studied thoroughly in many various fields such as domestic politics (Alpan 2016; Aydın-Düzgit 2016; Cebeci 2016; Ökten-Sipahioğlu 2017), civil society (Kaliber 2016; Boşnak 2016), gender equality policy (Soyaltın-Collela and Süleymanoğlu-Kürüm 2021), the rule of law (Saatçioğlu 2016), media freedom (Yılmaz 2016), education policy (Onursal-Beşgül 2016), citizenship policy (Soyaltın-Collela and Akdeniz-Göker 2019) and migration policy (Kaya 2021). Although studies on de-Europeanization of the TFP are rare (see Rodoplu 2019; Ovalı 2015 for good examples), other concepts such as 'divergence' (Torun 2021) or 'anti-Western populism' (Kaliber and Kaliber 2019) had also been used to denote the depreciation of the EU as a foreign policy anchor in this period.

This turning away from the EU anchor had been intertwined with Turkey's descent into authoritarianism. Various domestic and foreign elements accelerated this process and fuelled the authoritarian twist such as the Gezi Park protests, the failure of the Kurdish peace process, the contestation between the AKP and the Gülenists and, last but not least, the failed coup attempt on 15 July 2016 in which the Gülen Movement is known to have played an essential role (Esen and Gümüşcü 2017; Yavuz and Erdi Öztürk 2020). This wave of authoritarianism endowed the AKP with populism, mainly through the use of religion instrumentally and objectively and stark opposition to the West. In this context, Turkey pushed itself to pursue a more religious, nationalist and aggressive foreign policy in the latter half of the 2010s, relatively weakening its historical relationship with the West. Although this situation helped the AKP consolidate its base of electoral support in domestic politics (Öztürk 2021a), it caused many political circles to raise eyebrows and deterioration of bilateral political relationships with Europe as elsewhere.

Thus, during this period, it was also possible to observe a process of de-Europeanization in the realm of TFP. The 2010s and the course of Arab Spring, in particular, proved to create an unpredictable turn. With the Arab Spring, Ahmet Davutoğlu's foreign policy and claim to be the mediator began to crumble in the same place it began: The Middle East, primarily within the course of turbulent regime changes in Egypt and Syria (Vuksanovic 2017). Turkey committed a series of miscalculations in its approach towards Syria, believing that the regime would collapse within a few months in the face of mounting societal opposition and international pressures (Kösebalaban 2020, 341). As Öniş points out, 'Turkey has over-engaged itself in Syria, contributing to further instability and undermining both its own interests and its international image in the process' (Öniş 2014, 211). Turkey's 'trade-oriented' and soft-power approach in foreign policy has been replaced by a 'security-oriented' one (Tziarras 2018, 597). The Syrian politics of Turkey demonstrated that it was drifting away from the soft power of diplomacy and dialogue and the EU norms (Rodoplu 2019, 5).

Another aspect of the de-Europeanization of the TFP in this period was the hijacking of the EU conditionality in foreign policy by the migration crisis. The EU had followed the 2015 refugee crisis–*Turkey Deal*[1] of 18 March 2016 which implied enforced border-control measures by Turkey and a strict re-admission of refugees trying to reach the EU territories via Turkey. The visa liberalization process, which had earlier been introduced as a strong tool for Turkey's compliance with the EU *acquis* in the field of migration, was instrumentalised through this Deal and turned into a 'bargaining chip' (Kaya 2021) between Turkey and the EU, contributing to issue-based cooperation between Turkey and the EU (as already discussed above) and a concomitant de-Europeanization trend.

The 2010s also witnessed Turkey and the EU having clashes over the Cypriot and Turkish drilling activities in the Eastern Mediterranean. The ongoing tension between Ankara and Athens over gas reserves and maritime rights in the East Mediterranean has flared up in July after Turkey put out a Navtex that it was sending its Oruç Reis research ship to carry out a drilling survey in waters close to the Greek Island of Megisti (Kastellorizo). The specific route of Oruç Reis provided the East Mediterranean quarrel - already escalating since 2019- with a tripartite structure, the other two footings being the Cyprus issue and the Aegean dispute (Alpan 2020). After a video conference on 14 August, the EU foreign ministers issued a declaration, reaffirming the EU's full solidarity with Greece and Cyprus and underlining that sovereign rights of EU member states must be respected (EEAS 2020). It has also been aired many times by EU High Representative Josep Borrell that Turkey's drilling activities in the East Mediterranean might face punitive measures.

All in all, Turkey's de-Europeanization in domestic governance has had a direct effect on the ways in which Turkey's *soft power* has taken form in the 2010s. The link between domestic politics and foreign policy is an extensive theoretical debate going beyond the limits of the research questions of this paper. Nevertheless, it suffices to say that Turkey's descent into authoritarianism in the domestic sphere led to a more radical recalibration of the TFP, characterized mainly by the re-inscription of the West as the 'other' of Turkey (Kaliber and Kaliber 2019, 2). This foreign policy discourse has introduced the 'essentially different and morally higher Islamic' Turkish self-vis-à-vis the essentially inferior and threatening Western other (Alaranta 2015, 31). Added to this picture was the securitization of relations with neighbour countries such as Syria and Greece, which led to the reshaping of Turkey's soft power approach, endowed with more intense references to religion, nationalism, personal links with the political leaders and economic ties. There cannot be a better realm than the Balkans to project this varied soft power approach, which the following sections will scrutinize.

Setting the background of a multifaceted and intricate relationship: Turkey and the Balkans

'Ottoman Empire was a Balkan Empire, but Turkey is an independent state. Therefore, Turkish policymakers should understand that they are not representing the Ottoman Empire anymore. Indeed, using culture, history, language, and religion are the main tools of the contemporary foreign policy, but having hegemonic and imperial desires is a different issue.'

In our interview in 2018, one of the leading scholars of the University of Sofia's Political Science Department underlined the relationship between the Ottoman Empire and Turkey as such, pointing out the need on the part of Turkey not to act like its predecessor in the region. Indeed, various studies about the history of the relationship between the Ottoman Empire and the Balkans focus on various aspects of this relationship. One of the most significant points underlined in these studies is the particular characteristics of imperialist and Western identity of the Ottoman state, rendering the acquisition of territory, political influence and networks of economic relations in the Balkan geography possible, mainly through cultural and religious interaction (İnalcık and Faroqhi 1997; Mazower 2001). This argument also gets confirmed when we consider that the collapse of the Ottoman Empire began with its loss of influence in the Balkans and that the foundation of the Republic of Turkey became possible thanks to the efforts of military officers coming from the Balkans. It is worth noting here that there are significant differences between how the Balkan states and Turkey describe this case during the Ottoman era.

After the foundation of the Turkish Republic, the rapid and relatively permanent rectification of 'problems of the past' between Turkey and the Balkan states mainly owed to Turkey's determination of its own position and regional role from a realist perspective. Turkey defined itself as a medium power and sought to maintain good relations with both Western and Eastern powers (Çalış and Bağcı 2003). Turkey had never abandoned the Balkans but pursued diplomatic relations as equal nations. The wave of migration that began during the Ottoman era and continued into the early Republican era undoubtedly nourished the religious, cultural and economic relations between Balkan and Turkish societies (İçduygu and Sert 2015). This situation persisted consistently throughout the Cold War era, even though Turkey diverged with many Balkan states, including Yugoslavia, on different issues.

The first breaking point in Balkan-Turkish relations appeared after the 1980s when Turgut Özal came to power with his Motherland Party (*Anavatan Partisi*-ANAP) and through the impact of the Cold War (Demirtaş, 2013). It was also underlined by a North Macedonian member of parliament in late 2019:

'For the Balkan people, Özal always stays in a different and special position because of his close relations with us'.

The Balkans had a special position in the foreign policy that Özal crafted by integrating - though to a limited extent- economics, culture and religion. Many Muslim and non-Muslim thinkers, politicians and religious figures in the region have noted that Özal's Turkey maintained relatively closer relations with the Balkan region than before. During the Özal era, it is clear that Turkey engaged with the Balkans through official diplomatic channels and introduced controversial structures to the region, such as the Gülen Movement (Rašidagić and Hesova 2020). However, Özal's sudden death, the complexities that emerged at the end of the Cold War and the convoluted nature of Turkey's domestic politics caused Turkey to become an actor perceived to a relatively lesser extent in the Balkans in the 1990s. Nevertheless, Turkey always sought to make its presence in the region known in such situations as the Bosnian War and other special issues. In the 1990s, for example, Turkey maintained its top-down and bottom-up diplomatic work through its mobilization of many transnational apparatuses – particularly the Diyanet – in countries such as Bosnia, Serbia, North Macedonia and Albania. We can assert that Turkey's use of its soft power, public diplomacy efforts and fostering of relations with the regional public dates back much earlier than the AKP era and are remnants of the circumstances that formed particularly during the Özal era.

However, the AKP and Erdoğan occupy a unique position in the region. Almost all the individuals we spoke to during the fieldwork articulated that Erdoğan and his associates know the region very well and that their good relations in the Balkans have persisted in a multifaceted manner since the 1990s, as confirmed by one of the local imams from Serbian Sandžak region back in March 2016:

'We knew Erdoğan before the 2000s, and I can say that even when he was a mayor of Istanbul, he was dealing with the issues of the Balkans.'

Moreover, ever since he served as the Istanbul mayor, Erdoğan has been working with individuals from the Balkan region or who have family ties to the area. This contributed to his reputation in the Balkans and familiarized him with the region. After coming to power, Erdoğan's economic development program and the pro-Europe language he employed and his claim that democracy and religious freedom could co-exist elevated his profile to an attractive position for the Balkan people, who were eager to 'return to' Europe in search of economic growth. For example, in a 2018 interview with former Albanian Foreign Minister Genc Polo, he argued:

'Erdoğan, the pro-Europe entrepreneur, was one of the most important partners for the Balkans in the early 2000s.'

Numerous political actors reiterated this sentiment. With the impact of this positive environment, Turkey began to assume a more active role in the region through institutions such as the Diyanet, TIKA (Turkish Cooperation and Coordination Agency) and the Yunus Emre Institute. It was certainly not only through these institutions that Turkey began to amass influence during this period. In this context, structures emerged in the region that operated as education institutions and student dormitories and worked on other matters relating directly to the local communities.

It would be difficult to claim that this atmosphere disappeared and was fully inverted after 2010. During our research in the region, we witnessed how perceptions of Turkey varied, with most of the Muslim political elite viewing the AKP's Turkey positively while others harboured suspicions. However, despite this apparent difference, two points and related ruptures were echoed as primary determinants of the Balkan-Turkish relations in recent years by almost all interviewees: Turkey's own domestic politics, as well as the departure of Turkey and the Balkans from the ideals of the EU respectively, have an influence on the relations between two parties in the 2010s, the period we now turn to.

Turkey and the Balkans in the 2010s: rupture or continuity?

As already scrutinized above, TFP in the 2010s has mainly been shaped by various developments and the novel policy tools adopted by the foreign minister, Ahmet Davutoğlu, who assumed the position in 2009. Coming from an academic background, Davutoğlu sought to implement in TFP the concepts he had adopted in his own line of thinking. In his view, Turkey should be elevated to a key role by implementing a proactive foreign policy, first in the region and then elsewhere in the world. The country should achieve this elevation in global affairs by being bound to the religion, culture, and other normative values it had inherited from the Ottoman Empire (Özkan 2014). Irrespective of whether this view was successful or not, it indicated a breaking point for the Balkans. While the Turkish public thought that Turkey's presence in the Balkans grew as a result of the historical ties, it was claimed in the Balkans, particularly by the elites, that Turkey was once again seeking to establish a hegemony like it had during the Ottoman period or was transitioning towards a neo-colonialist policy (Bebler 2017). Political figures throughout the region certainly began to articulate this viewpoint more frequently. For example, between 2016 and 2018, when Davutoğlu was still a member of the AKP and somewhat maintained his influence, most of our interviewees claimed that Davutoğlu's doctrine failed to understand the sensitivities of the Balkans, was crafted through calculations of Turkey's domestic politics and excessively used elements of soft power.

This period has also witnessed Turkey's rapid departure from the ideals of the EU and the descent into authoritarianism, as already scrutinized in previous sections. In this respect, Turkey's overall de-Europeanization at the domestic level has had a direct effect on the ways in which Turkey's *soft power* has taken form in the Balkans in the 2010s. A former government minister whom we interviewed in Albania in 2018 confirmed this view:

'In the past, there was a more democratic Turkey, one that had close relations with Europe. I would like to say that this was the case during Erdoğan's initial years. But the chemistry has changed; now, there is a more oppressive Turkey that lacks good relations with the West. Turkey is certainly a part of us – we still have many economic, cultural and political ties. But we would like to see not this Turkey but the other Turkey as an active partner in our region. There are certainly many actors in the Balkans who like and want this new Turkey.'

This quote demonstrates the degree to which Turkey's domestic politics and its corresponding relations with the EU are important in its relationship with the Balkans, as already discussed in the previous section. Nevertheless, Turkey's soft power approach still lingering in the Balkans is confirmed by almost all of our interviewees, which is epitomized through three dimensions, which we will scrutinize in the following section.

Turkey's 'soft power' in the Balkans: three dimensions

Normative soft power: the use of religion synthesized with nationalism

During our fieldwork, it did not go unnoticed while discussing Erdoğan's Turkey that the issue is mostly stirred for activities conducted in the domain of religion. Most of our Muslim interviewees were relatively pleased with Turkey's implementation of a religious foreign policy synthesized with nationalism, while our non-Muslim interviewees found this approach excessive. Additionally, some Muslim actors expressed that the growing element of religion in foreign policy after 2016 was somewhat more than necessary. For example, a Kosovar Muslim political actor, interviewed online platform in 2020, said:

'The fact that Turkey has introduced both religion and nationalism into every activity it has conducted in the region in recent years has compelled people to ask the question of how and in what manner any policy will be produced if not through the use of religion and nationalism. Moreover, some groups define this policy as Islamist foreign policy, which is not very good for Turkey's image in the region.'

As we mentioned above, this viewpoint is not too uncommon, but there is a clear precedent for this. As has been already scrutinized above, Turkey began to directly assume a more active role in the Balkans in the 1990s through official and unofficial religious institutions. Turkey's Diyanet began to establish various bureaucratic and official representative offices as well as craft agreements throughout the Balkans, particularly in Bulgaria, Albania and North Macedonia. Additionally, structures such as the Gülen Movement and the Sulaimani Jamia began operating in the region as a natural result of the need arising after the Cold War. In the Balkan region, where nationalism and religion are such important elements (Aktürk and Lika 2020), these initiatives were met with relative appreciation in the 1990s and early 2000s. As a result, these institutions, directly and indirectly, served the Muslims in the region. There are three underlying reasons for Turkey's use of religion synthesized with nationalism in its recent foreign policy in the Balkans.

Firstly, the economic predicament that grew after 2011 in Turkey's domestic policy precipitated a loss of power for Turkey's ruling party, whose desire to preserve its electoral base compelled AKP elites to adopt a foreign policy synthesized with nationalism domestically and internationally. We can call this *the boomerang effect* (Liotta 2002). The AKP used the influence it had engendered in the Balkans through religion and its mass support to explain how powerful Erdoğan had become in domestic politics. For example, Erdoğan was able to hold rallies in Bosnia before elections, and he sought to demonstrate to the Turkish public that he was preserving Islam – or, more accurately, the Islam of Turkey – internationally by putting into operation mosques that TIKA and the Diyanet had restored in Serbia's Sanjak region. This undoubtedly relates to the reflection in the Balkans of the global struggle Turkey entered with Saudi Arabia, the United Arab Emirates, Iran and other Muslim countries.

Secondly, on a more international note, when populist and oppressive regimes began to administer the AKP's Turkey and the Balkans, as was noted above, the more instrumental use of religion began to emerge. This situation is fundamentally consistent with the historical practice of some authoritarian leaders' using religion as a tool of domestic and foreign policy. Similar examples are found in Muslim regions and elsewhere in the world (Kuru 2019; Koesel 2014). As these countries further departed from the ideals of the EU, they began to use religion more often and more excessively. We reached this conclusion following the interviews we conducted with political elites, and this is an indicator of how religion was used as a political force.

Last but not least, the use of religion synthesized with nationalism as a tool of foreign policy in the Balkans, especially after 2015 and 2016, is a struggle experienced within Turkey and s over its borders (Öztürk, 2019). The contestation between the AKP and the Gülen Movement that had mainly been prevalent after 2012 culminated in the bloody coup attempt in Turkey on 15 July 2016(Öztürk 2018), and the Gülenists were forced to disperse themselves throughout the diaspora following this process (Watmough and Erdi Öztürk 2018; Yavuz 2018). Although this has been reflected everywhere in the world, the circumstances in the Balkans also spread into the realm of religion. The most fundamental reason for this was the fact that the Gülenists were already quite influential in the Balkans, whom the AKP desired to pacify through religion, Turkishness and other identity-based discourses. For example, an important figure in Albanian politics interviewed in 2020 argued:

'After 2014, the two movements accused one another of not being Muslim, of fraud, especially after 2016. This eventually carried the political struggle to the mosques and the religious organisations.'

This essentially summarizes the interviews we conducted as well as our fieldwork. AKP governments, while coercing the Balkan countries to outlaw the activities of the Gülenists, seek to leave no place for the movement in the relatively civil religious space. While doing so, it uses the Diyanet, an official state apparatus, and religious organizations that have indirect relationships with the AKP. It has begun to establish relationships with local umbrella religious institutions and community organizations and demonstrate its own religious reach in the region. It is worth noting that this excessive use of religion and nationalism pleased prominent segments of society in the Balkans that espoused Islamic values such that these largely deterministic policies do not have an entirely pejorative dimension.

The material soft power: Turkey's economic investments in the region

'Turkey and its institutions thankfully have always been by our side. Through floods, earthquakes and other natural disasters, it is always Turkey that is first to run to us. Additionally, Halkbank, Ziraat Bank and other institutions are here with us. Your Turkey is here in more areas than I can count. We can see its investments. Believe me, these are not new, but they began to become more visible in the AKP era.'

The above quote came from an Orthodox clergyman we met with in 2017 in the North Macedonian capital of Skopje. This and similar views have spread through nearly all the Balkan states. We can comfortably say that the economic dynamics during the AKP era constituted one of the main elements of Balkan-Turkish relations. The direct investments in the Balkans constitute the most important leg of Turkey's economic presence in the region. Since the 2000s, there has generally been an increase in Turkey's investments in the Balkans. In 2016, a total of $200 billion in investments from Turkey entered 11 countries in the region. This was the highest investment total after the amounts recorded in 2011, 2012 and 2015, respectively (Ekinci 2017, 8–19).Additionally, Turkey provides direct and indirect investments to the region through TIKA, the Yunus Emre Institute, the Diyanet, TOKI and similar institutions. In this regard, Turkey has been developing its own foreign trade capacity while strengthening its connections with the Balkans in various manners.

The economic relations Turkey crafted in the Balkans during the AKP era after 2002 can be divided into two separate policies: one that was maintained directly through state apparatuses and another that was maintained through commercial operations with business leaders close to the state. In this regard, we can actively see organizations such as Cengiz Construction and Albayrak Holding, which are close to the state or to AKP members, in sectors ranging from construction to telecommunications (Öztürk 2021a, 118). This certainly pertains to the balances in Turkey's domestic politics and the outward reflection of these balances. It is evident based on this background that Turkey is making itself more visible in the region through indirect and direct investments while maintaining aid activities to guarantee its influence over various segments of society. And although this may allow Turkey to be perpetually visible in various domains in one way or another, Turkey engages in economic activity in the backdrop of the European Union and countries such as the United States, United Kingdom, China and Russia. However, this does not mean that Turkey lacks influence or is ineffective. The trade Turkey maintains with Western Balkan states constitutes only a small amount of the €145 billion ($165 billion) of foreign trade with the European Union; its visibility is, in fact, very high.

For example, although Turkey's share of Serbia's foreign trade represents only 3.5% of the total, it has managed to enter the ten countries that have the highest levels of trade, almost going completely unnoticed (see Pacariz 2022 in this volume). Additionally, in Serbia, Turkish construction firms are building 20 electric power stations that they will subsequently operate. Turkey is among the top three countries for foreign trade with Kosovo (see Hoti, Bashota and Sejdiu 2022 in this volume). However, the economic crisis Turkey encountered after 2018 has had a negative impact on these figures. The Turkish lira's loss of value resulted in a negative impact on the expenditures of the Turkish government, and many experts concur that this situation severely limited the resources that Turkey had allocated for its activities in the Balkans. But although it may appear that Turkey's economic recession will reduce its investments in the Balkans, Turkey's influence still seems to be significant in the region, according to our observations and the data at hand. However, two basic problems emerge in this regard.

The first problem becomes apparent when comparing Turkey's economic investments with those of the EU and the United States in that it has relatively fewer investments that are aimed at producing added value and are future-oriented. Turkey, which typically operates more often in the construction sector and similar fields, works in the Balkan economic space through direct and indirect assistance from the government, originating from its domestic authoritarian structure. Under these circumstances, it does not compete directly with countries with much larger economies such as China and the United Kingdom.

The second problem relates to the direct and indirect economic assistance that Turkey has made through the state rather than economic investment. In this context, we find statements and impressions regarding Turkey's engaging in operations that pertain more often to Sunni Muslim societies or to issues that relate directly to them. During the interviews we conducted in 2017, the head mufti of Bulgaria said that Turkey had provided them with both financial and immaterial support during the AKP era, while Bektashi Leader Baba Mondi, whom we interviewed in Tirana, complained that they had not received any support despite their requests. Prominent among the basis for this difference is the identity change that Turkey has experienced domestically.

Personalized soft power: neo-patrimonialism and leadership-based relations

Turkey increasingly started to be defined as a neo-patrimonial country after 2013 and especially after 2016, placing Erdoğan at the centre and, concurrently, his family and inner circle growing stronger in proximity to him (Uğur-Çınar 2017; Yılmaz and Bashirov 2018; Cengiz 2020). As it further distances itself from the EU, Turkey has ignored criteria such as merit and entitlement and instead been governed through an understanding of politics that is administered domestically and internationally through the notion of leadership proximity. This reinforces the decisiveness of the leader. While this certainly does not create a greater degree of decisiveness in political relations with more developed, Western nations, it does have a certain predictive value in Balkan states in which strong men are in power and the ruling administration determines the foreign policy. And the influence that Erdoğan has engendered over the Muslim population in the Balkans represents a greater element of pressure over these leaders. Bosnia and Herzegovina, Serbia and Bulgaria are among the most striking examples in this context. We discussed above both how Turkey used religion and nationalism as an instrument in these countries and which groups rose to economic prominence. The matter of proximity to the leaders of these countries is relevant in all these cases. However, there are varying determining factors in these countries.

On 20 May 2018 when Erdoğan and the Office of the President in Turkey were unable to receive permission to hold political rallies in European capitals, Bosnia and Herzegovina and Bakir Izetbegovic, one of the country's prominent politicians, hosted Erdoğan. In the venue where he held a political rally, Izetbegovic referenced Erdoğan, claiming that God had sent him to the Muslims. This discourse indicates deeper connections than a mere populist slogan. The field research we conducted in the region demonstrates a more profound degree of collaboration between Erdoğan's family and that of Izetbegovic that ties their countries together. On the one hand, Turkey actively uses state institutions and banks in Bosnia and Herzegovina through the support of the Izetbegovic family, and on the other hand, Izetbegovic receives support from Erdoğan and his family in his own domestic politics. For example, Izetbegovic's family members host the openings of structures and institutions that Turkey has restored. Bakir Izetbegovic's wife Sebija resides as the director of the Sarajevo City Hospital, which TIKA put back into operation. Although the cases we highlighted may appear to be purely symbolic, the leaders and their relatives clearly occupy key positions of power structures starting from decision-making mechanisms at the highest peaks of the state spreading downwards. Moreover, these leader-oriented understanding of governance discursively and materially support one another.

In this context, we can say that an intricate relationship has emerged between Balkan leaders and Erdoğan. While Balkan leaders attended special celebrations, including wedding ceremonies, for Erdoğan's family, Erdoğan also was present as a key guest on occasions that Balkan leaders sought to use as political propaganda. It is clear that Balkan leaders have established some degree of proximity with Erdoğan in a rhetorical and image-based sense. The blazer jackets they wear, their discourse regarding making their countries great and powerful and the populist language they most often use demonstrate their political similarities. Additionally, their support for major projects and their desire to develop their countries in fields such as construction that provide little added value also highlights the practical dimensions of this similarity.

Conclusion

The Balkans have always been a significant region for TFP. While the region was ruled by the Ottoman Empire until the nineteenth century, since the foundation of the Republic, it has been a neighbouring region of the country with deep-running historical, cultural and social ties. This geographical and cultural proximity has been the pretext of what had been dubbed as 'Turkey is back in the Balkans', a motto which had preoccupied the TFP agenda since the 2000s. This article, departing from the claim that TFP had clearly deviated in the 2010s from its soft power approach, intertwined with a twist of de-Europeanization, argued that this divergence had been crystallized in a particular way in Turkey's approach to the Balkans during the same period. The de-Europeanization trend in Turkish politics as well as in the TFP (mainly intertwined with rising authoritarianism in the country) led to a soft power approach in the Balkans endowed with highly nationalist, religious, economic and neo-patrimonialist elements. Through more than 80 semi-structured interviews with political actors, diplomats, religious leaders, scholars and journalists in Turkey as well as in the Balkans, the article aimed to explore the crux of Turkey's soft power in the Balkans by deciphering various dimensions of soft power. The salience of soft power approach to the Balkans mainly owed to the use of religion synthesized with nationalism within the relations (*normative soft power*) and Turkey's economic investments in the region (*material soft power*) as well as neo-patrimonialism and personal relations between President Erdoğan and the political leaders in the region (*personalized soft power*). This thorough analysis is crucial to underline that soft power is not always that 'soft' and should be scrutinized more critically and always with a pinch of salt. Theoretically speaking, *soft power* exists when a country becomes attractive to a wide range of actors where the influence is fielded. Our field research showed that Turkey's *soft power* showed itself in the Balkans through the three dimensions elaborated above. Nevertheless, some respondents also pointed out the lack of it (such as the Bektashi leader who complained about not taking any support from Turkey). Therefore, there could always be a dissonance between the analytical framework we use to understand *soft power* and its practical use.

On a different note, the main takeaway of the interviews in the region proved to be that the aforementioned trend of de-Europeanization on the part of Turkey would run the risk of detaching the country from the Balkans as well, debilitating its influence and reliability in the region. Another crucial finding of the interviews has been that TFP in the region is never deemed only about foreign policy. Our respondents perceived the domestic developments in the Turkish political scene to boil down to Turkey's foreign policy approach to the Balkans. This is not a new story since Robert Putnam already argued back in 1988 that domestic politics and international relations are often inextricably entangled, and (the then) existing theories -particularly 'state-centric' ones do not adequately account for these linkages (Putnam 1988). All in all, the way in which Turkey's foreign policy approach to the Balkans, as well as other regions, is intermingled with the domestic factors and political processes is a task that definitely deserves particular attention, which needs to be scrutinized in further research endeavour.

Note

1. The Deal, which was announced by the European Council and Turkey, aimed to end irregular migration from Turkey to the EU, stipulated that 'all new irregular migrants crossing from Turkey into Greek Islands as from 20 March 2016will be returned to Turkey' and 'for every Syrian being returned to Turkey from Greek Islands, another Syrian will be resettled from Turkey to the EU taking into account the UN Vulnerability Criteria' (European Council 2016).

Acknowldgement

Authors would like to thank Senem Aydın-Düzgit and Kemal Kirişçi for their valuable comments on the earlier versions of this article.

Disclosure statement

No potential conflict of interest was reported by the author(s).

Funding

For this research, Başak Alpan benefited from funding offered by the Jean Monnet Network, 'Linking the Europe at Periphery (LEAP)', supported by the European Commission (Project number: 612019-EPP-1-2019-1-TR-EPPJMO-NETWORK).

References

Aknur, M, and T. Durmuşlar. 2019. Turkey's changing security environment and transformation of Turkish foreign policy. *Dokuz Eylül Üniversitesi Sosyal Bilimler Enstitüsü Dergisi* 21, no. 4: 1355–76. doi:10.16953/deusosbil.567894.

Aktan, S. 2018. AB'den Türkiye'ye Suriye Çağrısı: Tek Taraflı Askeri Adım Atmayın. *Euronews*, available at: https://tr.euronews.com/2018/12/17/ab-den-turkiye-ye-suriye-cagrisi-tek-tarafl-askeri-adim-atmayin (accessed December, 2021).

Aktürk, Ş and I. Lika. 2020. The puzzle of Turkish minority representation, nationhood cleavage, and politics of recognition in Bulgaria, Greece, and North Macedonia. *Mediterranean Politics* 1–28. doi:10.1080/13629395.2020.1750269.

Alaranta, T. 2015. *National and state identity in Turkey: The transformation of the Republic's status in the international system*. New York and London: Rowman and Littlefield.

Alpan, B. 2016. From AKP's 'conservative democracy' to 'advanced democracy': Shifts and challenges in the debate on 'Europe'. *South European Society and Politics* 21, no. 1: 15–28. doi:10.1080/13608746.2016.1155283.

Alpan, B., 2020. The Cyprus Question in 2019. In *Year 2019: World politics and Turkish foreign policy*, ed. Z. Alemdar, and S. Akgül-Açıkmeşe, 22–23. Avaialbe at http://wfp14.org/en/our-work/almanac/ (accessed December 2021).

Alpan, B. 2021. Europeanisation and EU-Turkey relations: Three domains, four periods. In *EU-Turkey relations: Theories, institutions and policies*, ed. W. Reiners and E. Turhan, 107–38. Switzerland: Palgrave.

Athanassopoulou, E. 1994. Turkey and the Balkans: The view from Athens. *The International Spectator* 29, no. 4: 55–64. doi:10.1080/03932729408458069.

Ayata, B. 2014. Turkish foreign policy in a changing Arab world: Rise and fall of a regional actor. *Journal of European Integration* 37, no. 1: 95–112. doi:10.1080/07036337.2014.975991.

Aydın-Düzgit, S. 2016. De-Europeanisation through discourse: A critical discourse analysis of AKP's election speeches. *South European Society and Politics* 21, no. 1: 45–58. doi:10.1080/13608746.2016.1147717.

Aydın-Düzgit, S. and A. Kaliber. 2016. Encounters with Europe in an era of domestic and international turmoil: Is Turkey a de-Europeanising candidate country? *South European Society and Politics* 21, no. 1: 1–14. doi:10.1080/13608746.2016.1155282.

Aydın, M. and S. Açıkmeşe. 2007. Europeanisation through EU conditionality: Understanding the new era in Turkish foreign policy. *Journal of Southern Europe and the Balkans* 9, no. 3: 263–74. doi:10.1080/14613190701689944.

Baczynska, G., and J. Chalmers. 2020. Exclusive: EU fumes at Turk migration 'blackmail', mulls more money for Ankara. *Reuters*. 3 March, available at: https://www.reuters.com/article/us-syria-security-eu-turkey-exclusive/exclusive-eufumes-at-turk-migration-blackmail-mulls-more-money-for-ankara-idUSKBN20Q2EK (accessed December, 2021).

Başer, B., and A. Erdi Öztürk. 2017. *Authoritarian politics in Turkey: Elections, resistance and the AKP*. London: Bloomsbury Publishing.

Bebler, A. 2017. Turkey's imperial legacy and the conflict potential in the Balkans. *Defense & Security Analysis* 33, no. 4: 308–19. doi:10.1080/14751798.2017.1377368.

Bieber, F. 2018. Patterns of competitive authoritarianism in the Western Balkans. *East European Politics* 34, no. 3: 337–54. doi:10.1080/21599165.2018.1490272.

Boşnak, B. 2016. Europeanisation de-Europeanisation dynamics in Turkey: The case of environmental organisations. *South European Society and Politics* 21, no. 1: 75–90. doi:10.1080/13608746.2016.1151476.

Çalış, Ş. and H. Bağcı. 2003. Atatürk's Foreign Policy Understanding and Application. *Sosyal Ekonomik Araştırmalar Dergisi* 3, no. 6: 195–228.

Cebeci, M. 2016. De-Europeanisation or counter-conduct? Turkey's democratisation and the EU. *South European Society and Politics* 21, no. 1: 119–32. doi:10.1080/13608746.2016.1153996.

Cengiz, F.Ç. 2020. Proliferation of neo-patrimonial domination in Turkey. *British Journal of Middle Eastern Studies* 47, no. 4: 507–25. doi:10.1080/13530194.2018.1509693.

Coşkun, B. B., S. Doğan, and M. Demir. 2017. Foreign policy as a legitimation strategy for the AKP's hegemonic project of the "New Turkey". In *Authoritarian politics in Turkey: Elections, Resistance and the AKP*, ed. B. Bahar, and A. Erdi Öztürk. Bloomsbury Publishing.

Davutoğlu, A. 2009. Speech at the handover ceremony of office of foreign ministry, Ankara, 2 May, available at: http://www.mfa.gov.tr/devlet-bakani-ve-basabakan-yardimcisi-sayin-ali-babacan-iledisisleri-bakani-sayin-ahmet-davutoglu_nun-devir-teslim-vesilesiyle.tr.mfa (accessed December, 2021).

Davutoğlu, A. 2011. Speech at the Izmir chamber of commerce, 9 April, available online as video at: https://www.youtube.com/watch?v=OwNNilTkTbY (accessed December, 2021).

Demirtaş, B. 2013. Turkey and the Balkans: Overcoming prejudices, building bridges and constructing a common future. *Perceptions: Journal of International Affairs* 18, no. 2: 163–84.

Domaradzki, S., 2019 *Wymiary deeuropeizacji–Dimensions of De-Europeanization*, 155–173.

EEAS. 2020. Video conference of foreign affairs ministers: Main outcomes. 14 August, available at: https://eeas.europa.eu/headquarters/headquarters-homepage/84103/video-conference-foreign-affairs-ministers-main-outcomes_en (accessed December, 2021).

Ekinci, M.U. 2017. Türkiye-Balkanlar ilişkileri. *SETA Analiz* 204: 12.

Esen, B., and Ş. Gümüşcü. 2017. Turkey: How the coup failed. *Journal of Democracy* 28, no. 1: 59–73. doi:10.1353/jod.2017.0006.

European Council. 2016. EU-Turkey statement 18 March 2016: available at https://www.consilium.europa.eu/en/press/press-releases/2016/03/18/eu-turkey-statement/(accessedDecember, 2021).

İçduygu, A., and D. Sert. 2015. The changing waves of migration from the Balkans to Turkey: A historical account. In *Migration in the Southern Balkans*, eds. Vermeulen, H., M. Baldwin-Edwards, and R. Boeschoten. 85–104. Cham: Springer.

İnalcık, H., and S. Faroqhi. 1997. *An economic and social history of the Ottoman Empire*. Vol. 1. Cambridge: Cambridge University Press.

Kaliber, A. 2016. De-Europeanisation of civil society and public debates in Turkey: The Kurdish question revisited. *South European Society and Politics* 21, no. 1: 59–74. doi:10.1080/13608746.2016.1152656.

Kaliber, A., and E. Kaliber. 2019. From de-Europeanisation to anti-Western populism: Turkish foreign policy in flux. *The International Spectator* 54, no. 4: 1–16. doi:10.1080/03932729.2019.1668640.

Kaya, A., 2021. Closing the door to migrants and refugees: Assessing justice in the EU-Turkey statement. In *The EU's External Governance of Migration*, 61–78. Routledge.

Kaya, A., 2021. Europeanization and de-Europeanization of Turkish asylum and migration policies. In *EU-Turkey Relations*, 347–372. Cham: Palgrave Macmillan.

Koesel, K.J., 2014. *Religion and authoritarianism: Cooperation, conflict, and the consequences.* Cambridge: Cambridge University Press.

Kösebalaban, H. 2020. Transformation of Turkish foreign policy toward Syria: The Return of Securitization. *Middle East Critique* 29, no. 3: 335–44. doi:10.1080/19436149.2020.1770450.

Kuru, A.T. 2019. *Islam, authoritarianism, and underdevelopment: A global and historical comparison*. Cambridge: Cambridge University Press.

Lavrič, M. and F. Bieber. 2021. Shifts in support for authoritarianism and democracy in the Western Balkans. *Problems of Post-Communism* 68, no. 1: 17–26. doi:10.1080/10758216.2020.1757468.

Liotta, P.H. 2002. Boomerang effect: The convergence of national and human security. *Security Dialogue* 33, no. 4: 473–88. doi:10.1177/0967010602033004007.

Mazower, M. 2001. *The Balkans: From the end of Byzantium to the present day*. London: Phoenix.

Müftüler-Baç, M. and Y. Gürsoy. 2010. Is there a Europeanisation of Turkish foreign policy? An addendum to the literature on EU candidates. *Turkish Studies* 11, no. 3: 405–27. doi:10.1080/14683849.2010.506734.

Noutcheva, G. and S. Aydin-Düzgit. 2012. Lost in Europeanisation: The Western Balkans and Turkey. *West European Politics* 35, no. 1: 59–78. doi:10.1080/01402382.2012.631313.

Nye, Joseph S. 1990. Soft power. *Foreign policy* 80: 153–171.

Oğuzlu, T. 2016. Turkish foreign policy at the nexus of changing international and regional dynamics. *Turkish Studies* 17, no. 1: 58–67. doi:10.1080/14683849.2015.1136088.

Ökten-Sipahioğlu, B. 2017. Shifting from Europeanisation to de-Europeanisation in Turkey: How AKP instrumentalized EU negotiations. *The Turkish Yearbook of International Relations* 48: 51–67.

Öniş, Z., 2014. Turkey and the Arab revolutions: Boundaries of regional power influence in a turbulent Middle East. *Mediterranean Politics* 19, no. 2: 203–219.

Onursal-Beşgül, Ö., 2016. Policy transfer and discursive de-Europeanisation: Higher education from Bologna to Turkey. *South European Society and Politics* 21, no. 1: 91–103. doi:10.1080/13608746.2016.1152019.

Ovalı, Ş. 2015. The Global financial crisis and de-Europeanisation of Turkish foreign policy. *Hellenic Studies* 23, no. 1: XX.

Özkan, B. 2014. Turkey, Davutoğlu and the idea of pan-Islamism. *Survival* 56, no. 4: 119–40. doi:10.1080/00396338.2014.941570.

Öztürk, A.E. 2019. An alternative reading of religion and authoritarianism: The new logic between religion and state in the AKP's New Turkey. *Southeast European and Black Sea Studies* 19, no. 1: 79–98. doi:10.1080/14683857.2019.1576370.

Öztürk, A.E., 2021a. Turkey's post-2016 foreign policy drivers: Militarisation, Islam, civilisation and power, *ELIAMEP Policy Papers* 58.

Öztürk, A.E. 2021b. *Religion, identity and power: Turkey and the Balkans in the twenty-first century*. Edinburgh: Edinburgh University Press.

Öztürk, A.E. and S. Akgönül. 2019. Turkey: Forced marriage or marriage of convenience with the Western Balkans? In *The Western Balkans in the world*, ed. F. Bieber and N. Tzifakis, 225–40. London: Routledge.

Putnam, R. D., 1988. Diplomacy and domestic politics: the logic of two-level games. *International organization* 42, no. 3: 427–460.

Radaelli, C. M., 2003. The Europeanization of public policy. In *The politics of Europeanization*, 320.

Rašidagić, E.K. and Z. Hesova. 2020. Development of Turkish foreign policy towards the Western Balkans with focus on Bosnia And Herzegovina. *Croatian International Relations Review* 26, no. 86: 96–129. doi:10.37173/cirr.26.86.4.

Saatçioğlu, B. 2016. De-Europeanisation in Turkey: The case of rule of law. *South European Society and Politics* 21, no. 1: 133–46. doi:10.1080/13608746.2016.1147994.

Solana, J., 2017. All that glitters is not gold: the re-use of securities collateral as a source of systemic risk. PhD diss., University of Oxford.

Soyaltın-Collela, D. and E. Akdeniz-Göker. 2019. De-Europeanisation and equal citizenship in Turkey: The case of Circassians. *International Spectator* 54, no. 4: 62–77. doi:10.1080/03932729.2019.1666233.

Soyaltın-Collela, D. and R. Süleymanoğlu-Kürüm. 2021. Enlargement strategy of the EU: A framework for analysis for the (de-)Europeanisation in Turkey. In *Feminist framing of Europeanisation: Gender equality policies in Turkey and the EU*, ed. R. Süleymanoğlu-Kürüm and F.M. Cin, 19–40. London: Palgrave.

Szerencsés, L., 2021. Inclusion and repression in Turkey's diaspora policies in Kosovo as a tool of loyalty building in religious circles. *Diaspora: A Journal of Transnational Studies* 21, no. 2: 188–208. doi:10.3138/diaspora.21.2.2021.05.25.

Tanasković, D. 2012. Turkey and the Balkans: Old traditions, new aspirations. *Israel Journal of Foreign Affairs* 6, no. 2: 51–62. doi:10.1080/23739770.2012.11446502.

Tonra, B., 2013. *Europeanisation and EU foreign policy: A genealogy and survey*. London: UCD School of Politics and International Relations.

Torun, Z. 2021. From convergence to divergence: The compatibility of Turkish and EU foreign policy. In *EU-Turkey relations: Theories, institutions and policies*, ed. W. Reiners and E. Turhan, 323–46. London: Palgrave.

Tziarras, Z. 2018. Erdoğanist authoritarianism and the 'new' Turkey". *Southeast European and Black Sea Studies* 18, no. 4: 593–98. doi:10.1080/14683857.2018.1540408.

Uğur-Çınar, M. 2017. Embedded neopatrimonialism: Patriarchy and democracy in Turkey. *Social Politics: International Studies in Gender, State and Society* 24, no. 3: 324–43. doi:10.1093/sp/jxx009.

Vuksanovic, V., 2017. The Western Balkans could be the first casualty of a 'connectivity war' between the EU and Turkey. LSE European Politics and Policy (EUROPP).

Watmough, S.P. and A. Erdi Öztürk. 2018. From 'diaspora by design' to transnational political exile: The Gülen Movement in transition. *Politics, Religion and Ideology* 19, no. 1: 33–52. doi:10.1080/21567689.2018.1453254.

Yavuz, M.H. 2018. A framework for understanding the intra-Islamist conflict between the AK party and the Gülen movement. *Politics, Religion and Ideology* 19, no. 1: 11–32. doi:10.1080/21567689.2018.1453247.

Yavuz, M.H. and A. Erdi Öztürk. 2020. Guest editors' introduction: Islamism, identity and memory: Turkey under Erdoğan. *Middle East Critique* 29, no. 3: 237–43. doi:10.1080/19436149.2020.1770439.

Yılmaz, G. 2016. Europeanisation or de-Europeanisation? Media freedom in Turkey (1999-2015). *South European Society and Politics* 21, no. 1: 147–61. doi:10.1080/13608746.2016.1148102.

Yılmaz, İ. and G. Bashirov. 2018. The AKP after 15 years: Emergence of Erdoğanism in Turkey. *Third World Quarterly* 39, no. 9: 1812–30. doi:10.1080/01436597.2018.1447371.

A delicate balancing act: Turkish-Bulgarian relations within the context of foreign and domestic politics

Emilia Zankina

ABSTRACT

The article examines Turkish-Bulgarian relations and the way they play into domestic politics in Bulgaria and Turkey, as well as at the EU level. Turkish-Bulgarian relations are complex and burdened with a long and complicated history that has left affected populations on both sides of the border and an array of political actors that argue over and exploit that history. In addition, Turkish-Bulgarian relations represent a delicate balancing act, as they take place within the context of a complex international political environment and growing tensions between Turkey and the EU. I argue that in order to understand current dynamics in bilateral relations, we must examine them through three lenses: 1) EU-Turkish relations and Bulgaria as an agent in this dynamic, 2) domestic politics in Bulgaria and the way bilateral relations are influenced and exploited by domestic political actors, and 3) domestic politics in Turkey and the potential benefit bilateral relations and political rhetoric towards Bulgaria can bring to Erdogan's ruling party.

Turkish-Bulgarian relations are complex and have a long history. In addition to being neighbouring counties with close economic ties, Turkey and Bulgaria share some common cultural characteristics and a burdened past – a result of five-century domination of the Ottoman Empire over the Bulgarian territory and population. Consequently, there is a sizable Turkish minority in Bulgaria and a broad spectrum of policies by the Bulgarian state since independence in the late 19th century that aim to 'deal' with that minority (Dimitrov 2000). Similarly, there is a large diaspora of Bulgarian Turks in Turkey, a large part of who maintain strong ties with Bulgaria (Parla 2009) but who are also voters in Turkey. With the collapse of communist rule in Bulgaria, ethnic Turks found political representation in the face of the Movement for Rights and Freedoms (MRF). MRF has benefited from the ethnic Turkish vote on both sides of the border and has been among the most stable political parties in the last 30 years, enjoying representation in every parliament, as well as access to executive positions and government.

While Turkey was considered a belligerent state during the Cold War in line with Moscow's directive, bilateral relations have been friendly and flourishing since the fall of communism (Demirtaş-Coşkun 2001). Bulgaria looked at Turkey as 'an asset in courting the US over NATO enlargement' (Bechev 2012, 139) and, indeed, Turkey was among the strongest advocates for Bulgarian membership to NATO. With Bulgaria joining the EU in 2007, Bulgarian-Turkish relations have taken on yet another level of complexity. In recent years, the Bulgarian government has tried to play a mediating role in the ever more tense relations between Turkey and the EU, especially on pressing topics such as refugees, human rights, and energy. Thus, in turn, Turkey has come to view Bulgaria as a potential ally in the EU arena. Furthermore, Russia has often come into the mix of bilateral relations, as well as relations with the EU, adding yet another layer of complexity given the strong pro-Russian sentiments among many Bulgarians.

This article argues that in order to understand current dynamics in Bulgarian-Turkish relations, we must examine them through three lenses: 1) EU-Turkish relations and Bulgaria as an agent in this dynamic, 2) domestic politics in Bulgaria and the way bilateral relations are influenced and exploited by domestic political actors, and 3) domestic politics in Turkey and the potential benefit bilateral relations and political rhetoric towards Bulgaria can bring to Erdogan's ruling party. After a brief review of scholarship on the topic, the article provides background on the context of Bulgarian-Turkish relations and examines each of the abovementioned aspects. This article uses qualitative descriptive analysis based on review of literature, media sources, and official data sources.

Bulgarian-Turkish relations in the scholarly literature

Scholarship on Turkish-Bulgarian relations falls into several related categories. A significant part of this scholarship focuses on Bulgarian ethnic Turks from a minorities studies perspective. Studies range from examining specific historical periods such as ethnic Turks during communism (Mahon 1999) or the renaming process (Mihail and Kalionski 2008) to focusing on broader topics such as the history of Muslim and other minorities (Eminov 1997), the rights of Muslim minorities (Simeon et al. 2015) or state policies towards Muslim minorities (Ivanova 2007). Others like, Parla (2009) take on an interesting angle by examining nostalgia among Bulgarian ethnic Turks who emigrated to Turkey and their connection to Bulgaria as their birthplace.

Some studies explicitly focus on how domestic policies and bilateral relations between Bulgaria and Turkey define the fate and status of ethnic Turks in Bulgaria. Dimitrov (2000) provides a historical account of state policies, including bilateral agreements and arbitration, towards the ethnic Turkish minority from independence to the collapse of communist rule. Köksal (2006) focuses on policies towards minorities in the process of nation-building in Turkey and Bulgaria, while Petkova (2002) examines how domestic policies towards ethnic Turks influence bilateral foreign relations. Neuberger (1997) explores the 'Turkish question' in the process of shaping the modern Bulgarian nation, touching on the way post-communist political dynamics have been influenced by the presence of an ethnic Turkish minority and its particular history.

Other studies focus exclusively on political dynamics and the political representation of ethnic Turks in Bulgaria, as opposed to cultural, anthropological, or historical perspectives. Spirova (2016) analyses the ethnic Turkish party, the Movement for Rights and Freedoms (MRF), from a political party and party system perspective. Ganev (2004) examines ethnic relations and ethnic political representation as defined by the constitutional framework. Zankina (2010) analyses the MRF through the lens of political elites theory and elite transformation.

A growing scholarship examines Turkey's ambitions in the Balkans, including Bulgaria, and its relations with Balkan countries formerly under Ottoman rule (Bechev 2012, Bechev 2019a, 2019b,; Öztürk 2021; Öztürk and Fırat Büyük 2019). Öztürk provides a detailed account of Erdogan's tactics to strengthen Turkey's influence in the Balkans through soft power. In particular, he examines the use of culture and religion and the infiltration by Turkish religious organizations in the Balkans. In his analysis of Albania, Bulgaria, and North Macedonia, Öztürk traces, among other things, the evolution of Bulgarian-Turkish relations and the notable change that occurred with the ascent of Erdogan and his party to power. His account provides a sobering analysis of power politics and is in sharp contrast to previous studies which praised the 'exemplary relations' between the two countries in the 1990s (Demirtaş-Coşkun 2001). Bechev (2019a) agrees that Erdogan has used soft power to assert Turkey's influence on the Balkans, including through the instrumentalization of Islam. He argues, however, that Turkey is not trying to undermine EU influence and Western order but trying to take advantage of it. What becomes immediately evident in the literature is that Erdogan and his party have taken on a much more deliberate approach towards the Balkans, instrumentalizing past legacies, cultural affinities, economic and religious ties.

Scholarship related to Bulgarian-Turkish relations in the various categories mentioned above illustrates the complex context within which these relationships exist and evolve. Regardless of the particular disciplinary approach and topic, all studies emphasize the multiple factors that come into play and the multiple levels and actors involved. This article contributes to our knowledge by emphasizing this complexity. The goal is to illustrate how domestic, foreign, and EU-level policies interplay in Bulgarian-Turkish relations and create a complex setting that political actors need to navigate through and delicately balance.

Past legacies and current dynamics

According to the latest census, ethnic Turks constitute 8.8% of the population in Bulgaria and are the second largest ethnic group in Bulgaria (NSI 2011). Ethnic Turks live predominantly in rural areas and are concentrated in several regions of the country – only 37.7% live in urban centres, and 63.7% are concentrated in 8 regions (Kardzhali, Razgrad, Targovishte, Shumen, Silistra, Dobrich, Russe, Burgas). Turkish is the mother tongue for 9.1% of respondents, while 10% identify as Muslim.

By contrast, there are an estimated 1 million people in Turkey of Bulgarian Origin, a quarter of whom still maintain Bulgarian citizenship (Tzekov 2017). They are concentrated primarily in the northwest of the country and are settlers from various migration waves in the past century. Over the past 20 years, between 25,000 and 92,000 people have voted in Bulgarian parliamentary elections in Turkey (Hristova 2021; Central Electoral Commission). This is a relatively small percentage of the overall population in Turkey of Bulgarian origin, as older generations of migrants have not necessarily maintained Bulgarian citizenship. Of those eligible to vote, many engage in the so-called 'voting tourism' – a term coined to describe Bulgarian Turks from Turkey who hold Bulgarian citizenship and travel to Bulgaria on election day to vote in parliamentary, presidential, EU parliament, and even local elections.

Bulgarian Turks on both sides of the border are a legacy of the Ottoman Empire and the ensued migration waves following Bulgarian independence, as well as a series of forced or voluntary migrations during the communist regime and in the troubled years of the democratic transition. Following independence in 1878, Bulgaria was left with 'a sizable Turkish minority, amounting to between a fifth and a quarter of the population' (Eminov 1997, 71), with one-third of the population being Muslim – mostly Turkish but also Pomak, Tatar, and Roma (Köksal 2006, 506). Before the communist coup in 1944, Bulgarian governments adopted various strategies to 'deal' with the Turkish minority, from forced emigration and bilateral agreements on protection of minorities to hegemonic control 'aiming to maintain the political and economic supremacy of the ethnic Bulgarian majority and keep the Turks in an inferior position.' (Dimitrov 2000, 4). There were no attempts to integrate or assimilate the Turkish population into Bulgarian society during that time. Rather policies aimed at marginalization and exclusion (Mahon 1999). This changed with the advent of the communist regime in 1944 and the ideology of a transnational communist society, calling for integration on a non-ethnic principle. In the early years of the regime, policies were aimed at bringing the Turkish minority into the socialist society, though some cultural freedom was still allowed – with newspapers in Turkish being published at the local level and Turkish being taught as a subject matter in some cities with large concentrations of ethnic Turks. Parallel to that, forced immigration was still pursued – about 155,000 Bulgarian Turks were accepted by Turkey between 1949 and 1951 in escape from the forced collectivization of land, as well as an additional 130,000 between 1968 and 1978 as part of a family reunification agreement between Bulgaria and Turkey (Zhelyazkova 2021). However, the focus was on raising the standard of living of the Turkish minority. While the gap between ethnic Bulgarians and ethnic Turks significantly decreased by the 1980s, improved economic conditions tended to strengthen rather than weaken the ethnic identity of Bulgarian Turks (Dimitrov 2000, 6). The strong ethnic identity combined with a higher birth rate than ethnic Bulgarians provided an opportunity to the Bulgarian Communist Party (BCP) to portray the Turkish minority as a 'threat'. Communist regimes often engaged in ultra-nationalist policies, especially in countries with ethnic minorities, in an attempt to gain legitimacy by exploiting nationalist rhetoric. The communist regime in Bulgaria similarly played the nationalist card at a time when economic stagnation and disillusionment with communist ideology, as well as lack of support by the new leadership in Moscow, shook the legitimacy of the communist regime to an unprecedented degree (Zankina 2010). Within this context and fearing for losing its grip on power, Todor Zhivkov – the longest-standing communist dictator in Eastern Europe, embarked on the most extreme nationalist undertaking in Eastern Europe in the 1980s – the renaming process.

The renaming process, also known as the 'revival process' (възродителен процес), was a forced assimilation campaign that took place between 1984 and 1985 and resulted in the forced change of names of some 800,000 Bulgarian Turks (Mihail and Kalionski 2008). Preceded by smaller renaming campaigns of Muslim minorities in the 1960s and 1970s, the assimilation campaign was justified through a systematic redefinition of the Bulgarian nation and the claim that Turks (and other Muslim minorities) were, in fact, ethnic Bulgarians who were forcefully converted to Islam under the Ottoman rule and who needed to 'revive' their original roots. Furthermore, it was cynically declared that 'they voluntarily and spontaneously wanted their Bulgarian names back as a symbolic 'rebirth of their Bulgarian nationality' (Mahon 1999, 157). Soon after its start in 1984, the assimilation campaign escalated into what was essentially a military operation, resulting in several hundred civilian casualties (Ganev 2004, 68). However, the campaign was met with growing unrest by ethnic Turks, culminating in the first mass protests during the communist regime in May 1989. The immediate government response was a change in policy from forced assimilation to strongly encouraged voluntary exile, bordering on ethnic cleansing. Turkish president at the time, Turgut Özal, initially embraced the migrants with rhetoric emphasizing the common ethnic identity and historical roots. When the communist regime opened the borders with Turkey, a mass exodus of Bulgarian Turks ensued, also known as the 'great excursion.' Turkey found itself overwhelmed with the wave of migrants. Unable to accommodate all those piling at the border, Turkey closed its border. With over 360,000 Bulgarian Turks exiled to Turkey and many more stuck at the border, the mass exodus caused a full-blown international crisis in the summer of 1989 and a special session of the UN Security Council. Eventually, about 150,000 of those exiles returned to Bulgaria after the collapse of the communist regime. The renaming process and the ensued protests and international outcry became a significant factor in the collapse of the communist regime in Bulgaria. Moreover, it led to the strengthening of ethnic group identity and political mobilization of the Turkish minority (Dimitrov 2000; Mihail and Kalionski 2008; Zankina 2010).

The start of the democratization process brought immediate improvement in the status of ethnic Turks in Bulgaria and in bilateral relations. The communist party publicly apologized and restored the names of ethnic Turks. Over the following decade, laws and policies were adopted that steadily improved the treatment of the Turkish community and ethnic minorities in Bulgaria (Petkova 2002). Most importantly, ethnic Turks were able to gain political representation through the MRF.

Founded in 1990, the MRF represents the Turkish minority in the country, although it has always included ethnic Bulgarians in both its leadership and its membership in order to comply with the Bulgarian constitution, which bans ethnic parties.[1] It has been among the most enduring and successful political parties, present in all parliaments since 1990, with a share of the vote and seats often well above the proportion of the Turkish minority in the country (Spirova 2016). It has participated in three government coalitions since 2001, and, in addition, it has played an important role in two governments in the 1990s. The MRF positions itself as a liberal party in the centre of the political spectrum, part of the Liberal International and the Alliance of Liberal and Democrats for Europe (ALDE) in the European Parliament. The MRF has enjoyed steady representation in the European Parliament with 2–4 MEPs since 2007. The party traces its origins to the clandestine Turkish National Liberation Movement of Bulgaria, operating during the renaming process, whose founder Ahmed Dogan was imprisoned before 1989 for dissident activity. The MRF has been dominated by the persona of its founder, Dogan, who stepped down as leader of the party in 2013 but who continues to exert influence over the party leadership. The party maintains 'notoriously close ties with its members and supporters, and party discipline in and out of parliament is high' (Spirova 2016, 156).

The MRF has monopolized the ethnic Turkish vote in Bulgaria and among Bulgarian Turks in Turkey, despite internal conflicts and splinter parties' attempts to challenge MRF's dominance. Many Bulgarian politicians have further credited it for not radicalizing the ethnic Turkish community, especially at a time when former Yugoslavia was torn by ethnic wars, and for actively contributing to ethnic peace in the country (Dimitrov 2003; Spirova 2016). At the same time, the MRF has become synonymous with corruption, patronage, and clientelistic networks. The most controversial MRF figure is Delyan Peevski – a media mogul known for corruption schemes, control of the security services, and media for personal gain and power brokerage. His attempted appointment as director of the Bulgarian secret service in 2013 triggered mass protests that lasted over a year. Ultimately, the MRF has come to be widely perceived as part of the 'corrupt status quo', becoming a target of the latest 2019–2021 protests and the 'protest' parties that emerged and entered parliament in 2021. Those include Change Continues, There is Such People, Democratic Bulgaria, and Stand Up! We are Coming! (priorly known as 'Stand Up! Thugs Out!).

The MRF has had a varied relationship with the government in Ankara. Erdogan was harshly criticized by MRF leader, Ahmed Dogan, for being a dictator and sentiments towards Erdogan among Bulgarian Turks have been mixed at best (Shikerova 2020a). Erdogan, in turn, has tried to undermine the position of Dogan and the MRF in Bulgaria, actively supporting the splinter parties of Lyutvi Mestan and Kasim Dal (Bedrov 2020; Öztürk 2021; Shikerova 2020a).[2] It is only recently that this relationship has improved, and Erdogan has shown inequivalent support for the MRF (discussed below). The relationship between Ankara and the MRF plays a part in the larger context of EU-Turkish relations and the way in which Turkey's bilateral relations with Bulgaria and various political actors in Bulgaria can be utilized to further Turkish interests at the EU level. The MRF, with its steady representation at the European Parliament, is a case in point. However, as argued below, such influence goes well beyond Erdogan's relations with the MRF.

A delicate balancing act: EU-Turkish relations and Bulgaria in between

Since the fall of communism, Bulgarian-Turkish relations have been friendly and ever closer in terms of trade and tourism, as well as in the international arena. Turkey is among Bulgaria's top 5 trading partners and the only non-EU country on that list (NSI). Turkey is the top destination for Bulgarian tourists (NSI). Both countries are members of NATO, and, until recently, Bulgaria had been a strong supporter of EU membership to Turkey (Shuster 2017).

With Erdogan coming to power, Bulgarian-Turkish relations have also been defined by the personal relationship between Erdogan and Boyko Borissov, who served as prime minister (with brief interruptions) between 2009 and 2021. Borissov has dedicated a lot of time and effort to portray himself as a mediator between Turkey and the EU and the one among EU leaders who can find the best approach towards Erdogan (Bedrov 2020). Borissov has visited Erdogan multiple times during his tenure and has even been criticized for becoming 'Erdogan's henchman' (Dimitar and Popp 2020). Indeed, Borissov has repeatedly and consistently defended Erdogan in the EU arena. He publicly defended Erdogan in October 2019 when the EU accused Turkey of not keeping its end of the 2016 migration deal, and he sided again with Erdogan in his attack on French President Marcon in relation to caricatures of the prophet Mohammed (Mitov 2021).

Most striking was Borissov's cooperation in the persecution of Erdogan's political opponents. Following the attempted coup in Turkey in July 2016, Erdogan embarked on vengeful persecution of Gülen supporters. The Bulgarian authorities assisted these efforts and extradited seven Gülen supporters who had escaped to Bulgaria, among whom Turkish businessmen Abdullah Büyük. Later investigations proved these extraditions to be in violation of international norms (Dimitar and Popp 2020; Shikerova 2020b). The Bulgarian state was subsequently convicted in the European Court of Human Rights for failing to provide asylum and legal protection to Büyük. Such conviction happens at the backdrop of other EU states refusing extradition of alleged Gülen supporters.

In January 2018, Bulgaria took over the Presidency of the Council of the European Union. One of the four priorities of the Bulgarian presidency was security and stability, with EU-Turkish relations being a key element. Borissov took the opportunity of holding the EU presidency and having a strong personal relationship with Erdogan to organize an EU-Turkey Summit in Bulgaria in March 2018. In the context of rising tensions between Turkey and the EU, the summit was awaited with high hopes by all sides. The topics on the agenda included cooperation on migration and terrorism, the rule of law in Turkey, Turkey's actions in the Eastern Mediterranean and the Aegean Sea,[3] and Turkey's involvement in Syria. For Turkey, the pressing issues were visa-free movement for its citizens, the revival of EU accession talks, and an upgrade of the EU-Turkey customs union. But the summit ended on a bitter note and, according to European Council President Donald Tusk, 'didn't achieve any kind of concrete compromise' (Sidlo 2018). Nevertheless, Borissov congratulates himself on securing Erdogan's support and cooperation on migration and energy and infrastructure projects (Mitov 2021).[4]

Tensions between Turkey and the EU continued to escalate, and in December 2020, the EU discussed sanctions against Turkey related to gas drilling in Cypriot-claimed waters. At the summit, Merkel and Borissov openly opposed sanctions against Turkey, despite a strong push by many member states. Consequently, the EU took a much softer stance granting Turkey another grace period (Bedrov 2020; Michalopoulos 2020). This is but the latest example of how Erdogan has skilfully exploited his relationship with select European leaders, including Borissov, to protect Turkish interests at the EU level.

Turkey as a factor in Bulgarian domestic politics

Given the large Turkish minority in Bulgaria, Bulgarian-Turkish relations have always had a significant impact on domestic politics. As Dimitrov argues when analysing the factors that led to the renaming process, 'In a situation where the Turkish minority could look towards a neighbouring country, Turkey, as its 'mother-country', the state of Bulgaria's relations with Turkey was clearly a significant determinant of Bulgarian policy (Dimitrov 2000, 4). Historically, Bulgarian policy towards Turkey has been mainly determined by the fact that there is a large ethnic Turkish minority in the country. By the same token, Turkish policy towards Bulgaria has always been interpreted within that context and often seen as an attempt to interfere with domestic politics in Bulgaria and influence in one way or another the ethnic Turks in the country. Turkey and Erdogan, in particular, have been accused more than once of meddling in Bulgarian internal affairs. Alleged interference has also been exploited by nationalist parties and other political actors, including the President of the Republic Rumen Radev. Accusations of Turkey interfering in domestic politics has helped various political actors in the country mobilize voters by exploiting nationalist and anti-Turkish rhetoric – from nationalist parties such as Ataka, the Internal Macedonian Revolutionary Organization (IMRO), or the National Front for Salvation of Bulgaria (NFSB) to the Bulgarian Socialist Party and centre-right parties. The votes of Bulgarian Turks on both sides of the border have further been influenced by dynamics in bilateral relations.

Although the MRF holds a monopoly over the ethnic Turkish vote in the country, there have been challenges to such dominance, including by Erdogan himself. Following a Russian plane incident in 2015, the MRF leader at the time, Lyutvi Mestan, issued a declaration in support of NATO's fellow member, Turkey. Following this declaration, Mestan was expelled from the MRF and Dogan (who is often accused of being an instrument of Russia)[5] strongly criticized his pro-Turkish, and by default anti-Russian, declaration (Bedrov 2020). Subsequently, in 2016, Dogan and Delyan Peevski were banned from entering Turkey, while Erdogan showed explicit support for Lyutvi Mestan's new splinter party DOST. However, since then, relationships between Erdogan and the MRF have smoothened out, even if Dogan is still banned from entering Turkey. The culmination of this shift of direction was demonstrated at the 2020 MRF party conference, where Erdogan appeared in a video message addressing the MRF delegates. In his address, he expressed full support for the MRF as the unquestionable defender of the rights of ethnic Turks in Bulgaria and the legitimate representative of their vote in Bulgaria. He further expressed support for Borissov, hinting at a potential coalition in the upcoming elections between Borisov's party GERB (Citizens for European Development of Bulgaria) and the MRF (Bedrov 2020). Finally, he expressed criticism towards Delyan Peevski, thus, attempting to dictate intra-party affairs.

Erdogan's virtual appearance at the MRF conference is a precedent. Never before has a Turkish head of state or head of government participated in a high forum of a Bulgarian political party (Bedrov 2020). This symbolic action served to signal that the 'division has ended' and to legitimize the MRF as the sole representative of the ethnic Turkish vote in Bulgaria, thus delegitimizing any contenders for that vote. But there is more than just symbolism. The MRF also relies on support from Turkish authorities in Bulgarian elections when it comes to organizing the voting of Bulgarian Turks in Turkey. Recent changes to the Bulgarian electoral law have removed the cap of 35 sections in a non-EU country, making cooperation by Turkish authorities even more critical. In the July 2021 early parliamentary elections, there were 121 sections, compared to 35 in the April 2021 parliamentary elections, even if the increase in votes was very modest (Mediapool 2021). The November 2021 elections, however, brought almost 90,000 votes from Turkey, constituting over a quarter of the votes for the MRF. This is in stark difference to the 29,609 votes from Turkey registered in the July 2021 elections – a result as many would argue of Turkey's active involvement in Bulgarian elections through vote mobilization of the Bulgarian diaspora in Turkey (Angelov 2021). In addition to mobilized voters in Turkey, thousands of Bulgarian Turks travel to Bulgaria on election day – the exact number being hard to estimate.

Bulgarian-Turkish relations and MRF's interaction with the government in Turkey, in particular, have also served to fuel nationalist rhetoric and support for nationalist parties. An illustration of the sensitivities surrounding bilateral relations is a 2018 scandal over a statement made by Erdogan. At a rally in a Turkish city, Erdogan stated that the Bulgarian city of Kardzhali, which is predominantly populated by ethnic Turks, finds itself 'in the spiritual boundaries of Turkey' (Gatev 2018). The statement resulted in an outcry in public opinion and a harsh reaction by the Bulgarian Foreign Ministry.

Nationalist parties have been quick to jump at any opportunity to criticize Turkey, as well as any domestic actors related to Turkey. They often label official visits between Bulgarian and Turkish officials as interference in Bulgaria's national affairs. As nationalist parties have been continuously represented in parliament since 2005 and a nationalist coalition participated as a junior partner in the 2017–2021 government, their actions go far beyond rhetoric and have a real influence on government policies. Nationalist parties were firmly against removing the cap on electoral sections for non-EU countries, including Turkey, calling the change 'treason' (Trud 2021). They are also against allowing political agitation in a language other than Bulgarian – an issue that has been very contentious and that they have been able to define. Most striking and extreme are their actions around election day, which include blocking the Bulgarian-Turkish border to prevent 'voting tourism', i.e. Bulgarian Turks travelling to Bulgaria in order to cast their vote. The most recent of such blockades took place during the early parliamentary elections in July 2021. Media reports from the border, as well as various actions aiming to block the border crossing of buses from Turkey, are an inseparable part of Bulgarian elections.

The nationalists have strongly condemned Erdogan's virtual address at the MRF conference. Their criticism was even stronger in relation to a recent delegation of MRF's to Turkey. Most importantly, this rhetoric has spread beyond nationalist parties and has become quite common for more moderate political actors as well. For example, a visit of MRF leadership with Erdogan right before the early elections in July 2021 provoked harsh criticism in Bulgaria. President Radev criticized MRF leader Karadayi for his strong nationalist rhetoric in favour of Turkey and especially for his statement in which Karadayi called Turkey a 'homeland' (Nikolov 2021).

But nationalist parties are not the only ones to criticize Turkey and the MRF. President Radev was even more critical of Erdogan's address to the MRF conference this year, labelling it 'interference with the electoral process in Bulgaria' and alluding to similar interference in the 2017 parliamentary elections (Svobodnaevropa 2020). In preparation for the November 2021 parliamentary elections (the third in the country in seven months) and presidential elections held in conjunction, the Interior Ministry strongly criticized Turkey, summoning its ambassador, for interfering in Bulgarian elections by mobilizing voters in Turkey in support of the MRF. The criticism was further backed up by protests in front of the Turkish embassy in Sofia (Svobodnevrop.bg 2021).

Non-nationalist parties have also exploited anti-MRF rhetoric. One of the most notable examples is an activist action by Hristo Ivanov, co-chair of Democratic Bulgaria and former minister of justice, at Rosenets. Rosenets is a beach area that is technically public, although Ahmed Dogan has illegally privatized the area and constructed a palace in the vicinity. The area is heavily guarded by the National Security Service which has no legal reason to protect Dogan, who is no longer an MP nor a party leader. In a spectacular action, Hristo Ivanov and a group of activists coasted on the beach and videotaped the harsh treatment by the National Security Service. The action was widely broadcast on social media, causing a public uproar. Ivanov has called Rosenets 'the "black hole" in the rule of law in Bulgaria' (Andreev 2020). One of the protest parties, Democratic Bulgaria, is old wine in a new bottle – a new coalition of already known political actors who have managed to rally the urban middle-class in large cities, gaining parliamentary representation following the April and July 2021 elections. The Rosenets action served as a significant boost and a powerful mobilizing factor for Hristo Ivanov and Democratic Bulgaria. He, as well as the leaders of other protest parties, have labelled the MRF the 'corrupt status quo' that needs to be uprooted from political and economic life. Ivanov and other protest parties have tried to reach out to emigrant communities in Turkey and 'steal' some of MRF's votes. Despite such attempts, MRF's dominance with emigrants in Turkey remains unchallenged.

It seems Borissov has been the only one among Bulgarian politicians not to criticize Erdogan. In fact, he visited Erdogan right before the July 2021 early parliamentary elections when he was no longer serving as prime minister – an act that has provoked numerous speculations and criticisms. The official reason for Borissov's visit to Turkey is to meet with emigrant organizations there. Most commentators saw this as an attempt to lobby with Erdogan for the votes of the Bulgarian Turks in Turkey (Milcheva 2021; Mitov 2021). Public statements made after the meeting, however, cover a much broader scope, including the close cooperation between Erdogan and Borissov on migration and the EU migrant flow deal – a message that was clearly addressed at the EU. Erdogan has been quite open about his support for Borissov, calling him 'my trusted friend and brother' (Mitov 2021). It is argued he would like to see his 'friend and brother' hold on to power, as this would serve Erdogan well both in Bulgaria and at the EU level (Milcheva 2021).

Overall, bilateral relations, Bulgarian Turks on both sides of the border, and the very existence of the MRF, have provided fruitful ground for nationalist parties and beyond to engage in anti-Turkish and anti-MRF rhetoric for political ends.

What Bulgaria has to offer: domestic politics in Turkey

Although Bulgaria is a small country and not as significant in terms of overall Turkish trade flows as larger EU countries, its strategic position as a neighbour and a NATO and EU member state renders it important to Turkish domestic and international politics. As already mentioned above, Bulgaria (and Borissov in particular) has been a faithful advocate for Turkey at the EU level. Borissov has also assisted Erdogan in handling domestic opposition even when other EU member states have condemned Erdogan's persecution of Gulenists. What else can Bulgaria provide to Erdogan?

According to former MRF member and critic of Dogan, Orhan Ismailov, Erdogan is hoping to get the votes of Bulgarian Turks in future Turkish elections (Shikerova 2020a). Although Erdogan's Justice and Development Party (AKP) currently holds 288 seats in the 600-seat National Assembly, its support in the northwest of the country is low. Bulgarian Turks concentrated primarily in this region traditionally vote for the Republican People's Party (CHP) – the oldest party in Turkey and the main opposition party to the AKP. Maintaining close relationships with the MRF, which dominates the vote of Bulgarian Turks on both sides of the border, can help legitimize the AKP party and increase support by Bulgarian Turks in Turkey for Erdogan, especially in the northwest of the country. In the past, the MRF has been very critical of Erdogan and has actively advocated against supporting his party (Tsekov 2017). During the 2017 constitutional referendum in Turkey, the MRF urged Bulgarian Turks to vote against the 18 amendments that aimed to consolidate Erdogan's hold on power and transform Turkey from a parliamentary into a presidential republic. Although the referendum passed with 51% of the votes, the northwest regions of the country voted against it. Dogan labelled the change 'transforming Turkey from a Kemalist Republic into a sultanate' and accused Erdogan of 'reinstating and legitimizing Neo-Ottomanism' (Bedrov 2020). With the warming of relations between Erdogan and the MRF, such criticisms are in the past. The symbolic acts by Erdogan and the MRF in the past year signal to Bulgarian Turks in Turkey to support the AKP.

Neo-Ottomanist rhetoric is another factor that makes Bulgaria relevant. Erdogan has been repeatedly accused by Western political analysts for the shift in Turkey's foreign policy, which increasingly aimed to restore the Turkish influence of the Ottoman Empire over old Ottoman territories. Critics have termed this shift Neo-Ottomanism – a charge that, some argue, has increased Erdogan's popularity among Turkish people, who want to make peace with their historical roots, including their Ottoman heritage, as well as with some Muslim communities in the Balkans (Şebnem Oruç 2021). Erdogan has been spreading his Neo-Ottoman and pan-Turkic rhetoric both at home and abroad. In a recent statement he argued that 'The Republic of Turkey [...] is also a continuation of the Ottomans. Of course, the borders have changed. Forms of government have changed. [...] But the essence is the same, the soul is the same, even many institutions are the same' (Şebnem Oruç 2021). His visits to Sarajevo, for example, exemplify his great emphasis on the common Muslim identity and Ottoman past. Similarly, in Bulgaria he has pointed to the common Ottoman past in references to 'spiritual borders' and statements such as, 'I want to assure you that even though I am far away, my heart is with you', delivered at the MRF conference. Indeed, many Turks in Bulgaria relate to Turkey as the 'motherland' and to the pan-Turkic idea that all Turkish minorities are part of a larger ethnic community (Mahon 1999, 154). Erdogan is benefiting from this identity both in Bulgaria and in the Western Balkans, where 'ties run deep at the political, economic, and societal levels' (Bechev 2019b). When addressing the Balkans, Erdogan, Öztürk (2021) argues, speaks simultaneously to two audiences – his domestic political base, but also 'other Muslim societies and the people leading them, among whom he sought to burnish his credentials as a defender of Islam on the global stage' (29).

However, Bechev argues, Turkey's objective is not to recreate the Ottoman Empire in the Balkans, which is far beyond the country's resources and capacity (Bechev 2019b). Instead, what we see, he says, is a shift from multilateralism to bilateralism in foreign relations. Erdogan has managed to build relations with leaders from countries that are majority non-Muslim, which is a big achievement, especially at a time when Europe is ripe with disagreement on a number of issues and in the wake of Brexit. Bechev suggests, Erdogan is using the Balkans to make a case that he is the leader of the wider (Sunni) Muslim community in Europe and the Middle East – a message that is primarily addressed to his electorate in Turkey and only secondly to Muslims abroad. When it comes to foreign policy, Neo-Ottomanism is therefore the packaging, not the substance. In that context, reference to Bulgaria and Bulgarian Turks as part of a pan-Turkic community play into Erdogan's domestic strategy and rhetoric.

Conclusions

This article provides a context for Bulgarian-Turkish relations that looks at the various factors and actors involved and the multi-layered aspect of relations between the two countries. Beyond strictly bilateral relations, interactions between Bulgaria and Turkey matter a great deal for the EU and its strategic policy towards Turkey and the region; they matter to domestic audiences in Bulgaria and Turkey alike, and they matter to ethnic minorities on both sides of the border. Furthermore, such relations form an important part of the political debate and individual party positions in Bulgaria and, to some extent, in Turkey as well.

To Bulgarians, Turkey has many faces. It is vehemently hated when it comes to Ottoman-time massacres and the fight for independence and national identity. It is dearly loved when it comes to tourism, economic relations, and culture – from the delicious Turkish restaurants throughout the country to the Turkish soap operas and colourful Turkish phrases still very much present and used in vernacular Bulgarian. And, when it comes to the EU and Russia, opinions and actions vary greatly – Turkey being viewed at times as a loyal and much-needed partner and at times as an authoritarian country that cynically pursues its self-interest at the expense of its allies and neighbours. If anything, Turkey is quite complex and so are its relations with the Balkan nations and with Bulgaria. The present article tries to unravel some of this complexity by analysing Bulgarian-Turkish relations through a multidimensional lens. The focus is on this multidimensionality rather than on any single individual factor.

The interaction between domestic, foreign, and EU policies and processes is the key subject of this special issue (Alpan and Öztürk 2022). Another no less important theme is the shift in Turkey's domestic and foreign policy with Erdogan's ascent to power. Erdogan's rule has been characterized by a deliberate and strategic engagement in the Balkans, including in Bulgaria, and increased use of Turkey's soft power aiming to strengthen Turkey's influence in the region. Some argue the shift signals greater ambitions of reclaiming Ottoman-era influence (Yavuz 2020). Others see this shift as a tactical move aimed to engage the EU (Bechev 2019a, 2019b). The Bulgarian case provides a good illustration of the latter. That Turkey has employed soft instruments and religion in Bulgaria through transnational religious organizations is now well documented (Öztürk 2021). Such activities, however, have had limited impact beyond the ethnic Turkish minority. While in other Balkan countries, Turkish religious influence may also serve as mobilizing factor against EU integration, this is not the case in Bulgaria – a member of the EU since 2007 and a country with still very low levels of Euroscepticism (Stoyanov and Kostadinova 2020). What is more interesting in my view is Erdogan's success in convincing certain Bulgarian political elites to act as advocates of Turkish interests at the EU-level. Such success has not necessarily been achieved because of historical ties and kinship relations, but, often times, despite them. Some may argue Erdogan has found a clever way to dictate terms and influence EU policy from within. Others may see Bulgaria's unique position and long, even if highly controversial, history and ties with Turkey as a unique opportunity for a dialogue between Turkey and the EU. Bulgaria in turn is in a delicate position of having to tango with a powerful neighbour, maintain good ethnic relations at home, and abide by EU-level decisions on European relations with Turkey (such as on energy and migration, for example). Ironically, this delicate balance is anything but new. Turkey and Europe (or at least specific European countries) have often been at odds throughout past decades and centuries and Bulgaria has often been stuck in between. Stuck in many ways too – geopolitically, economically, and civilisationally.

Keeping in mind the long-term perspective and Turkey's many faces (not just to Bulgarians, but beyond) it is important to have an understanding that goes beyond current criticisms of Erdogan and his regime. Recent authoritarian shifts notwithstanding, Turkey remains among the most democratic and secular Muslim countries, as well as a buffer between Europe and a much more radical form of Islam. As Bechev argues in his latest book (Bechev 2022), Turkey's democratic instincts are resilient and its economic ties to Europe are as strong as ever. Therefore, we must look beyond Erdogan and we must view EU-Turkish relations as a two-way street. The questions we should ask are not only how Turkey has changed its course when it comes to the EU and the Balkans or whether this shift promotes anti EU-tendencies, but also what Europe has done to keep Turkey and its population as allies and what it should do in the future to make sure they do not drift even further apart. The role that Turkey takes on in the region is no less defined by Turkey itself, as it is defined by European countries and the EU.

Notes

1. In October 1992, 93 MPs from the Bulgarian Socialist Party (the successor of the communist party) submitted a petition to the newly established Constitutional Court demanding MRF be declared unconstitutional. The petition rested upon the newly adopted Bulgarian Constitution which outlawed political parties formed on an ethnic, racial, and religious basis. After several months of deliberation, the Constitutional court rejected the petition and affirmed the constitutionality of MRF. See, Ganev (2004).
2. Kasim Dal was expelled from the party in 2011 over disagreements with Dogan. Lyutvi Mestan took over the MRF in 2013 when Dogan stepped down, but was expelled from the party in 2015, again, over disagreements with Dogan.
3. In mid-February, an Italian oil company drill ship commissioned by the Cypriot government to explore natural gas resources in disputed waters south-east of Cyprus was confronted by a Turkish warship. The following month, two Greek soldiers were imprisoned after trespassing onto Turkish territory near the border town of Edirne. The soldiers claim they got lost in bad weather during a border patrol. Ankara, however, imprisoned them on suspicion of espionage. The EU called Turkey's actions 'illegal' and stood behind Cyprus and Greece. See, Sidlo (2018).
4. Referring to gas pipelines 'Balkan Stream' and 'Turkish Stream', as well as to highway construction.
5. Ahmed Dogan was proven to have extensively collaborated with the communist regime and the Bulgarian secret services in the 1980s. See, Zankina (2010). This is one reason why he has been often accused of holding a pro-Russian position in post-communist politics. See, Darik News (2015), Iliev (2019).

Disclosure statement

No potential conflict of interest was reported by the author(s).

References

Alpan, B., and A. Erdi Öztürk. 2022. Turkey and the Balkans: Bringing the Europeanisation/ De-Europeanisation Nexus into Question. *Southeast European and Black Sea Studies* 22, no. 1: (forthcoming).

Andreev, A. 2020. Срещу 'черната дупка' в правовата държава България - Христо Иванов на 'Росенец' [Against the 'black hole' in the rule of law in Bulgaria – Hristo Ivanov at 'Rosenets']/ Deutsche Welle, July 8, 2020. Available at: https://www.dw.com/bg/%D1%81%D1%80%D0% B5%D1%89%D1%83-%D1%87%D0%B5%D1%80%D0%BD%D0%B0%D1%82%D0%B0-% D0%B4%D1%83%D0%BF%D0%BA%D0%B0-%D0%B2-%D0%BF%D1%80%D0%B0%D0% B2%D0%BE%D0%B2%D0%B0%D1%82%D0%B0-%D0%B4%D1%8A%D1%80%D0%B6% D0%B0%D0%B2%D0%B0-%D0%B1%D1%8A%D0%BB%D0%B3%D0%B0%D1%80%D0% B8%D1%8F-%D1%85%D1%80%D0%B8%D1%81%D1%82%D0%BE-%D0%B8%D0%B2% D0%B0%D0%BD%D0%BE%D0%B2-%D0%BD%D0%B0-%D1%80%D0%BE%D1%81%D0% B5%D0%BD%D0%B5%D1%86/a-54090589

Angelov, G. 2021. Напрежение между Турция и България: хронологията на един скандал [Tensions between Turkey and Bulgaria: The chronology of a scandal], Deutsche Welle, November 19, 2021. Available at: https://www.dw.com/bg/%D0%BD%D0%B0%D0%BF%D1% 80%D0%B5%D0%B6%D0%B5%D0%BD%D0%B8%D0%B5-%D0%BC%D0%B5%D0%B6% D0%B4%D1%83-%D1%82%D1%83%D1%80%D1%86%D0%B8%D1%8F-%D0%B8-%D0% B1%D1%8A%D0%BB%D0%B3%D0%B0%D1%80%D0%B8%D1%8F-%D1%85%D1%80%D0% BE%D0%BD%D0%BE%D0%BB%D0%BE%D0%B3%D0%B8%D1%8F%D1%82%D0%B0-% D0%BD%D0%B0-%D0%B5%D0%B4%D0%B8%D0%BD-%D1%81%D0%BA%D0%B0%D0% BD%D0%B4%D0%B0%D0%BB/a-59876034

Bechev, D. 2012. Turkey in the Balkans: Taking a Broader View. *Insight Turkey* 14, no. 1: 131–46.

Bechev, D. 2019a. Turkey's Policy in the Balkans. Continuity and change in the Erdoğan Era. *Südosteuropa Mitteilungen*, no. 5–6: 34–45.

Bechev, D. 2019b. Turkey's Policy in the Balkans: More than Neo-Ottomanism. Istituto per gli Studi di Politica Internazionale. April 19, 2019. Available at: https://www.ispionline.it/it/pub blicazione/turkeys-policy-balkans-more-neo-ottomanism-22835

Bechev, D. 2022. *Turkey Under Erdogan: How a Country Turned from Democracy and the West.* Yale University Press. https://yalebooks.co.uk/display.asp?k=9780300247886I

Bedrov, I. 2020. Ердоган и ДПС. Откъде идва и накъде отива една изненадваща подкрепа на Турция [Erdogan and the MRF: Where does it come from and where does it go a surprising support by Turkey]. Sovobdnaevropa.bg, December 14, 2020. Available at: https://www.svobod naevropa.bg/a/30998466.html

Central Electoral Commission. Official data available at: cik.bg

Darik News. 2015. Медиите в Турция: Лютви Местан подкрепя НАТО, Доган – Русия [Turkish media: Lyutvi Mestan supports NATo, Dogan – Russia, December 25, 2015. Available at: https://dariknews.bg/novini/sviat/mediite-v-turciq-lyutvi-mestan-podkrepq-nato-dogan-rusiq-1539426

Demirtaş-Coşkun, B. 2001. Turkish-Bulgarian relations in the post-cole war era: The exemplary relationship in the Balkans. *Turkish Yearbook* 32: 25–60.

Dimitar, G., and M. Popp. 2020. How Bulgaria's prime minister Borisov became Erdoğan's henchman, *Der Spiegel*, September 11, 2020. Available at: https://www.spiegel.de/ausland/tuerkei-und-bulgarien-wie-bojko-borissow-zu-recep-tayyip-erdogans-handlanger-wurde-a-00000000-0002-0001-0000-000172993232

Dimitrov, P. 2003. Митовете на българския преход [The Myths of the Bulgarian Transition] Ciela.

Dimitrov, V. 2000. In Search of a Homogeneous Nation: The assimilation of Bulgaria's Turkish minority, 1984–1985. *Journal on Ethnopolitics and Minority Issues in Europe* 1, no. 4: 1–22.

Eminov, A. 1997. *Turkish and other muslim minorities of Bulgaria*. London: Hurst & Co.

Ganev, V. 2004. History, politics and the constitution: Ethnic conflict and constitutional adjudication in postcommunist Bulgaria. *Slavic Review* 63, no. 1: 66–89. 10.2307/1520270.

Gotev, G 2018. Bulgaria reacts to disturbing statement by Turkey's Erdogan. Euractiv, May 14, 2018. Available at: https://www.euractiv.com/section/global-europe/news/bulgaria-reacts-to-disturbing-statement-by-turkeys-erdogan/

Hristova, A. 2021. Гласовете в Турция са с почти една пета повече от април, ДПС добавя едва 6 хиляди [Votes from Turkey are almost one fifth more compared to April, MRF adds a mere 6,000]. Dnevnik.bg, July 14, 2021. Available at: https://www.dnevnik.bg/izbori_2021/2021/07/14/4232749_glasovete_v_turciia_sa_s_pochti_edna_peta_poveche_v/

Iliev, A. 2019. Русия ли е тайният кукловод на България? [Is Russia the secret puppeteer in Bulgaria?]. Investor.bg, April 25, 2019. Available at: https://www.investor.bg/ikonomika-i-politika/332/a/rusiia-li-e-tainiiat-kuklovod-na-bylgariia-281214/?page=3

Ivanova, Evgenia. 2007. Islam, State and Society in Bulgaria: New Freedoms, Old Attitudes? Journal of Balkan and Near Eastern Studies, 19, no.1: 35–52.

Köksal, Y. 2006. Minority policies in Bulgaria and Turkey: The struggle to define a nation. *Southeast European and Black Sea Studies* 6, no. 4: 501–21. 10.1080/14683850601016390.

Mahon, M. 1999. The Turkish minority under communist Bulgaria—Politics of Ethnicity and Power. *Journal of Southern Europe and the Balkans* 1, no. 2: 149–62. 10.1080/1461319990841396.

Mediapool.bg. 2021. Резултатите от Турция: Три пъти повече секции, а гласовете са почти същите [The results from Turkey: Three times as many sections, but the results are almost the same, July 13, 2021. Available at: https://www.mediapool.bg/rezultatite-v-turtsiya-tri-pati-poveche-sektsii-a-glasovete-sa-pochti-sashtite-news324147.html

Michalopoulos, S. 2020. Merkel and Borissov blocked EU sanctions against Turkey at summit: Sources. *Euroactiv*, December 11, 2020. Available at: https://www.euractiv.com/section/global-europe/news/merkel-and-borissov-blocked-eu-sanctions-against-turkey-at-summit-sources/

Mihail, G., and A. Kalionski. 2008. *The "Revival Process." Muslim Communities and the communist Regime: Policies, Reactions and Consequences* (in Bulgarian), Ciela.

Milcheva, E. 2021. Борисов при Ердоган: защо беше тази изненадваща среща? [Borissov visting Erdogan: Why this surprising meeting?], Deutsche Welle, July 5, 2021. Available at: https://www.dw.com/bg/%D0%B1%D0%BE%D1%80%D0%B8%D1%81%D0%BE%D0%B2-%D0%BF%D1%80%D0%B8-%D0%B5%D1%80%D0%B4%D0%BE%D0%B3%D0%B0%D0%BD-%D0%B7%D0%B0%D1%89%D0%BE-%D0%B1%D0%B5%D1%88%D0%B5-%D1%82%D0%B0%D0%B7%D0%B8-%D0%B8%D0%B7%D0%BD%D0%B5%D0%BD%D0%B0%D0%B4%D0%B2%D0%B0%D1%89%D0%B0-%D1%81%D1%80%D0%B5%D1%89%D0%B0/a-58159515

Mitov, V. 2021. "Моят верен приятел и брат Бойко". Как Борисов спечели симпатията на Ердоган ['My trusted friend and brother Boyko. How Borissov earned Erdogan's sympathy]. Svobodnaevropa.bg, July 8, 2021. Available at: https://www.svobodnaevropa.bg/a/31345014.html

National Statistical Institute. 2011. Census 2011. Available at: https://www.nsi.bg/census2011/

Neuberger, M. 1997. Bulgaro-Turkish encounters and the reimagining of the Bulgarian nation (1878–1995). *East European Quarterly* 31, no. 1: 1–18.

Nikolov, K. 2021. Tensions in Bulgaria flare up after Turkish-Bulgarian party meets Erdogan. *Euractiv*, July 9, 2021. Available at: https://www.euractiv.com/section/politics/short_news/tensions-in-bulgaria-flare-up-after-turkish-bulgarian-party-meets-erdogan/

Öztürk, A.E., and H. Fırat Büyük. 2019. The role of leadership networks in Turkey–Balkan relations in the AKP era. *Turkish Policy Quarterly* 18, no. 2: 118–27.

Öztürk, A.E. 2021. *Religion, Identity and Power: Turkey and the Balkans in the Twenty-First Century*. Edinburgh, UK: Edinburgh University Press.

Parla, A. 2009. Remembering across the border: Postsocialist nostalgia among Turkish immigrants from Bulgaria. *American Ethnologist* 36, no. 4: 750–67. 10.1111/j.1548-1425.2009.01208.x.

Petkova, L. 2002. The ethnic Turks in Bulgaria: Social Integration and Impact on Bulgarian - Turkish relations, 1947–2000. *The Global Review of Ethnopolitics* 1, no. 4: 42–59. 10.1080/14718800208405112.

Şebnem Oruç, M. 2021. 'Neo-Ottomanism' and Erdoğan: Comparisons, facts. Daly Sabah, February 24, 2021. Available at: https://www.dailysabah.com/opinion/columns/neo-ottomanism-and-erdogan-comparisons-facts

Shikerova, G. 2020a. "Гласовете на изселниците и Борисов". Какво получава Ердоган след сближаването с ДПС [The voices of emigrants and Borissov. What does Erdogan get after getting closer to MRF]. Svobodnaevropa.bg, December 15, 2020. Available at: https://www.svobodnaevropa.bg/a/31000453.html

Shikerova, G. 2020b. "Слагаха ми качулка, стреляха". Какво се случи с хората, които България върна на Ердоган [I was hooded and shot upon. What happened to the people Bulgaria returned to Erdgoan]. Svobodnaevropa.bg, July 28, 2020. Available at: https://www.svobodnaevropa.bg/a/30747946.html

Shuster, K. 2017. Turkey-EU relations: Which countries are for or against Turkish accession? *Deutsche Welle*, September 6, 2017. Available at: https://www.dw.com/en/turkey-eu-relations-which-countries-are-for-or-against-turkish-accession/a-40381533

Sidlo. 2018. Katarzyna. Post-varna EU-Turkey relations. Neither a break-through, nor a break-up. *showCASE*, no. 71.

Simeon, E., P. Makariev, and D. Kalkandjieva. 2015. Christianity, Islam, and human rights in Bulgaria. In *Religion and human rights*, ed. H.-G. Ziebertz and G. Črpić, 1–17. Switzerland: Springer International Publishing.

Spirova, M. 2016. Movement for rights and freedoms in Bulgaria: Beyond the ethnic vote. In *Ethnic Minorities and Politics in Post-Socialist Southeastern Europe*, ed. S.P. Ramet, Cambridge University Press, Cambridge, UK. 154–69.

Stoyanov, D., and P. Kostadinova. 2020. Bulgarian political parties and European integration: From anticommunism to Euroscepticism. *European Politics and Society* 22, no. 2: 222–36. 10.1080/23745118.2020.1729050.

Svobodnaevropa.bg. 2020. Радев: Поздравлението на Ердоган към ДПС е заявка за намеса в изборите [Radev: Erdogan's greeting to MRF is an attempt for electoral interference]. December 19, 2020. Available at: https://www.svobodnaevropa.bg/a/31009162.html

Svobodnaevropa.bg. 2021. Кабинетът и протестиращи обвиниха Турция в намеса в българските избори [The cabinet and protesters accused Turkey of interference in Bulgarian elections]. November 18, 2021. Available at: https://www.svobodnaevropa.bg/a/31567867.html

Trud. 2021. 'Българските патриоти': ДПС извърши национално предателство в Турция. Прокуратурата да се самосезира! ['The Bulgarian Patriots: MRF committed national treason in Turkey. The prosecution should be self-initaited!]. Trud.bg, July 7, 20201. Available at: https://trud.bg/%D0%B1%D1%8A%D0%BB%D0%B3%D0%B0%D1%80%D1%81%D0%BA%D0%B8%D1%82%D0%B5-%D0%BF%D0%B0%D1%82%D1%80%D0%B8%D0%BE%D1%82%D0%B8-%D0%B4%D0%BF%D1%81-%D0%B8%D0%B7%D0%B2%D1%8A%D1%80%D1%88%D0%B8-%D0%BD%D0%B0%D1%86%D0%B8%D0%BE%D0%BD%D0%B0%D0%BB%D0%BD%D0%BE-%D0%BF%D1%80%D0%B5%D0%B4%D0%B0%D1%82%D0%B5%D0%BB%D1%81%D1%82%D0%B2%D0%BE-%D0%B2-%D1%82%D1%83%D1%80%D1%86%D0%

B8%D1%8F-%D0%BF%D1%80%D0%BE%D0%BA%D1%83%D1%80%D0%B0%D1%82%D1%
83%D1%80%D0%B0%D1%82%D0%B0-%D0%B4%D0%B0-%D1%81%D0%B5-%D1%81%
D0%B0%D0%BC%D0%BE/

Tsekov, N. 2017. Българските турци и плановете на Ердоган [Buglarian Turks and Erdogan's Plans]. Deutsche Welle, April 13, 2017. Available at: https://www.dw.com/bg/%D0%B1%D1%8A%D0%BB%D0%B3%D0%B0%D1%80%D1%81%D0%BA%D0%B8%D1%82%D0%B5-%D1%82%D1%83%D1%80%D1%86%D0%B8-%D0%B8-%D0%BF%D0%BB%D0%B0%D0%BD%D0%BE%D0%B2%D0%B5%D1%82%D0%B5-%D0%BD%D0%B0-%D0%B5%D1%80%D0%B4%D0%BE%D0%B3%D0%B0%D0%BD/a-38408655

Yavuz, M.H. 2020. *Nostalgia for the Empire: The Politics of Neo-Ottomanism*. New York, NY: Oxford University Press.

Zankina, E. 2010. *Transformation of the Bulgarian Political Elite in the Period of Transition: Its Impact on the Transition Process*. Doctoral Dissertation, University of Pittsburgh

Zhelyazkova, A. 2021. Защо Турция е майка родина на българските турци? [Why Turkey is a motherland for Bulgarian Turks]. Marginalia.bg, August 20, 2021. Available at: https://www.marginalia.bg/aktsent/zashto-turtsiya-e-majka-rodina-na-balgarskite-turtsi/?fbclid=IwAR1mjsVHcOOOaybzGIjuWo9e5hOdm8kGGWQhnxzhdV_5Ta3TfmXUFLXrXiI

Securitizing the Aegean: de-Europeanizing Greek–Turkish relations

Nikos Christofis ⓘ

ABSTRACT
Turkish foreign policy has experienced a profound transformation in the nearly two decades since the Justice and Development Party (Adalet ve Kalkınma Partisi, AKP) came to power. In its first decade (2002–2011), the AKP government sought to consolidate, promote, and implement its agenda through the use of soft power while also aligning Turkey with the West and EU conditionality. However, since 2011 domestic and international developments have led Ankara to pursue a 'logic of strategic autonomy.' Since the failed coup attempt in July 2016 – which reinforced a trend towards resecuritization in Turkish foreign policy – relations with the EU in general and Greece, in particular, have grown more complicated, leading to a militarized and increasingly tense situation in the region. Against this backdrop, the present article analyses the rekindling of the 'Aegean Cold War' since 2016, focusing principally on the Aegean, Cyprus, and the refugee crisis and the EU's ambivalent policy towards Turkey and Greek–Turkish relations in general.

Introduction

Turkish foreign policy has experienced a profound transformation over the two decades that the Justice and Development Party (Adalet ve Kalkınma Partisi, AKP) has been in power. In the first decade of the AKP's administration, the 'logic of interdependence' constituted the key driving force of foreign policy, and Turkey was firmly anchored to the Western democratic order in terms of its identity and normative credentials in addition to its institutional commitments in the economic and security realms. In contrast, in the post-2011 era, Ankara has followed a 'logic of strategic autonomy' in its foreign policy approach (Önis 2021, 3).

Against this background, following the strategy developed by former Prime Minister and Foreign Secretary, Ahmet Davutoğlu in his influential book *Strategic Depth* (*Stratejik Derinlik*) (2001),[1] Ankara has pursued a soft power approach, albeit an ambivalent one (Öztürk 2020) in diverse regions, perhaps most notably in the Balkans (Alpan 2016). Davutoğlu's ideas still seem to influence Ankara's foreign policy decision-making in its active promotion of Sunni Islam and its apparent vision of a new world order in which Islam is a central part of the neoliberal order and where Turkey acts as a major representative of the global Muslim *ummah*. The Balkans, with a considerable Muslim population and historical ties with the Ottoman past, has been pivotal in that respect, especially since the 2010s when the AKP sought ways to promote and implement its agenda in the framework of 'neo-Ottomanism' (Yavuz 2020; Çandar 2022).

As Öktem (2010, 46) argues, Turkish presence under the AKP rule started to increase the visibility of Islam in the Balkans mostly through the increasing presence and activity of Turkish institutions.[2] However, this promotion of Sunni Islam has been enhanced over the past decade or so through popular Turkish television shows and soap operas (Bošković et al. 2015), as well as other cultural activities, educational and information linkages mostly with Sunni groups in the region. As Öztürk and Akgönül (2020, 226) rightly point out, what is essential here, is that all these activities and practices 'are supported by the AKP and promote the ideas of the party, [and] still have remarkable influence'. As far as foreign policy is concerned, the AKP's policies came at the expense of conducting 'proper' international relations (Haynes 2007, 33).

The above observation can be easily discerned in Turkey's relations with Greece, which presents a 'deviation' to the rest of the Balkans in the sense that it is already an EU and NATO member with a more stable economy and democracy than some of the other countries in the Balkan region. Furthermore, since 2016 Greece has sought to regain its leading role in the region as the mediator country shepherding Balkan countries along the path to EU accession and advancing Greek economic and diplomatic interests (Panagiotou and Tzifakis 2021). This presents, as expected, also a conflict of interest with Turkey.

Complicating Greek–Turkish diplomatic relations have been developments in the energy sector. The gas resources discovered in the Mediterranean Sea over a decade ago have upset the geostrategic balance in the region and pushed Greek–Turkish relations into a new phase. Indeed, since 2016, Greek–Turkish relations have centred on the great potential for economic gains in Mediterranean energy. Here, disputes over sovereignty – exemplified by Turkey's Mavi Vatan (Blue Homeland) doctrine – have subsumed (but also refreshed) older flashpoints, like the Aegean and Cyprus issues, and the newer concerns over refugees and migration.

When it comes to the bilateral relations with Greece, on the one hand, Turkey's transformation to a militarized, or even yet, securitized, foreign policy in the region put the relations between the two countries at odds and revived age-long hatred in public opinion where Turkey is being presented again as a 'ruthless' expansive country. On the other hand, this foreign policy shift demonstrates precisely the effects of Turkey's de-Europeanization process since the early 2010s on Turkey's relations with Western countries and institutions, particularly the US and the EU (Alpan and Ozturk 2022). These two developments are interconnected as Greece is not what perhaps can be called a 'typical' Balkan country. Greece sees itself, or stresses more, its European, rather than (also) its Balkan characteristics, which presents limitations to Ankara's policies in the region and potentially forces Ankara to seek other paths to achieve its goals.

Yet, as Greece seeks to regain its older status as a vital player for EU enlargement in the Balkans while remaining the epicentre of Europe's debt and refugee crises (Bieri and Nechev 2016; Panagiotou and Tzifakis 2021), several questions arise. What is the endgame of Ankara in regards to Greece? What are the factors that determine

Turkey's scope of activity towards Greece? How do Greek actors and public opinion respond to Turkey's newly-emerging activism in the region? What is the role of Turkey in the region, and how has it shifted since the beginning of the 2000s? And finally, how does the Europeanization/de-Europeanization nexus work within Greek–Turkish relations?

Greek–Turkish relations: A history of repeated and enduring enmity?

Looking at the long run of Greek–Turkish relations, the 'overall record is rivalry less than two-thirds of the time, with good neighbourly relations comprising a third' (Heraclides 2019, 3). This rivalry partly reflects the way national identities in both countries have been socially constructed (Özkırımlı and Sofos 2008). After all, national identity is defined not only from 'within' (the features that fellow-nationals share in common) but also from 'without' – namely, distinguishing and differentiating the nation from other nations or ethnic groups (Triandafyllidou 1998). Against this background, this dialectical relationship between identity and otherness advances a better understanding of those mechanisms through which the national 'other' is constructed together with national identity since the hypothesis of a 'positive national self' needs and reinforces a 'coherent other' (Millas 2019).[3]

During the Cold War and until 1999, the relationship between the two countries was considered a classic 'adversarial dyad' or 'enduring rivalry' between neighbours (Heraclides 2019, 3). After 1999, however, a period of rapprochement brought about by both countries' Europeanization process undergirded a generally peaceful period in the Aegean. Although the rapprochement was already in motion before devastating earthquakes in 1999 hit both countries hard, the disaster encouraged détente (Kadritzke 2000) and reinforced the underlying diplomatic rapprochement (Ker-Lindsay 2001) that lasted until early 2016. Since then, a series of developments have again put relations under strain. We seem to be witnessing a revival of the 'Aegean Cold War' (Ifantis 2005, 379) that recalls 'a history of obsessive symbolic and pragmatic tensions, a history of repeated and enduring enmity' (Karakatsanis 2014, xi).

Following the impasse of the 1980s and in particular, the Davos Peace Process in 1988 – although its contribution in the bilateral relations should not be underestimated – came a new era in bilateral relations and the involvement of issues such as the extent of territorial waters, national space, continental shelf, and others, which were minor issues until the 1990s in the Aegean Sea. In particular, it illustrated the crucial significance of EC/EU signals and involved the participation of state actors and civil society, and non-governmental organizations (NGOs). As Önis and Yilmaz (2008, 124), note in regards to the Davos Peace Process

> It was quite clear that without positive signals for Turkish membership from the EC/EU, the incentives for the state actors, in particular, to engineer a radical breakthrough in bilateral relations would be quite limited.

This stands true considering the series of crises the countries went into the following decade, including both major (such as the Imia/Kardak crisis in January 1996 and the diplomatic episode concerning the leader of the PKK, Abdullah Öcalan in Nairobi), and minor (such as the declaration of the Joint Defence Doctrine between Greece and Cyprus over the extension of Greek territorial waters, an action considered as *casus belli* by Turkish Prime Minister Tansu Çiller in October 1994, and the S-300 crisis in Cyprus in 1998) crises.

The Madrid Declaration in July 1997, in the aftermath of the Imia/Kardak crisis, appeared as the first step in putting an end to the warlike climate of the period with the two countries agreeing to refrain from the use of force and to respect each other's vital interests in the Aegean (Tsakonas and Dokos 2004, 107). Although distrust and suspicion remained highly salient, the post-Madrid shift highlights the significant impact of the EU in changing the foreign policy behaviour of adversaries and facilitating rapprochement through the process of Europeanization (Önis and Yilmaz 2008).

Against this background, as Turkey's European orientation was directly linked to Greece's deliberate policy of keeping the doors of the EU closed, Costas Simitis' rise to lead the Pan-Hellenic Socialist Movement (PASOK) in 1996 brought certain changes to Greece's strategic priorities, most notably a willingness to question the intensifying arms race, which was reinforcing Greek–Turkish competition and burdening an already tense and fragile bilateral security agenda (Athanasopoulou 2021). This change in Greek policy orientation opened the way to Ankara's EU accession with the Dublin and Luxemburg summits, in 1996 and 1997, respectively, according to which it was agreed to discuss Turkey's candidacy given that the latter would not stand as an obstacle to Cyprus' EU process. The process of Europeanization (and the Helsinki summit in particular) was a watershed for Turkey, albeit not without problems and challenges (Nicolaidis 2001). Cyprus remained a thorny issue in Greek–Turkish relations and one of the critical obstacles in the way of Turkey's EU vocation. This process coincided with the emergence of a new political actor on the Turkish political stage, which still dominates the country's politics.

The AKP: between Europeanization and de-Europeanization

By the time the AKP government came to power in 2002, the Helsinki summit had already set the pace of a series of political and economic reforms. For example, the country's Accession Partnership in March 2000 highlighted the short and medium-term priorities that needed to be addressed to satisfy the Copenhagen criteria. These included extended citizenship rights, freedom of expression, and prohibitions against torture. In addition, finding a comprehensive settlement to the Cyprus Question was a fundamental priority. Furthermore, needed reforms were extended to the economic sphere to transform Turkey's 'soft state' – characterized by populism, corruption, and endemic fiscal instability – into an effective regulatory state that would lay the foundations of sustained economic growth without the recurrence of crises, the historical norm in Turkey (Önis 2005, 11).

Indeed, the period 2000–2005 was one of democratic conditionality for Turkey, triggering a shift in state-society relations throughout the Turkish political landscape (Alpan 2021, 115). Moreover, it was that period that 'changes in political organisation . . . [and] changes in structures of meaning and people's minds' (Olsen 2002, 926; also quoted in Alpan 2021, 108) were front and centre in the process of Turkey's convergence with EU, in which the latter affected the domestic policy and politics of the former. Against this backdrop, the EU, through the impact of accession, has had a desecuritization effect on Turkey, and the EU's de-securitizing impact has been noted both domestically, in particular on the Kurdish issue and political Islam, and in Turkey's foreign policy like the Cyprus issue (Açıkmeşe 2013, 303).

Following the EU's conditionality, a series of further political and economic reforms, jointly crafted by the IMF and the Turkish authorities after the 2001 financial crisis, was already underway. This paved the way for an economic upturn that the AKP government was only too willing to claim credit for, and for which it gained massive approval both at home and abroad. Similarly, during the government's first term, the political reforms were also introduced and promoted to fulfil EU conditionality, a sine qua non of desecuritization. As Aras and Karakaya-Polat note:

> [T]his process of desecuritization is the result of the European Union accession process and concomitant step toward democratization, a transformation of the political landscape, and the appropriation of EU norms and principles in regional politics (quoted in Açıkmeşe 2013, 304).

Although it turned out that these political reforms were significant to pave the way for the AKP to consolidate its power domestically and act with enhanced legitimacy and become instances of counter-conduct[4] that the AKP used to pursue its own agenda (Cebeci 2016, 126), Turkey has made significant strides in fulfiling the Copenhagen political criteria and aligning its legislation with the EU. Yet, as Aydın-Düzgit (2012, 1) rightly points out, as the accession process has progressed, debates on the desirability of Turkish accession have intensified in the EU, and opposition has been increasingly based on the grounds that Turkey poses a profound challenge to the European project given the perceived ambiguities over its 'Europeanness'. The reactions and opposition mainly came from former French President Nicolas Sarkozy and German Chancellor Angela Merkel, who has asserted that Turkey's democracy, geography, history, culture, and the mindset of its politicians as well as its people qualify it as a non-European state that is ill-suited to become an EU member.

On top of that, domestic developments in Turkey, particularly the severe economic crisis since the end of the 2000s, prevented the EU from demonstrating the same enthusiasm and support for Greek–Turkish rapprochement as it did during its initial stages. This, however, did not stop the two countries from continuing their efforts to achieve amicable and stable relations while official circles in Greece were still supporting Turkey's EU prospects. For example, Georgios Katrougalos, Greece's foreign minister during the Syriza-Anel coalition government, stated that 'We're among the few European countries that still believe in that', referring to Turkey's long-stalled accession bid (Barigazzi 2019). Yet, as Onar and Anastasakis have argued (2013, 402), since the end of the 2000s, Greece and Turkey have faced intense internal challenges originating from different domestic changes. For Greece, the economic crisis has weakened its diplomatic and economic power and undermined its negotiating power vis-à-vis Turkey in difficult bilateral issues.

In contrast, by its economic growth, Turkey has been the more confident partner in the Turkish–Greek framework and has had a much more active and influential foreign policy agenda. Yet, along with the EU's reluctance to discuss Turkey's accession process, if there was ever any sincere intention, things started to change in the Turkish front, impacting its relations with Greece. This change gave space for negative perceptions and distrust towards Turkey to fester within Greek public opinion, which generally failed to take into account international developments and accepted uncritically the line put out by successive Greek governments (Christofis and Logotheti 2018; Christofis et al. 2019; Frangonikolopoulos 2019, 29).

Crucially, EU leverage was also empowering for the AKP, especially in curbing the military's predominance in Turkish politics. The Turkish Armed Forces refrained from opposing political reforms, especially because they did not want to hamper the EU harmonization process (Cebeci 2016, 216). This undoubtedly helped the AKP consolidate its power and pursue its political agenda without major restraints. In executing that agenda, the AKP government explicitly drew on the rhetoric of Europeanization/democratization, which explains Ankara's stance on foreign policy issues, particularly Greece and Cyprus, through a pro-European foreign policy discourse, making constant references to 'European norms and expectations to express Turkey's willingness to reach a viable solution' in Cyprus (Kaliber 2012) even as late as the mid-2010s when EU–Turkish relations had worsened.

By the early 2010s, however, Turkey had already given signs of change. The AKP's hegemony has been consolidated, and all previous reforms and steps towards democratization have proven tactical moves to take hold of society. The 2010 constitutional amendments, in particular, were presented as a crucial step in Turkey's EU accession and were supported vocally by liberal actors who saw them as moves towards further democratization (Cebeci 2016, 126). Since then, it has been evident that these reforms were instruments opportunistically employed in the AKP's struggle to conquer the state and suppress dissidence (Jongerden 2020).

Now, if Europeanization is understood as the convergence between Turkey and EU standards, as well as the overall and in-depth transformation of the political scene, this is likely to occur when there are possible shifts in relations of dominance. According to Olsen (2002, 926), that is, 'when there is a willingness and possibly an ability to challenge an established hegemony and win back a more central role at the global scene'. In light of the AKP hegemony over Turkey's politics and the EU's double-standard policy towards Turkey, the EU lost its place as 'a normative/political context and as a reference point' in domestic politics and debates (Aydın-Düzgit and Kaliber 2016, 5). The Arab uprisings in 2011 and Turkey's elevation to being a 'model' country for the MENA region saw the EU reference point attenuate even further and accelerated Turkey's de-Europeanization process. On the foreign policy front, this process proved to be contributing to Turkey's 'geographic imagination' and the formulation of a new foreign policy agenda, which can be considered part of the 'normalization' of Turkish politics and the identity that the AKP is trying to construct (Aras and Polat 2007; Aras and Fidan 2009), an identity that through its foreign policy is empowered through a civilizational mission (*62. Hükümet Programı*) with Ottoman cultural tradition and Sunni priorities at the core.

Empowered by the prestige the AKP was receiving in the Muslim world, a new historical narrative (Kalın 2011, 11) promoting Turkey as a central country in the capitalist world-system (Hendrick 2013, 241) was constructed. This foreign policy reconfiguration, which painstakingly tried to present Turkey as a 'central' state (Davutoğlu 2004), resulted in due course to its securitization, which rests upon an audience that is willing to grant the Turkish government a right to violate rules and international law (Wæver 2000, 251; also, 2011). Hence, by implication, securitization is prioritized above 'normal politics'. Given the AKP's shift to authoritarianism, political manipulation through the media and even legal sanctions and restrictions show that society's approval is not granted through negotiation and free discussion but by imposition and manipulation (Kaliber 2009, 112).

To that end, a series of events, including the Gezi Park protests in 2013, the collapse of the relationship between the AKP and the Gülen Movement the same year, and the impasse of the Kurdish peace process, accelerated the country's securitization. In addition, two more events should be added here: the failed coup attempt in July 2016 and the constitutional referendum in April 2017. The latter two, in particular, were unfolding in parallel with widening divisions with the West (Kirişçi 2018, 184) and the adoption of a militarized/securitized foreign policy. Concerning the EU–Turkey relationship, in particular, Kirişçi (2018, 172) argues that

> the EU's failure to respond to the coup attempt promptly and lend support to the government, led to resentment in Turkey, aggravated by the European Parliament's recommendations in November 2016 to suspend Turkey's membership negotiations.

In other words, the emphasis on militarization/securitization, Islam, civilization, and power, contributed to, and indeed accelerated, Turkey's de-Europeanization and allowed the AKP to adopt a more assertive foreign policy resorting to military force to an unprecedented degree (Öztürk 2021) after 2016 with direct consequences for Greek–Turkish relations and the overall stability in the Eastern Mediterranean.

Securitizing the Eastern Mediterranean and expanding assertions of Turkish sovereignty

The deposits of oil and natural gas discovered in the late 2000s off the coast of Cyprus have raised the stakes in the Eastern Mediterranean region. Moreover, Turkey's bid to assert itself as a pivotal regional power has grown not only concerning the MENA region but also to the Eastern Mediterranean (Bechev 2022, 182–183).

Against this background, and as signs of pragmatism and earnest attempts in Turkey's pursuing membership in the EU were still evident (Kirişçi 2018, 186), the two communities of Cyprus initiated a new peace process in 2015 that came tantalizingly close to a solution in 2017. The negotiations, however, deadlocked as crucial sticking points continued to hamper compromise. Key issues were power-sharing in a proposed federal government, territorial concessions by the Turkish Cypriots, the status of Turkish settlers, and property rights. Failure to agree led to the collapse of the negotiations in Crans Montana, Switzerland, in summer 2017. A fair share of responsibility for the negotiation deadlock has been analysed elsewhere (Christofis and Logotheti 2021; Heraclides 2021), but what is of equal importance here is the new realities presented not only for Cyprus but also Greek–Turkish relations writ large.

Concerning Cyprus, the Turkish Cypriot community was put in an awkward position when its new leadership had to negotiate with the Greek Cypriots and balance vis-à-vis the Turkish government and its aspirations. Against this background, the 'motherland saviour' discourse of the past remained a symbol of subordination, transforming in form but not in substance. It is now becoming evident in a more authoritarian, paternalistic and peremptory character. But, on the other hand, it has resulted in an acceleration of a 'normalization of partition' of the island through the right-wing Greek Cypriots' hard-line policies of the Nicos Anastasiades government, more evident after the negotiation impasse in the summer of 2017 (Ioannou 2020).

Given the disagreement concerning its Exclusive Economic Zone (EEZ) and the status and rights of the self-proclaimed Turkish Republic of Northern Cyprus, Cyprus plays a pivotal role in the Eastern Mediterranean region, as it does in Greek–Turkish relations. The failure of the talks in 2017 and the subsequent securitization of the issue by Ankara proved anew that Cyprus remains one of the central 'discursive battlefields' in the highly polarized Turkish political scene. The centrality stems from the heavy securitization of the Cyprus issue by Turkey's foreign and security policy establishment, which censors any genuine alternative. The result has been the perpetuation of statist rhetoric, evident also in the New Democracy (ND) party that came into power in Greece in 2019, 'substantially contributing to the institutionalization of a regime fetishizing such concepts as security, stability, and "national sensitivities"' (Kaliber 2009, 113).

Hydrocarbons in the Cyprus basin (as everywhere) could well prove more curse than blessing or at least bring much strife before any benefit is derived (İşeri 2019, 257). For Cyprus, the promise that untapped energy from the seafloor holds out has only intensified the interest of outside players in a divided country whose politics are already complicated enough. While natural gas has not been an explicit part of negotiations over a possible solution so far, it has become a source of strategic leverage for all parties and thus lurks just below the surface. Furthermore, the gas and oil discoveries have provided additional reasons for cooperation between the countries of the region to exploit resources for mutual gain, but at the same time, by intensifying Turkey's sense of being encircled.

Against this backdrop, the present situation in Cyprus reveals two seemingly paradoxical, but in all actuality, complementary conditions that feed Ankara's sense that it is beset by 'encirclement' – namely, the existence of a vital and imminent threat to Turkey's national security and Cyprus being an integral part of Turkey's defence. In fact, the 'encirclement syndrome' has been instrumental in depicting the extent to which the Cyprus dispute constitutes an urgent threat to the survival of the Turkish nation and state (Kaliber 2009, 114), and one that

[R]e-invented [the Eastern Mediterranean] as a regional—or in some cases sub-regional—context where Turkey's security calculations and interests on Cyprus should be situated. In the new rhetoric, the Eastern Mediterranean has signified not only the diversification and multiplication of threats, but also emerging opportunities for economic development and the prospect of becoming an activist, regional power for Turkey (Kaliber 2009, 106).

It becomes clear that the ideological construction of the Eastern Mediterranean is of immense importance as it can reveal the construction of security issues or the instrumentalization of real threats through which geopolitical orientation is reshaped and specific policies are implemented (Moudouros 2021b). As has been the case since the 1950s, politics regarding Cyprus always have repercussions for Greece, too, as the issue carries national connotations for both countries. If there is a difference today compared with the past, it is that the Eastern Mediterranean region serves as a bridge between the

AKP (and Erdoğan specifically) and nationalist factions advocating that Ankara upgrade its naval power and assert, as well as extend, its maritime sovereignty (Bechev 2022, 185) through the Mavi Vatan doctrine. Crucially and worryingly, the doctrine reveals these factions' primary threat to Turkey in the region: Greece.

The Mavi Vatan Doctrine and the Greek–Turkish relations

As a relatively new foreign policy approach, the so-called Mavi Vatan doctrine has been supported by a parliamentary alliance between the ruling AKP and the Nationalist Action Party (MHP) that began in 2015 (but became official in 2016) and the security bureaucracy and the *ulusalcı*/Eurasianist strand in Turkish politics. In this way, far-right ideas espoused by the new allies of the AKP found expression through the state apparatus. Nevertheless, the concept itself is attributed to the ultranationalist left, having been developed by a retired admiral, Cem Gürdeniz.

In short, Mavi Vatan is most often used as a shorthand expression for Ankara's maritime claims in the Eastern Mediterranean that extend Turkish sovereignty beyond agreed borders, and therefore, 'popularise the political goal of treating the seas surrounding Turkey as "homeland territory"' (Moudouros 2021b, 467). Central to these interests is the presence of large deposits of natural gas off the coast of Cyprus, 'the lion's share of [which] lies within what Turkey interprets is its exclusive economic zone' (Gingeras 2020). The coining of the term, as Gingeras points out, ultimately represents more than an act of political branding, as '[t]o a large extent, it signals a somewhat dramatic shift in doctrine within Turkish political and military circles'. For his part, Admiral Gürdeniz 'asserts that Washington intends to undermine Turkey's sovereignty in coalition with other regional powers' (Gingeras 2020). To Gürdeniz, as well as others, Greece is central to this alliance, and like in the past, Greece is allying with Western imperial powers, thus emerging as the most threatening of Turkey's neighbouring countries. In other words,

> the coup attempt contributed to the intensification of the ideological convergence between AKP and MHP, precisely because it mobilised in a direct and intense way the historical phobia of a large section of the Turkish right-wing — conservative spectrum: the fear that the Turkish nation was in danger 'of remaining without a state, a homeland and a religion' (*devletsiz, vatansız, dinsiz*) (Moudouros 2021b, 462)

Adar and Toygür argue that, since 2016, Turkish foreign policy has been based on two assumptions:

> First, because of the lack of solidarity during the 2016 attempted coup and the US partnership with the PYG/YPD in northern Syria against ISIS, Ankara believes it can no longer fully trust its Western partners. Second, it regards the West as in terminal decline owing to the retreat of liberalism and the power vacuum created by the US withdrawal from its multilateral commitments under the Trump Presidency (Adar and Toygür 2020, 2).

While it is not clear how Turkish foreign policy will develop in relation to its neighbours or the West, it is becoming abundantly clear that there will be increased tension in the Eastern Mediterranean, at least for the foreseeable future. Erdoğan's presidential address commemorating the founding of the Republic of Turkey on 29 October 2019 is quite revealing in that respect. Towards the end of his remarks, President Erdoğan surprised the audience by announcing that he would now be going live to Lieutenant Colonel Engin

Ağmış, aboard the Turkish naval frigate *TCG Gökçeada* operating in the Eastern Mediterranean. Addressing the president directly on a split TV screen before the country, Ağmış delivered a short, prepared statement to the camera, introducing himself as the vessel's captain and detailing its mission in the 'blue homeland'.[5] As he wound up his remarks before passing back to President Erdoğan, Ağmış said the following:

> I submit that we are ready to protect every swath of our 462 thousand square meter blue homeland with great determination and undertake every possible duty that may come (Gingeras 2020).

The decision to insert this live relay from a military officer in command of a Turkish naval vessel in the Eastern Mediterranean in a presidential address on the anniversary of the founding of the modern Turkish state was no coincidence. Nor was the content of Lieutenant Colonel Ağmış' remarks about the 'blue homeland' and the way it was expressed vis-à-vis specific geographical dimensions and in a way that underlined the competition in the Eastern Mediterranean and Turkey's 'rights and interests' there. It was, in sum, a highly symbolic performance designed to send a message about the willingness of the Turkish state to assert influence and, indeed, sovereignty in areas outside its politically defined borders (Moudouros 2021a, 8).

This was followed up by an 'emotional' article in *Yeni Şafak* by a pro-government journalist, İbrahim Karagül, as follows:

> The concept of the blue homeland is a wonderful definition. It is a beautiful expression that has changed the codes of our consciousness that shaped, once again, our understanding of the homeland.[6]

Turkey's 'geostrategic dogma' expressed through the Mavi Vatan doctrine legitimizes various politics, including those of national security. According to Bilgin's (2012, 153–154) analysis, this is exemplified by the primacy of geography in defining policies, the 'unique' geographical location of Turkey, its central location constituting 'the hinge of the world island that is made up of three continents' (Bilgin 2012, 154), but also the prospect of its 'encirclement by enemies', all of which are activated in times of crisis.

Greek–Turkish relations in crisis

A crisis in bilateral relations emerged right after the coup attempt at a time when the coalition government led by the leftist Syriza, and the far-right Anel (Independent Greeks) was in power. Amidst a domestic Greek economic crisis that would test the mettle of any administration, the Syriza-Anel coalition had to confront two thorny foreign policy issues that would also mark the beginning of the tense relations of the two countries: the 'harbouring' of Gülenist defectors who had fled to Greece and sought asylum after the coup attempt, and Ankara's agenda to revise the Treaty of Lausanne, a topic that continues to bubble under the surface.

In regard to the former, hours after the coup attempt, eight Turkish military personnel with ties to the Gülen movement fled to Greece seeking political asylum. This action was followed then with Ankara's demand from Greece to extradite 'the eight', as they came to be known, but Athens, abiding by Greek and international law and required the Greek authorities to open an asylum case (Christofis et al. 2019), refused to act according to

Ankara's demands. The intense discussions between representatives from both countries the following days ended with Turkey suspending its bilateral migrant readmission deal with Greece in June 2018 with the Turkish Foreign Minister Çavuşoğlu stating that Turkey will keep pressuring Greece on this issue in the future.

This incident came to add to Ankara's assertive statements regarding the revisionism of the Treaty of Lausanne, an issue that the Greek government regarded as an alarming burst of Turkish irredentism. As Tziarras notes, Turkey's revisionist geopolitical agenda abroad (including illegal maritime operations within Cyprus' EEZ) has exacerbated Greek and Greek Cypriot fears vis-à-vis Turkey that was already present because of the latter's role in Cyprus (Tziarras 2021, 41). The Lausanne Treaty signified the victory of the nationalist movement in Anatolia led by Mustafa Kemal and his associates against the European imperialist powers (1919–1922), and therefore, has been celebrated since then as one of the greatest achievements of the founder of Turkey. Now, the treaty has been seriously challenged by the AKP, and Erdoğan himself, who claims that Mustafa Kemal gave up Turkish sovereignty and shrunk the country. By implication, the criticisms towards the treaty target Greece also. As Erdoğan argued in one of his statements, 'we [Turks] gave away the [Aegean] islands', implying that Turkey is still struggling with the delimitation of what have long been thought settled borders (Christofis et al. 2019). Such statements, but also in-person meetings during Erdoğan's visit to Athens, were countered by his Greek counterpart, Prokopis Pavlopoulos, by affirming the validity of 'the Treaty of Lausanne [that still] defines the territory and the sovereignty of Greece, and of the European Union, and this treaty is non-negotiable. It has no flaws; it does not need to be reviewed or updated'.[7]

Mainstream media and governing political circles in Greece made constant references to Turkey's provocative and expansionist policies reminiscent of past times, fuelling negative public opinion towards Turkey and reinforcing the dominant view that Turkey will again use force to address international concerns (like in 1974 in Cyprus). Thus, the argument goes, any EU prospect should be out of the question. On that latter point, the findings of a recent study conducted by a team led by Ioannis N. Grigoriadis on behalf of the Greek think-tank ELIAMEP on Greek–Turkish views are interesting and revealing.[8]

While public opinion demonstrated several positive points of convergence, the interesting fact the study showed is that there is a divergence when it comes to the issue of Turkey's EU accession. Specifically, just 20.2% of Greeks surveyed support Turkey's EU accession (with 51.8% against), while, in the Turkish case, the percentage in support reaches 53.6% (with 18.5% of Turks opposed). Furthermore, concerning the domestic political situation in Turkey, the questionnaire asked: 'If Greece and Turkey were to face serious problems, which country would receive the support of world public opinion?' Interestingly, in response, just 3.8% of the Greeks and 5.9% of the Turks replied 'Turkey', while 17.5% of the Greeks and 35.9% of the Turks said 'Greece' would garner the support of other countries.

In the years that followed, and as Cyprus issued licences to large oil companies like Exxon Mobil in March 2017 for additional exploration, policymakers in Ankara interpreted energy concessions as a bid to encircle Turkey and deprive it of vital resources, and as such decided to counter this development by the deployment of Turkish warships to watch over drilling activities in Cyprus's EEZ (Grigoriadis 2021). This was by no means an isolated incident, nor was the provocation of Greece through the signing in

2019 of an EEZ agreement with the Libyan Government of National Accord (GNA), which rides roughshod over Crete. Rather, this comes as a direct response to the coup attempt and the complete concentration of power under Erdoğan, who promoted this centralization as essential to 'resoldering' state structures and restoring state power after the 2016 crisis (Moudouros 2021a, 2021b).

Ankara's overtly confrontational foreign policy should be seen in this light, which is only intensified by 'a bipolar – if fragile – geopolitical order [that] emerged in the Eastern Mediterranean with Turkey as one of the poles and the cooperating states (Cyprus, Greece, Israel, Egypt, etc.) as the other' (Tziarras 2021, 30).

Against this background, Turkish revisionist policy gained new momentum and was perhaps most visibly expressed in November 2019 through a Memorandum of Understanding (MoU) that conjured a Turkey-Libya maritime boundary, based on a Turkish EEZ that runs off the coast of several of the Dodecanese islands and Crete. The MoU alarmed Greece even more about its sovereignty and territorial integrity, especially regarding maritime zones. Thus, the mounting rhetoric from Turkish officials about their intention to revise or upgrade the Treaty of Lausanne, the new Mavi Vatan naval doctrine that extends from the Black Sea to the Aegean and the Eastern Mediterranean, and several naval and military operations had Greece (and other regional states) deeply concerned (Tziarras 2021, 35).

For its part, Greece adopted a more dynamic foreign policy in the Eastern Mediterranean as it was left with 'no other recourse than to develop a closer interest in the regional conflicts and pursue a more proactive position in seeking bilateral agreements for delimitation of its maritime borders with its neighbours' (Grigoriadis 2020, 27). At the same time, policymakers in Ankara saw Turkey's exclusion from the EastMed Gas Forum and the alignment of both adversaries, such as Egypt, and Western partners with Greece and Cyprus as affirming the urgent need for self-reliance through two of the largest naval drills in its history called 'Blue Homeland' and 'Seawolf'.

Turkey's hostile and provocative actions were not left unanswered by the EU and international organizations, which took Greece and Cyprus's side. They adopted harsh language criticizing the Turkish government and imposing sanctions (albeit quite limited ones) on Turkey concerning its resumption of oil and gas drilling in EU member states' territorial waters. Furthermore, it led to the decision by the foreign ministers of the EU to impose travel bans and asset freezes on Turkish officials.[9] This triggered a scathing reaction from Turkey's president, who boasted about Turkey's military capacity to alter the map with Greece and insulted Emmanuel Macron, the French President, further escalating tensions between Turkey and the EU (Christofis 2021). At the same time, a few weeks later, the US was stating through the American Secretary of State, Mike Pompeo, that Turkish drilling is 'illegal' and 'unacceptable',[10] putting Turkish-Western relations to yet another test.

Amidst these developments, Greek–Turkish relations deteriorated on additional grounds, most notably on the refugee/immigration issue. Tensions between Greece and Turkey rose precipitously in February and March 2020 when thousands of refugees and immigrants attempted to storm the Greek-Turkish border at Pazarkule/Kastanies near Edirne, in what the Greek and other European governments deemed a deliberate attempt by Turkey to weaponize the refugee question against Greece and Europe (Grigoriadis

2020). For example, already in 2019, then EU Council President Donald Tusk sharply criticized Ankara's action stating that 'we will never accept [refugees being] weaponized and used to blackmail us [the EU]' referring to Erdoğan's threat to 'send 3.6 million refugees your [i.e., Europe's] way' (Christofis 2021).

Relations soured further in July 2020 following the decision of the Turkish administration to 'politicize' and convert the Hagia Sophia and Chora museums to mosques (Christofis 2020). Finally, tensions reached a new peak in Greek political, diplomatic and media circles in summer 2020, following the dispatch of *Oruç Reis*, a Turkish maritime research vessel, on an exploration mission southeast of the Greek island of Kastellorizo in the Eastern Mediterranean with Athens to respond by sending naval vessels to protest the *Oruç Reis'* research activities, confronting the exploration vessel's Turkish naval escort. This military escalation reached a peak on 12 August when the Greek frigate *Lemnos* collided with the Turkish frigate *Kemal Reis*, fortunately, without further escalation.

Conclusion

The (almost) weekly incidents in the Aegean, on issues related to maritime boundaries, rocks, and islets, search and rescue, national airspace, and flight information regions (FIR), have marked the rekindling of the 'Aegean Cold War'. Be it by accident or design, the Aegean issue involves immediate and grave repercussions and considerably increases the probability of an armed clash.

It has become evident that the inconsistent policy of the EU towards Turkey has not only undermined any possible solution in the Eastern Mediterranean but also demonstrates that its role in promoting regional cooperation and integration, and as an institution that functions as a conflict resolution agent, has been recently only minimal. As a result, for the past decade, the EU lost its normative force and its relations with Turkey, being perhaps at the lowest point during the AKP's administration, proved to be disastrous for the entire Eastern Mediterranean region, let alone for the 'troubled triangle' of Turkey, Greece, and Cyprus.

Against this background, Turkey's de-Europeanization since the early 2010s led to a militarized/securitized domestic and foreign policy that instrumentalized a discourse that holds Turkey 'captive' of its hostile neighbours. The Mavi Vatan foreign policy that continues to press Turkey's claims and challenges the sovereignty and rights of neighbouring Greece and Cyprus, gives Turkey, and Erdoğan himself, significant leverage in negotiations with Greece and the EU as a whole (Bechev 2022, 185). This becomes evident in Erdoğan's several anti-EU statements, which on several occasions contained not-so-veiled threats to Brussels. Indeed, apart from threatening to send millions of refugees to the EU if the latter persisted in calling out the Turkish military operation in Syria,[11] Erdoğan's threats extended to threats of sending ISIS prisoners held in Turkey towards Europe unless EU sanctions were lifted in response to Turkey's drilling for gas in the Mediterranean off Cyprus.[12]

Interestingly, recent developments show that a complete unbridgeable political rift was avoided, as Erdoğan called for a new Turkey–EU summit to relaunch ties[13] and discuss Eastern Mediterranean tensions. At the same time, Ankara and Athens have resumed talks easing months of tensions and agreed to gradually normalize their relationship through a series of exploratory talks in both capitals without however, bearing any fruit. These were followed by a high-level meeting between the foreign ministers of Greece and Turkey in May 2021, but a joint press conference in Ankara in May 2021 erupt into a public spat revealing that the only framework through which Greek–Turkish relations are workable is an EU framework that will mediate and provide a basic setlist of principles and conditions.

Notes

1. Since 2001, the book has gone through approximately 80 editions and been translated into several languages.
2. A number of Turkish transnational institutions, such as the *Diyanet* (Diyanet İşleri Başkanlığı/Presidency of Religious Affairs), TİKA (Turkish Cooperation and Coordination Agency/Türk İşbirliği ve Koordinasyon Ajansı), and others, have been the most active apparatuses of the AKP's Turkey in the Western Balkans, at least, since the mid-2000s (Bošković et al. 2015; Öztürk and Akgönül 2020; https://www.tika.gov.tr/en/news/analysis_turkeys_balkan_policy_not_interest_oriented-21145).
3. Threat perceptions on both sides of the Aegean are not symmetric. As Aydın (2004) notes, given the disparity between the two countries' history, resources and population, it is understandable that most Greeks consider Turkey a 'threat', but that Turks do not attribute priority to the 'Greek threat' in return. However, distrust created by 'living history' is a sense that is shared and continually reinforced on both sides of the Aegean.
4. Borrowing from Waever, Cebeci (2016) notes that '"counter-conduct" in the case of the EU's governmentality refers to those techniques employed by third countries to counter and resist the EU's imposition of its "silent disciplining power" on them'.
5. https://www.haberturk.com/gokceada-firkateyn-komutani-yarbay-engin-agmis-cumhuriyet-bayrami-resepsiyonu-na-canli-baglandi-2535477.
6. https://www.yenisafak.com/yazarlar/ibrahim-karagul/mavi-vatan-adini-butun-renkleriyle-sevdigim-vatan-2049447. See, also, Moudouros (2021b).
7. http://www.newgreektv.com/english-news/item/23913-how-global-mediareacted-to-the-turkish-president-s-visit-to-greece.
8. The polls were conducted by two distinguished polling companies in Greece and Turkey, MRB and KONDA, respectively, as part of a project by the research partnership between diaNEOsis, ELIAMEP and the Istanbul Policy Center (IPC). They took place between 19 and 21 February 2021 with the participation of 1,022 Greek and 1,142 Turkish citizens. As part of the same study, 12 in-depth interviews were conducted with Greek experts on Greek–Turkish relations. Ioannis N. Grigoriadis and Balta (2021).
9. https://www.consilium.europa.eu/en/press/press-releases/2020/02/27/turkey-s-illegal-drilling-activities-in-the-eastern-mediterranean-eu-puts-two-persons-on-sanctions-list/.
10. https://www.reuters.com/article/us-usa-greece-pompeo-mitsotakis-idUSKCN1WK04I.
11. https://apnews.com/article/Syria-Turkey-Greece-middle-east-international-news-2e2c94ededd1c5fa9dd49950c0068e9f.
12. https://apnews.com/article/214e7c236e414e59aae5db0025899533.
13. https://www.euractiv.com/section/global-europe/news/erdogan-tells-merkel-he-wants-turkey-eu-summit-by-july/.

Disclosure statement

No potential conflict of interest was reported by the author(s).

ORCID

Nikos Christofis http://orcid.org/0000-0001-7899-9959

References

AKP. *62. Hükümet programı.* 2014. Istanbul: AKP. September.

Açıkmeşe, S.A. 2013. EU conditionality and desecuritization nexus in Turkey. *Southeast European and Black Sea Studies* 13, no. 3: 303–23. doi:10.1080/14683857.2013.812772.

Adar, S., and İ. Toygür 2020. Turkey, the EU and the Eastern Mediterranean crisis: Militarization of foreign policy and power rivalry. SWP Comment. December 9 https://www.swp-berlin.org/en/publication/turkey-the-eu-and-the-eastern-mediterranean-crisis/ (accessed December 14, 2020).

Alpan, B. 2016. From AKP's 'conservative democracy' to 'advanced democracy': Shifts and challenges in the debate on 'Europe'. *South European Society and Politics* 21, no. 1: 15–28. doi:10.1080/13608746.2016.1155283.

Alpan, B. 2021. Europeanization and EU–Turkey relations: Three domains, four periods. In *EU-Turkey relations: Theories, institutions, and policies*, ed. W. Reiners and E. Turhan, 107–38. Cham: Palgrave.

Alpan, B., and A.E. Ozturk. 2022. Turkey and the Balkans: Bringing the Europeanisation/De-Europeanisation nexus into question. *Southeast European and Black Sea Studies* 22, no. 1 forthcoming. doi:10.1080/14683857.2022.2034385.

Aras, B., and H. Fidan. 2009. Turkey and Eurasia: Frontiers of a new geographic imagination. *New Perspectives on Turkey* 40: 193–215. doi:10.1017/S0896634600005276.

Aras, B., and R.K. Polat. 2007. Turkey and the Middle East: Frontiers of the new geographic imagination. *Australian Journal of International Affairs* 61, no. 4: 471–88. doi:10.1080/10357710701684930.

Athanasopoulou, E. 2021. Η Μετέωρη Πολιτική και Στρατηγική της Αθήνας προς την Τουρκία: Η Εσωτερική Παράμετρος της Συναίνεσης [Athens' undecided policy and strategy towards Turkey: The internal parameter of consensus]. In *Εξωτερική Πολιτική της Ελλάδας: Επιλογές & Προσδοκίες στον 21ο Αιώνα [The Foreign Policy of Greece: Choices & Expectations in the 21st Century]*, ed. E. Athanasopoulou, H. Tsardanidis, and E.T. Fakiolas, 51–110. Athens: Papazisis.

Aydın, M. 2004. Contemporary Turkish-Greek relations: Constraints and opportunities. In *Turkish-Greek relations: The security dilemma in the Aegean*, ed. M. Aydin and K. Ifantis, 21–52. London: Routledge.

Aydın-Düzgit, S. 2012. *Constructions of European identity: Debates and discourses on Turkey and the EU*. Basingstoke: Palgrave.

Aydın-Düzgit, S., and A. Kaliber. 2016. Encounters with Europe in an Era of domestic and international turmoil: Is Turkey a De-Europeanising candidate country?. *South European Society and Politics* 21, no. 1: 1–14. doi:10.1080/13608746.2016.1155282.

Barigazzi, J 2019. Greek foreign minister: EU should keep door open for Turkey. Politico. May 16 https://www.politico.eu/article/greece-fm-eu-should-keep-door-open-for-turkey-accession-bid/ (accessed July 12, 2020).

Bechev, D. 2022. *Turkey under Erdogan: How a country turned from democracy and the west*. New Haven: Yale University Press.

Bieri, M., and Z. Nechev. 2016. Time ot seize the Greek opportunity. *Policy Perspectives* 4/3: 1–4.

Bilgin, P. 2012. Turkey's 'geopolitics dogma'. In *The return of geopolitics in Europe? Social mechanisms and foreign policy identity crises*, ed. S. Guzzini, 151–73. Cambridge: Cambridge University Press.

Bošković, M.M., D. Reljić, and A. Vračić. 2015. Elsewhere in the neighborhood: Reaching out to the Western Balkans. In *Turkey's public diplomacy*, ed. B.S. Çevik and P. Seib, 99–120. Basingstoke: Palgrave.

Çandar, C. 2022. Turkey in Syria: A neo-Ottomanist or a nationalist moment for Erdoğan? In *The Kurds in Erdoğan's 'New' Turkey: Domestic and International Implications*, ed. N. Christofis, 199–217. London and New York: Routledge.

Cebeci, M. 2016. De-Europeanisation or counter-conduct? Turkey's democratisation and the EU. *South European Society and Politics* 21, no. 1: 119–32. doi:10.1080/13608746.2016.1153996.

Christofis, N. 2020. Η πολιτικοποίηση τη Αγίας Σοφίας: από το 'Ισλάμ στο έθνος' ως το 'έθνος στο Ισλάμ' [The politicization of Ayia Sofia: From the 'Islam in the nation' to the 'nation in Islam']. *Syghrona Themata* 149: 28–31.

Christofis, N. 2021. 'You sleep with the devil; you wake up in hell!' On the new EU–Turkey deal. *The Commentaries* 1, no. 1: 1–7. EU Turkey Civic Commission. April http://eutcc.net/wp-content/uploads/2021/04/Commentary-1_.Christofis_EU-Turkey_Refugee-Deal.pdf

Christofis, N., B. Baser, and A.E. Öztürk. 2019. The view from next door: Greek–Turkish relations after the coup attempt in Turkey. *The International Spectator* 54, no. 2: 67–86. doi:10.1080/03932729.2019.1570758.

Christofis, N., and A. Logotheti. 2018. Turkey in Syriza's foreign policy, 2015–2017. In *The role of the image in the Greek–Turkish relations*, ed. Z.M. Uzuner, 103–20. Frankfurt am Main: Peter Lang.

Christofis, N., and A. Logotheti. 2021. Between political survival and regional power: The justice and development party and Cyprus, 2002–2017. *British Journal of Middle Eastern Studies*: 1–18. doi:10.1080/13530194.2021.1903833.

Davutoğlu, A. 2001. *Stratejik derinlik*. Istanbul: Küre Yayınları.

Davutoğlu, A. 2004. Türkiye Merkez Ülke Olmalı. Radikal. 26 February.

Frangonikolopoulos, C.A. 2019. Turkey in the greek media: The need for a shift from confrontation – to peace-oriented journalism. In *Greece and Turkey in conflict and cooperation: From Europeanization to De-Europeanization*, ed. A. Heraclides and G.A. Çakmak, 224–37. London and New York: Routledge.

Gingeras, R. 2020. Blue homeland: The heated politics behind Turkey's new maritime strategy. *War on the Rocks*. June 20 https://warontherocks.com/2020/06/blue-homeland-the-heated-politics-behind-turkeys-new-maritime-strategy/ (accessed January 14, 2021).

Grigoriadis, I.N. 2020. The Eastern Mediterranean as an emerging crisis zone: Greece and Cyprus in a volatile regional environment. In *Eastern Mediterranean in uncharted waters: Perspectives on emerging geo-political realities*, ed. M. Tanchum, 25–30. Turkey: Konrad Adenauer Stiftung.

Grigoriadis, I.N. 2021. Greek–Turkish relations. In *Oxford handbook of Greek politics*, ed. K. Featherstone and D.A. Sotiropoulos, 613–30. Oxford: Oxford University Press.

Grigoriadis, I.N, and E. Balta. 2021. *Joint Greek-Turkish public opinion survey: Wave I*. Athens & Istanbul: ELIAMEP-DiaNEOsis and IPC. May 15.

Haynes, J. 2007. *Religion and development: Conflict or cooperation?*. Cham: Springer.

Hendrick, J.D. 2013. *Gulen: The ambiguous politics of market Islam in Turkey and the world*. New York: NYU Press.

Heraclides, A. 2019. Greek-Turkish relations and conflict: A bird's-eye view. In *Greece and Turkey in conflict and cooperation: From Europeanization to De-Europeanization*, ed. A. Heraclides and G.A. Çakmak, 3–12. London and New York: Routledge.

Heraclides, A. 2021. Ελλάδα, Ελληνοκύπριοι και Κυπριακό: Ένα Χρονικό Χαμένων Ευκαιριών [Greece, Greek Cypriots, and the Cyprus issue: A chronicle of lost opportunities]. In *Εξωτερική Πολιτική της Ελλάδας: Επιλογές & Προσδοκίες στον 21° Αιώνα [The foreign policy of Greece: Choices & expectations in the 21st century]*, ed. E. Athanasopoulou, H. Tsardanidis, and E. T. Fakiolas, 191–218. Athens: Papazisis.

Ifantis, K. 2005. Greece's Turkish dilemmas: There are back again. *South East European Studies* 5, no. 3: 379–94.

Ioannou, G. 2020. *The normalization of Cyprus' partition among Greek Cypriots: Political economy and political culture in a divided society.* Basingstoke: Palgrave.

İşeri, E. 2019. Turkey's entangled (energy) security concerns and the Cyprus question in the Eastern Mediterranean. In *Greece and Turkey in conflict and cooperation: From Europeanization to De-Europeanization,* ed. A. Heraclides and G.A. Çakmak, 257–70. London and New York: Routledge.

Jongerden, J. 2020. Conquering the state, subordinating society: A Kurdish perspective on the development of AKP authoritarianism in Turkey. In *Erdoğan's 'New' Turkey: Attempted coup d'état and the acceleration of political crisis,* ed. N. Christofis, 200–15. London and New York: Routledge.

Kadritzke, N. 2000. Greece's earthquake diplomacy. Le Monde diplomatique, June https://mon dediplo.com/2000/06/06greece (accessed June 14, 2021).

Kaliber, A. 2009. Re-imagining Cyprus: The rise of regionalism in Turkey's security lexicon. In *Cyprus: A conflict at the crossroads,* ed. T. Diez and N. Tocci, 105–23. Manchester: Manchester University Press.

Kaliber, A. 2012. Turkey's Cyprus policy: A case of contextual Europeanisation. In *Turkey and the European Union: Processes of Europeanisation,* ed. Ç. Nas and Y. Özer, 225–41. Surray: Ashgate.

Kalın, İ. 2011. Soft power and public diplomacy in Turkey. *Perceptions XVI, No 3:* 5–23.

Karakatsanis, K. 2014. *Turkish-Greek relations: Rapprochement, civil society and the politics of friendship.* London and New York: Routledge.

Ker-Lindsay, J. 2001. Greek-Turkish rapprochement: The impact of disaster diplomacy?. *Cambridge Review of International Affairs* 14, no. 1: 215–32. doi:10.1080/09557570008400339.

Kirişçi, K. 2018. *Turkey and the west: Faultlines in a troubled alliance.* Washington: Brookings Institution Press.

Millas, H. 2019. Greek–Turkish differences and similarities: National stereotypes and their implications. In *Greece and Turkey in conflict and cooperation: From Europeanization to De-Europeanization,* ed. A. Heraclides and G.A. Çakmak, 66–86. London and New York: Routledge.

Moudouros, N. 2021a. Η Ανατολική Μεσόγειος ως «Γαλάζια Πατρίδα»: «ωέες» γεωπολιτικές αντιλήψεις και ο συνασπισμός της «επιβίωσης του κράτους» στην Τουρκία [The Eastern Mediterranean as 'Blue Homeland': 'New' geopolitical perceptions and the coalition of 'survival of the state' in Turkey]. *Annual Review of History, Society, and Politics* 7: 7–30.

Moudouros, N. 2021b. "Blue Homeland" and Cyprus: The "Survival of the State" coalition and Turkey's changing geopolitical doctrine in the Eastern Mediterranean. *Vestnik RUDN. International Relations* 21, no. 3: 459–71. doi:10.22363/2313-0660-2021-21-3-459-471.

Nicolaidis, K. 2001. Europe's tainted mirror: Reflections on Turkey's candidacy status after Helsinki. In *Greek–Turkish relations in the era of globalization,* ed. D. Keridis and D. Triantafyllou, 245–77. Dulles: Brassey's.

Öktem, K. 2010. *New Islamic actors after the Wahhabi Intermezzo: Turkey's return to the Muslim Balkans.* Oxford: European Studies Centre; University of Oxford.

Olsen, J.P. 2002. The many faces of Europeanization. *Journal of Common Market Studies* 40, no. 5: 921–52. doi:10.1111/1468-5965.00403.

Onar, N.F., and O. Anastasakis. 2013. Sustaining engagement? On symmetries and asymmetries in Greek–Turkish relations. *Southeast European and Black Sea Studies* 13, no. 3: 401–06. doi:10.1080/14683857.2013.824669.

Önis, Z. 2005. Domestic politics, international norms and challenges to the state: Turkey-EU relations in the post-Helsinki era. In *Turkey and the European Union: Domestic politics, economic integration and international dynamics,* ed. A. Çarkoğlu and B. Rubin, 8–31. London: Frank Cass.

Önis, Z. 2021. Turkish policy in flux. *Turkish Area Studies Review* 38: 3–8.

Önis, Z., and Ş. Yilmaz. 2008. Greek–Turkish rapprochement: Rhetoric or reality? *Political Science Quarterly* 123, no. 1: 123–49. doi:10.1002/j.1538-165X.2008.tb00619.x.

Özkırımlı, U., and S. Sofos. 2008. *Tormented by history: Nationalism in Greece and Turkey.* London: Hurst.

Öztürk, A.E. 2020. The ambivalence of Turkish soft power in Southeast Europe. *Border Crossing* 10, no. 2: 111–28. doi:10.33182/bc.v10i2.1050.

Öztürk, A.E. 2021. *Religion, identity and power: Turkey and the Balkans in the twenty-first century.* Edinburgh: Edinburgh University Press.

Öztürk, A.E., and S. Akgönül. 2020. Turkey: Forced marriage or marriage of convenience with the Western Balkans? In *The Western Balkans in the world: Linkages and relations with Non-Western Countries*, ed. F. Bieber and N. Tzifakis, 225–40. London and New York: Routledge.

Panagiotou, R., and N. Tzifakis. 2021. Ο Μεταβαλλόμενος Ρόλος της Ελλάδας στα Δυτικά Βαλκάνια: Μεταξύ Απομόνωσης και Ρόλου Προστάτη [The changing role of Greece in the Western Balkans: Between isolation and the role of protector]. In *Εξωτερική Πολιτική της Ελλάδας: Επιλογές & Προσδοκίες στον 21ο Αιώνα [The foreign policy of Greece: Choices & expectations in the 21st century]*, ed. E. Athanasopoulou, H. Tsardanidis, and E.T. Fakiolas, 239–300. Athens: Papazisis.

Triandafyllidou, A. 1998. National identity and the 'other'. *Ethnic and Racial Studies* 21, no. 4: 593–612. doi:10.1080/014198798329784.

Tsakonas, P., and T. Dokos. 2004. Greek–Turkish relations in the early twenty-first century: A view from athens. In *The future of Turkish foreign policy*, ed. L.G. Martin and D. Keridis, 101–26. Cambridge: MA and London: The MIT Press.

Tziarras, Z. 2021. The stakes for Greece and Cyprus in the Eastern Mediterranean. In *The scramble for the Eastern Mediterranean. Energy and geopolitics*, ed. V. Talbot, 29–45. Milan: Ledizioni LediPublishing.

Wæver, O. 2000. The EU as a security actor: Reflections from a pessimistic constructivist on post-sovereign security order. In *International relations theory and the politics of European integration: power, security and community*, ed. M. Kelstrup and M.C. Williams, 250–94. London and New York: Routldge.

Wæver, O. 2011. Politics. *Security, Theory. Security Dialogue* 42, no. 4–5: 465–80. doi:10.1177/0967010611418718.

Yavuz, M.H. 2020. *Nostalgia for the Empire: The politics of Neo-Ottomanism.* Oxford: Oxford University Press.

Web

https://www.haberturk.com/gokceada-firkateyn-komutani-yarbay-engin-agmis-cumhuriyet-bayrami-resepsiyonu-na-canli-baglandi-2535477.

https://www.yenisafak.com/yazarlar/ibrahim-karagul/mavi-vatan-adini-butun-renkleriyle-sevdigim-vatan-2049447.

http://www.newgreektv.com/english-news/item/23913-how-global-mediareacted-to-the-turkish-president-s-visit-to-greece.

https://www.eliamep.gr/en/project.

https://www.consilium.europa.eu/en/press/press-releases/2020/02/27/turkey-s-illegal-drilling-activities-in-the-eastern-mediterranean-eu-puts-two-persons-on-sanctions-list/.

https://www.reuters.com/article/us-usa-greece-pompeo-mitsotakis-idUSKCN1WK04I.

https://apnews.com/article/syria-turkey-greece-middle-east-international-news-2e2c94ededd1c5fa9dd49950c0068e9f.

https://apnews.com/article/214e7c236e414e59aae5db0025899533.

https://www.euractiv.com/section/global-europe/news/erdogan-tells-merkel-he-wants-turkey-eu-summit-by-july/.

https://www.tika.gov.tr/en/news/analysis_turkeys_balkan_policy_not_interest_oriented-21145.

Foreign direct investment (FDI) as indicator of regime type: contemporary Serbian–Turkish relations

Sabina Pacariz (iD)

ABSTRACT
This paper investigates the relationship between regime type and foreign policy through the observational lens of the Serbian – Turkish bilateral relationship starting from 2009 to 2018. The approach was chosen to analyse sources of authoritarian power at the points of convergence between domestic and foreign policy, in a realm free from EU conditionality and the push towards liberal democracy. The article argues that investigating foreign direct investment (FDI) in hybrid regimes dependant on foreign capital provides more granular insight into the wielding and consolidation of incumbent power. An empirical examination of the mutual economic relations and the trajectory of the Turkish factory in Serbia indicate that, while Turkish FDI are of smaller financial worth than investments of EU actors, they are highly valuable in qualitatively portraying the complexity of political power. The paper employs the concept of hybridity more holistically to incorporate the regime ambivalence across the entire trio of politics, economy, and society, thus providing simultaneous insight into the embeddedness of informal mechanisms throughout formal institutions, the fusion of economic and political authorities, and the personalization of political power in Serbia. Process-tracing was the primary method of analysis. .

Introduction

In the light of mutual historical stereotypes and the developments in the Balkans during the infamous 1990s, thriving bilateral relations between Serbia and Turkey seem least likely. However, over the past few years, closer political and economic cooperation has been evident, especially with the consolidation of power in both countries respectively. It is intriguing how bilateral relations have evolved during the rule of Serbian President Aleksandar Vučić, a former radical nationalist turned vocal pro-European (Subotić 2017). Not only have the number of Turkish investments in Serbia increased considerably during Vučić's tenure, but he and Turkish President Recep Tayyıp Erdoğan have met frequently, including six meetings in 2017 alone. All these developments raise questions about the stakes of this sudden improvement. Is it a mere coincidence or deliberate outcome of the rising authoritarianism on both sides? After all, the complexity of the relationship has not changed. The often negative mutual stereotypes have been perpetuated over a long time and exploited by political and intellectual elites during the 1990s (Tanasković 1992, 1993; Jevtić 1993; Cigar 1994). Such perceptions include notions of enmity, danger, and a potential Muslim threat (Galijašević 2011; Dević 2016; Cigar 1994, 2003; Jevtić 2011). The resilience of such symbolism was illustrated during the 2017 state visit of Turkish President, Recep Tayyip Erdoğan, to Serbia, when Serbian President Aleksandar Vučić opened the press conference with: 'We should all bear in mind that it is no longer 1389 and Turkey is now a friend of Serbia' (Nova Srpska politička misao).

As already mentioned in the introduction to this special issue, Turkish involvement in the Balkans has often been considered as either rival or complementary influence to the EU (Alpan and Ozturk 2022). This article confirms the necessity for an independent and multidimensional analysis of Turkish involvement but takes a somewhat different perspective by turning the observation lens towards the domestic level. It uses the bilateral relationship with Turkey better to understand the consolidation of political power in Serbia. Serbia has mainly been studied through the perspectives of democratization (Bunce and Wolchik 2010; Bieber 20177, 2017b, Ramet, 2013 & 2017) and Europeanization (Subotić 2010; Vachudova 2014; Kmezić 2017; Džankić et al. 2019, Fagan & Wunsch, 2019, Sedelmeier, 2019). Its conflictual past also generated significant literature on transitional justice (Kostovicova and Bojicić-Dželilović 2006, Subotić, 2011, Gordy, 2013, Obradović-Wochnik, 2013). The most common recent notion to arise in this context has been 'stabilitocracy', which refers to a pattern of rule advanced by political elites in the Western Balkans to provide stability instead of democracy in exchange for legitimization by EU actors (Bieber 2018b &2020; BiEPAG 2017). While the role of the EU as the crucial international factor is indisputable for the study of Western Balkan regimes, this article argues that by switching attention to a foreign actor that does not impose conditionality and is a powerful regional force, we gain a closer insight into mechanisms that unfold more 'organically' ansd are thus more illustrative of the ruling regime. It is based on the contention that negotiations over inbound FDI from an economically capable country that is also authoritarian depict how bilateral arrangements are primarily embedded in informal networks, thus stripping power away from the formal institutions and accumulating it around the incumbents. Such practices blur the division of powers among the different sectors of the state and result in the concentration of political power, in this case, personified through the Serbian President, Aleksandar Vučić. The management of FDI eventually becomes a bargaining process for domestic influence. This analytical perspective has been far less prevalent in the academic literature on the Western Balkans, with scholars typically treating these factors (FDI and informal networks) as separate or unrelated phenomena. The present study aims to expand that discussion by emphasizing the salience of non-institutionalized arrangements in foreign policy that bolster the fusion and personalization of powers in hybrid regimes.

Unlike in many Balkan countries where Turkey has exploited religious ties with considerable comfort (Ozturk 2021), it wavered from such an approach in Serbia after the unsuccessful mediation for uniting the Islamic Communities (Slobodna Evropa). However, Turkey has recently shown ample economic and political involvement in this regional anchor country. Serbia's interest in deeper ties is not immediately evident, especially considering its EU candidacy and historical animosity towards Turkey. These queries are central in framing the principal line of inquiry: what brings the sudden change in the mutual relations? What kind of relationship exists between foreign policy and competitive authoritarian regimes? Are they mutually supportive? How are bilateral developments negotiated? Considering Serbian`s post-socialist configuration and the dependency on foreign capital, the paper is more precisely interested in the political economy aspects of such relationship, thus questioning how are FDI managed by the elites in competitive authoritarian regimes, and to what extent do FDI support the power of the incumbents? Has the relationship become institutionally more deep-seated? Does it subsequently buttress the regime type?

The conceptual framework rests on the third wave democratization literature and allocates particular attention to Offe`s triple transition of post-socialist societies (Offe, 1993). The article contends that transition to market democracies is not a linear process. The post-socialist states of the Western Balkan clearly illustrate the tendency to evolve into separate regime types that are neither fully authoritarian nor democratic and resemble market economies while having large properties controlled by the state that have formal rules and institutions, yet incumbents control processes via informal networks. Such hybridity across politics, economy, and society was enabled by the incumbents` fusion of power due to lacking controlling mechanisms; a possibility Offe warned us about at the very beginning of transition (Ibid.). The revamp of similar practices in the contemporary context can be observed in the privatization of state-owned companies, mainly through foreign brownfield investments. The details are further explained in the next section.

The research questions are analysed through empirical research of the economic relations between Serbia and Turkey in the period 2009–2018, particularly the initiation of a Turkish business that will later open the way for more Turkish FDI in Serbia, namely the 'Jeanci' factory. Applying a mainly qualitative approach, the findings indicate that incumbents in competitive authoritarian regimes exploit foreign relations with non-liberal actors to consolidate power domestically. And although the position of the incumbents is reinforced through such foreign policy, this power is not stable due to the non-institutionalized type of cooperation.

While looking at political developments on both sides, the article is primarily interested in how relations with Turkey serve as an alternative perspective in explicating power for the Serbian leadership. The research period is divided into two phases: the 'thawing phase' (2009–2013) and the 'honeymoon phase' (2014–2018). Somewhat hesitant relations marked the first phase, occasionally infused with mutual scepticism. Between 2009 and 2013, much diplomatic effort was invested in bringing the two countries closer, and economic cooperation was thin on the ground. The event that distinguished these two stages and caused a significant diplomatic crisis was President Erdoğan's official visit to Kosovo in 2013, where he infamously declared that 'Kosovo is Turkey, and Turkey is Kosovo' (Balkan Insight a). Though it seemed initially as if the statement might push relations to a new low, they improved considerably in the second phase, which saw a significant rise in Turkish investment in Serbia.

It is important to underline that the division to 'thawing' and the 'honeymoon phase' also coincides with changes in political leadership in both Turkey and Serbia. The thawing phase coincided with the prominent role of Ahmet Davutoğlu in Turkish politics, especially in foreign affairs. In interactions with Balkan countries, Davutoğlu prioritized relations to Muslim communities, which resulted in a somewhat reserved attitude towards Serbia. The opening of Turkish state agencies and the arrival of Turkish companies in Serbia lagged years behind the increase of such activity in Serbia's neighbours. While the infamous statement of Erdoğan in 2013 (Balkan Insight c) caused diplomatic setbacks, it was followed by an unexpected improvement in bilateral relations. Apparently, against all odds, bilateral relations entered their 'honeymoon' stage, which saw a tripling of trade exchange, a rising number of Turkish investments, and frequent high-level bilateral visits. The second stage co-occurred with the gradual consolidation of power for Vučić within his own political party and in state leadership (). In 2017, Vučić won the presidential elections but chose not to resign from his party presidency despite his new role (Predsednik). In Turkey, on the other hand, AKP leadership saw the withdrawal of Davutoğlu and the dominance of Erdoğan within the party and state echelons. Moreover, Turkey in 2017 moved to a presidential system, allowing Erdoğan an even larger power base (European Policy Centre). To sum up, a visible improvement of mutual relations coincides with the consolidation of power in both states. While the larger geopolitical context had a significant impact on increasing investors` interest in Serbia, the authoritarian inclinations should not be ignored either.

How do political, economic, and social hybridity support authoritarian rule?

Political power in Serbia has mainly been studied through the democratization and Europeanization literature (Schimmelfennig et al. 2005, Mungiu-Pippidi, 2012; Vachudova 2014; Džankić et al. 2019). As such, Serbia has been mistakenly categorized alongside post-socialist states with wildly different trajectories, as it did not face a 'democratic revolution' at the end of communism, which problematizes later concepts of 'democratic backsliding' and 'illiberal turn' (Hanley and Vachudova 2018; Vachudova 2019). These concepts cannot be applied to the continuous Serbian movement between different levels of authoritarianism (Pavlović 2004; Pavlaković 2005; Gordy 2004).

The democratization literature implies that the transition process entails a linear trajectory, the endpoint of which is market democracy (Fukuyama 1989; Blanchard and Layard 1991; Lipton et al. 1990). It attaches little importance to the possibility that some states will stall once reaching a particular stage then regress into authoritarianism, or like Serbia, develop into a different regime type (Pavlović 2016; Bieber 2020; Lavrič and Bieber 2021). Several authors have elaborated on the emergence of hybrid regimes but usually treat it as a sub-type either of democracy (Lauth 1997; Merkel 2004) or authoritarianism (Bunce and Wolchik 2010). Moreover, the 'hybrid regime' concept is often used interchangeably with 'competitive authoritarianism' (Levitsky and Way 2002, 2010). Problematically, these conceptualizations focus too much on the political sphere and neglect the all-important economic and social spheres. The regime change to market democracy is far from completed in Serbia; a phenomenon Offe predicted when warning about the dangers of simultaneous creation of markets, democratic institutions, and rules by the same privileged actors (Offe 1991). Therefore, the *presumptions of linear transition* and hybridity as *a distinctly political notion* are both disputable in the study of political power.

The influence of external relations over regime type in the Western Balkans has mostly been studied through the Europeanization perspective (Schimmelfennig et al. 2005; Subotić 2010, Mungiu-Pippidi, 2012; Vachudova 2014; Kmezić 2017; Džankić et al. 2019; Bieber 2020). The 'stability dilemma' (Wittkowski 2000) remained at the top of the EU's Serbia agenda throughout the post-communist period, largely overlooking democratization, let alone economic liberalization (Kostovicova and Bojicić-Dželilović 2006). Unlike in CEE, where enlargement motivated broad-based reform (Vachudova 2010), the EU focused on geostrategic motives in the Western Balkans (Bieber 2018b, 2020), producing rather cosmetic changes with a limited impact on political values (Subotić 2010, 2011). The recent concept of 'stabilitocracy', which this article also adopts as a useful rubric, emerged in the analysis of the EU's ambiguous role in reform in the Western Balkans and the ways that region's regimes have manipulated it to consolidate power (Bieber 2020; BiEPAG 2017). The article does not dispute the EU's crucial role in understanding Serbian regime dynamics but argues that by taking the conditionality factor out of the analysis, we can observe how the power processes unfold more organically.

Existing strands of research have all recognized Serbia's authoritarian inclinations but have so far failed to explain the influence of external actors other than the EU. Power is primarily observed in a limiting manner, either through the EU or the post-conflict scope, almost locking the regime into a stability-security paradigm. The insufficient focus on economic processes or other potential sources of power leaves the authoritarian mechanisms only partly exposed. Similarly, under-researched is the role of informality, not as a separate phenomenon, but as a binding thread across the foreign and domestic realms. While acknowledging this literature's contribution to exposing the illiberal aspects of the current regime, the article argues that wielding political power in Serbia is a more complex and dynamic process. The literature presents a somewhat truncated portrayal of the incumbent's regime, limiting their manoeuvring field to providing a façade of stability and provisional democracy approved by the EU. The lens of observation needs to be widened to include foreign actors other than the EU, look deeper into the domestic context, and acknowledge the critical importance of the triadic relationship among politics, economy, and society. In other words, understanding political power in Serbia demands a more sophisticated lens of observation that can both zoom out to include broader aspects of international politics and zoom in to uncover fine details in the tapestry of domestic power.

Conceptually, this article takes stabilitocracy as a starting point due to the importance it accords to the coalescence of the external and domestic contexts and its recognition of widespread authoritarian rule in the Western Balkans. The notion has arisen amidst debates on democratization and Europeanization in the region. It refers to a pattern of rule advanced by political elites in the Western Balkans to provide stability instead of democracy in exchange for legitimization by EU actors (Bieber 2018b &2020; BiEPAG 2017). However, the central concept used in the analysis is that of 'hybrid regime', borrowed from the aforementioned literature and modified to offer a more locally sensitive lens of observation. In the present research, hybrid regimes are typified by several features – namely, political, economic, and social hybridity.

Before detailing each of these features, It is crucial to draw attention to the work of Klaus Offe. In the very early stages of post-socialism, Offe warned of *a triple transition* in the region – that is to say, *simultaneous democratization, marketization* and *nation-state-formation* – which he referred to as 'capitalism by democratic design' (Offe 1991). The same narrow set of actors responsible for creating new rules and institutions and allocating material resources unrestrained by functional control mechanisms inevitably led to the triple transition being an elite-led process. The parallel transformations granted incumbents broad authority over political and economic developments, undermining the development of a class of independent capitalists to demand functional institutions to enforce the law and protect private property (Gould and Sickner 2008). The early winners of the transitions accumulated huge personal benefits, at great social cost (Hellman 1998; Grubiša 2005; Gallagher 2003 in Dolenec 2013), creating a 'democracy against itself' (Ramet and Wagner 2019). This article considers the unfettered power of incumbents in all three aspects of the transition from the very beginning as essential in understanding political power in Western Balkans regimes in the past and to the very present.

The ambivalence of the economic and social realms is often overlooked or tackled only marginally in the conceptualization of hybrid regimes. This article argues that they are critical components that constitute and shape political power in hybrid regimes. The tendency for the authoritarian rule is deeply embedded in the hybrid capitalism of these states, as well as the blurring of formal and informal mechanisms in their societies. The literature on the political economy of transition and informality are critical to conceptualize economic and social hybridity.

The economic resources of authoritarian power can be observed from two perspectives. Firstly, by looking at how the fusion of powers came into existence, for this results in long-lasting political and economic hybridity, secondly, by incorporating economic arrangements with the EU and the IMF to understand the peculiarities of Western Balkans integration into broader economic dynamics. In the following parts, economic and social hybridity is mapped through Western Balkan states' transition towards capitalism, corrupt privatization, the role of informality, and the recent exploitation of extractive institutions in public procurements and supervision and approval of FDI. The section ends by elaborating on the integration of the Western Balkans into the global economy via trade and investment.

Privatization in the Western Balkan states has largely favoured those closely connected to the regime who have grabbed state assets at bargain prices (Gallagher 2003 in Dolenec 2013). Hellman argues that post-socialist states' main challenge has been to restrain the early winners from the economic transition, as they have tended to accumulate huge private benefits at significant social costs (Hellman 1998). The grey zone of transitioning to capitalism granted incumbents wide authority over political and economic development, thus undermining the development of independent capitalists who would, in return, demand functional institutions that enforce the law and protect private property. Many new business owners were more interested in asset stripping than in the sustainable governance of newly privatized companies (Grubiša 2005).

The majority of influential private economic actors emerged under illiberal conditions, and so had an outsized influence on how the institutions of market democracy evolved. They eroded the rule of law by seeking exemptions and diminished development prospects under 'regular' conditions, thus forcing newly emerging economic actors into rent-seeking relations with the regime (Gould and Sickner 2008). The synchronicity of the triple transition thus ended in 'democracy against itself' (Ramet and Wagner 2019).

This model of discriminatory privatization and public procurement continued in later stages. The repeated combination of the fused power, state weakness, and informal networks enabled further subverting of the public good in the interest of elites (Fazekas and Tóth 2016). The novelty of contemporary regimes is the larger presence of foreign investors, so that established practices are now more frequently applied in the approval and supervision of FDI and the implementation of large-scale projects (Bieber 2020). This is another indication of the economic hybridity of these regimes, as the relative openness of markets allows foreign investors to enter and pursue novel opportunities, even as established elites tightly control actual economic governance.

Analysing the links between economic hybridity and authoritarian rule also requires inspection of processes of internationalization and integration of post-socialist economies into global currents. In the early 1990s, prosperous Western countries outsourced the processing of raw materials to European peripheries, taking advantage of the low wages and production costs. The rise in costs sparked an interest in FDI, which saw CEE and SEE countries' industrial and manufacturing sectors expand significantly (Kaser, 2019). However, investments in low-wage, labour-intensive industries risk creating Islands isolated from the rest of the economy, which barely contribute towards large-scale growth and development (Zysman and Schwartz 1998, in Kaser, 2019). Grabher argues that the overreliance on FDI, whereby newly opened 'branch plants' are integrated into industrial networks in other countries, produces disembodied regional economies (Grabherg 1994). Capitalist rationality is seldom transferred at the local level so that the host country develops a truncated form of 'capitalism without capitalists'.

A strong state and functional institutions are significant in defining the type of foreign capital attracted. In other words, minimal standards attract short-term investment (in lower volumes), whereas optimal standards bring capital-intense FDI (Kaser, 2019). Only the latter type leaves a positive imprint upon local wages and the overall economy. Additionally, the type of FDI shapes the growth model of regional economies, which in the SEE countries has meant credit-fuelled growth, underwritten by Western banks (Connolly 2012).

The fragility of this growth model was exposed during the Eurozone crisis. The already vulnerable Western Balkan states encountered new challenges in managing the state economy during the recession (Bartlett and Prica 2013, 2017a and b). Due to their 'candidate' status, the EU could not provide bailout funds or support measures, which then mutated into legitimizing illiberal regimes complying with austerity measures (Pavlović 2019). The economic concerns of the 'core states' dominated the EU's agenda towards the Western Balkans. Democratization was again pushed aside, this time in favour of economic stability. Awareness of the Western Balkan countries' economic dependence on foreign capital is thus crucial for understanding political power in these hybrid regimes.

Informality represents a key element of social hybridity in post-socialist regimes. Ledeneva defines informality as 'the world's open secrets, unwritten rules and hidden practices assembled in this project as "ways of getting things done"' (Ledeneva 2018, 1). Due to lack of market competition, informal networks and clientelism were reinforced during communism (Pickles and Smith 1998). Harders considers that the 'social contract of informality' exists in many developing countries, meaning that personalized relations based on social solidarity, material distribution and professional promotion have increasingly replaced enforceable citizen rights (Harders 2011, in Günay and Džihić 2016). While informality improves citizens' daily lives, it significantly undermines the social contract between the state and citizens.

Social hybridity is widely sustained through the blurred lines between formal and informal institutions. Coupled with economic and political hybridity, the blurring of these institutions creates a vast grey zone of exploitation for the ruling elites. The existing formal institutions function with a significantly decreased ability to apply checks and balances upon the regime (Bieber 2020). Numerous developments are negotiated through party membership, clientelist loyalty, and state capture. The enmeshing of formal and informal institutions in the Western Balkans is closely related to the fusion of political and economic power. Due to state capture and a circumscribed rule of law, all economic decisions become political as well (Kostovicova and Bojicić-Dželilović 2006).

Social hybridity needs to be fathomed through the types of property that informal networks organize, both material and discursive (Smith and Swain 1998). On the material level, the networks undertake relations among various institutions, while on the discursive level, they reinforce regulatory practices based on shared knowledge and understanding. The capacities of informal networks are pertinent to the three processes of wielding political power (concentration, transformation, and dispersion) in hybrid regimes (Zakošek, 1997). Consolidated authoritarian power can only be properly diffused on the material and symbolic (discursive) levels through the informal mechanisms that brought it into existence. It is dispersed throughout all spheres of politics, the economy, and society, in a personalized form, detached from formal institutions. The personalization and informalisation of power further increase non-transparent procedures and support authoritarian tendencies. Zakošek calls this phenomenon of the monopolization of power through personalization and erosion of formal institutions the 're-feudalisation of power' (1997). Dolenec opts for the term 'state politicisation' (Dolenec 2013) to emphasize state capture, patronage and clientelist practices, together with corruption and abuse of power.

As mentioned, the literature tends to downplay the importance of economic and social hybridity for the consolidation of political power in Western Balkan regimes. The triple transition perplexed economic and political powers. The significant number of 'recombinant properties' not wholly owned by the state or private entities (Smith and Swain 1998) created new extracting opportunities for the ruling elites. The properties were mostly sold to foreign investors through a mixture of state capture and informality. The leaders acted as brokers of state developments through various economic guarantees. Depending on the foreign partner, the guarantees stretched from abiding by austerity measures to accessing state-owned properties. The confluence of political, economic, and social hybridity enabled the elites to effectively 'privatise' the state.

Methods

The key method adopted in this research is process-tracing due to its ability to integrate several methods under one umbrella and undertake comprehensive within-case analysis for tracking agents' social behaviour (Bennett and Checkel 2015). A constructivist theoretical approach was chosen since power represents a 'negotiated order', where social actors shape external realities and continuously change rules, institutions, and meanings (Bryman 2008). The research design is predominantly qualitative. Most data was collected through elite interviews and complemented by desktop research of simple statistical data. A total of 23 semi-structured interviews were conducted with decision-makers on both sides of the relationship – that is, Serbian and Turkish officials, diplomats, mayors, investors, and experts of particular profiles.

The core objective of process-tracing is to identify the *causal mechanisms* located between causes and outcomes (cannot be conflated with either) which are specific to that particular process (Beach and Pedersen 2019). As Waldner points out, process-tracing is more than a narration of events, as it seeks to explain what has brought those events into existence (Waldner 2012). For this article, the raw empirical evidence was first assembled to set an initial outline of causes and outcomes. A further investigation was necessary to understand the components of power consolidation in what initially seemed like a chronological sequence of events.

Process-tracing allowed *collecting a plethora of information* on the incentives and capacities of key actors. On the other hand, it keeps one *cognizant of the context* in which these actors operated. An obvious switch was observable in Serbian–Turkish relations within the researched period, from a period of restraint and setbacks (a 'thawing' phase) to a 'honeymoon' phase. Many events occurred during the latter: Turkish factories started mushrooming in the south of Serbia, sales-oriented investors became more visible, the Yunus Emre Institute (YEI) opened, and the number of high-level bilateral visits multiplied. These various developments reflected different facets of foreign and domestic politics and did not follow the progressive change. Thus, an initial observation of the events outline failed to capture the interactions among actors or reveal the salience of particular contexts.

To capture the agency of elite representatives within this change, the collected observations were broken into smaller pairs of causes and outcomes, and the mechanisms connecting them were investigated. Intense scrutinizing was necessary before precise theoretical predictions of mechanistic evidence could be developed. The research period was disaggregated into smaller trios of causes–mechanisms–outcomes. Very often, the outcome of one trio became the cause for the next one, binding a new process and outcome. However, not all trios were connected linearly, as numerous events emerged simultaneously. This richness of variables and their relationship with the context made process-tracing a valuable choice. While the list is not exhaustive, the following processes were identified to be of key importance for the improvement of mutual relations: a) withdrawal of Davutoglu from Turkish leadership; b) consolidation of power around President Erdogan; c) EU emerging as Turkey's largest trading partner d) consolidation of power around Serbian Prime Minister (and later President) Vučić; e) intensified high bilateral communication; and d) powerful network of informal mechanisms controlling formal outcomes.

In summary, the process-tracing method was critical in identifying causality amongst the various actors, events, and outcomes. The empirical evidence from interviews was augmented with secondary data gathered from respective state agencies of statistics, financial institutions, scholarly articles, and analytical reports. The data was then observed in a holistic fashion, not as a simple sequence of results but as a sum of several parts that were analysed in depth. Applying process-tracing was crucial for connecting and theorizing the numerous events, thus proving highly suitable for studying the concentration of political power in hybrid regimes through the exploitation of international relations.

Serbian – Turkish economic relations from 2009 To 2018

The article empirically examined the starting of a Turkish FDI in Serbia, analysing how they navigated the administrative and informal hurdles of initiating a business in a hybrid regime. A general overview of economic relations is presented first to highlight the main features and dominant trends in the economic relationship. Then the case study of the Jeanci factory is presented, portraying the embeddedness of informal mechanisms throughout formal institutions, the enmeshment of economic and political authorities, and the degree of personalization of political power. The opening of this relatively small factory became the entry point for other Turkish investments and the gradual improvement of mutual relations. Such scrutiny illuminates the scope of Turkish economic influence in Serbia and provides insight into the domestic rule of law and the economic governance of the state. Understanding the drivers and patterns of investment offers better insight into the Serbian political economy under Aleksandar Vučić, exposing the fine print of relations among state institutions, independent investors, foreign actors, and domestic centres of power.

Serbia became a destination for Turkish investment a few years after other Balkan countries did. The signing of a Free Trade Agreement in 2009 (Uprava carine) improved the conditions for bilateral trade, as did the liberalization of the mutual visa regime in 2010. The political changes on both sides brought the two increasingly powerful presidents into closer cooperation, visible in frequent mutual visits (six during 2017) and intensified mutual relations. Several indicators show evident growth in Turkish economic engagement in Serbia in the last decade. One of them is the overall value of bilateral trade, which tripled between 2009 and 2018. Table 1 below depicts this upward trend.

According to the Serbian Business Registers Agency, in 2018, there were 605 active businesses owned by Turkish citizens/legal entities, of which 319 were trading and vehicle repair businesses, 79 in the manufacturing sector, 43 in tourism and hospitality, 42 construction related businesses, and 37 science and innovation-related businesses (Ibid.). While the number of newly opened factories, retail, and other Turkish companies grew, none of the large Turkish consortiums or holding companies entered the market

Table 1. Total volume of trade (imports and exports) between Serbia and Turkey (2009–2018).

Year	2009	2010	2011	2012	2013	2014	2015	2016	2017	2018
US$ (millions)	336	411	588	626	750	821	816	927	1,131	1,230

Note: Figures rounded to the nearest whole value. Source: National Statistics Agency of the Republic of Serbia, 2018.

Table 2. Ranking of Turkey among the top 20 foreign investors in Serbia 2011–2018, based on data from the National Statistics Agency of the Republic of Serbia, 2018.

Year	2011	2012	2013	2014	2015	2016	2017	2018
Rank	18th	15th	18th	17th	17th	17th	18th	19th

Table 3. Growth of Jeanci factory from 2013–2018.

Year	2013	2014	2015	2016	2017	2018
Number of employees	250	506	792	872	900	896
Profit (thousands of Serbian dinars)	406	937	1,275	1,500	1,459	1,602

Note: Figures rounded to the nearest whole value. Source: Business Registers Agency of the Republic of Serbia, 2018.

during the designated research period. At the end of January 2018, an Agreement for Promoting and Protecting Investments was signed between the two countries. In 2009–2010, Turkey did not even rank among the top 20 countries for FDI in Serbia – it entered the list only after 2011. Table 2 below indicates changes in Turkey's ranking as a source of FDI in Serbia between 2011 and 2018.

Prior to any formal incentives, broader geostrategic events pushed independent Turkish investors to re-consider Serbia. The Arab Spring and the outbreak of war in Syria (Kuyumcu and Kösematoğlu 2017), deteriorating relations with Israel, and Russian heavy economic sanctions after the downing of their military aircraft in 2015 (BBC News b), urged Turkish businesses were thus to seek new sites to produce and sell goods, as well as more viable transportation routes (Interview TUR2018_1, Interview TUR2018_2, Interview TUR2018_7, Interview TUR2018_16, Interview TUR2018_17). The political vulnerability naturally saw economic attention drift towards the more stable Western Balkans neighbourhood (Interview SRB2018_2, Interview TUR2018_1). Serbia's central geographical location in the Balkan Peninsula – namely its relative accessibility and decent road infrastructure – was essential for Turkish investors to consider Serbia, especially those planning to site new production facilities there (Interview TUR2018_16, Interview TUR2018_17, Interview SRB2018_2). As Serbia is placed in the middle of its easiest access route to the EU (Turkey's largest trading partner), it gained strategic importance for investors, significantly shortening the time and distribution costs. These factors largely contribute to the siting of Turkish production businesses along the main highways, usually brownfield investments in smaller towns in the south, which offer cheaper labour and often some pre-existing production facilities (Interview TUR2018_15, Interview TUR2018_17). Examples include the Jeanci factory in Leskovac, Teklas in Vladičin Han, Soylemez in Žitoradja, Aster Tekstil in Niš, and Kardem Orme in Smederevo.

Jeanci Factory – An Icebreaker For Closer Cooperation

This textile factory was officially registered in 2010 but became fully operational in 2013, employing 250 people (Business Registers Agency of the Republic of Serbia, 2021). The progression trajectory of Jeanci factory is illustrated on Table 3. It was opened in Leskovac, a town with a population of 138,000 in southern Serbia (Infomedia). It offered quite favourable conditions, such as proximity to the E-75 motorway and high labour potential (Interview TUR2018_1). The factory owner Taner Buyukcan aimed to double the profits and number of employees within a year, which required enabling high-capacity water tanks and a proportionally high electricity supply. Such technical preconditions could be provided in Serbia through special licences approved by governmental and municipal authorities. Instead, these seemingly routine administrative procedures led to a much larger jigsaw in Serbian–

Turkish relations. The procedures were initiated soon after a problematic diplomatic incident with Kosovo, complicating Turkish investors' business environment in Serbia. Some Serbian civil servants even openly stated that as long as Erdoğan made provocative statements, they could not help to obtain official permits (Interview TUR2018_1). The political climate was clearly unfavourable for Turkish investment and prompted Buyukcan's plans to withdraw the business due to administrative blockages.

At that point, Turkish diplomats had already dealt with various consequences of the political crisis and losing an investor would have complicated affairs even further, so the issue was soon taken to Serbia's highest leadership. In the words of one Turkish diplomat: 'It was embarrassing to call the Prime Minister for electricity and water supplies, but we had no choice. The investor was genuinely preparing to leave' (Interview TUR2018_11). Vučić promised to help on the condition that the factory fulfils all legal requirements and regular procedures. Jeanci completed all formalities and obtained the necessary water and electricity supplies within two weeks. The business soon began to grow, as illustrated in Table 3.

Buyukcan soon opened another factory in southern Serbia. The second factory was propelled by the political motives of Serbian high officials and opened the door for more Turkish investors. In the spring of 2014, Serbia suffered from heavy floods and landslides, followed by considerable human and material casualties. Many countries promptly provided humanitarian aid, including Turkey. A Donors Conference for Flood Relief in Serbia and Bosnia and Herzegovina was held in Brussels in July 2014, at which Turkey committed to provide €1.35 million in assistance. Meanwhile, Prime Minister Vučić asked his Turkish counterpart Davutoğlu to assist in finding investors for towns affected by the floods, and the initiative was soon transferred to the Turkish Embassy (Interview TUR2018_1).

Krupanj, a town of 17,860 people in western Serbia, was heavily devastated by the floods. Prime Minister Vučić contacted the Turkish ambassador several times to emphasize the difficult economic conditions in Krupanj, aggravated by the floods. An old, closed textile factory called 'Krupanjka' was located in the town that, if bought and re-opened, would create new jobs and decrease economic emigration. Vučić essentially signalled that bringing an investor to Krupanj would significantly change the attitude of Serbian authorities towards Turkey (Interview TUR2018_17).

In a period of fragile bilateral relations that included the recent cancellation of the public auction for Čačanska Banka (which Turkish Halk Bank won but was ultimately unable to agree on a final price), Ambassador Bozay could not pass up opportunities for improvement and promptly contacted Buyukcan. The odds of Buyukcan starting a factory in a town difficult to reach and far from main transportation routes were slim. Still, the perceived contribution to 'national wellbeing' convinced him nonetheless to proceed (Interview TUR2018_16). Krupanjka's official opening was in April 2015, a year after the floods. The ceremony featured numerous media, including broadcasts of Prime Minister Vučić, the Turkish ambassador, and the Turkish investor, altogether cutting red ribbons. Krupanj factory came to employ between 138 and 150 workers (N1). This facility has not made any considerable profit, and management has often treated it as a project of 'social responsibility' (Interview TUR2018_16).

However, this small factory opened a new chapter in mutual relations between Serbia and Turkey, enhancing trust at a high bilateral level. Turkish investors soon opened four other factories in Serbia (in Teklas, Soylemez, Kardem Orme, Aster Tekstil). At the same time, Halk Bank completed its launch, and the Turkish Cultural Institute 'Yunus Emre' was finally registered. According to Aleksandar Medjedović, the former president of the Turkish Foreign Economic Relations Board (Dış Ekonomik İlişkiler Kurumu, hereafter DEIK): 'Buyukcan's gain from the Krupanj factory cannot be fully explained in financial terms. It might not be the most lucrative business, but it opened all doors in Serbia' (Interview SRB2018_2).

In summary, Turkish business has been driven by larger geostrategic developments to seek new markets, which enabled Serbia to capitalize on its geographic and political position. The opening of a small factory tailored to Serbian political interests (Jeanci in Krupanj) emerged as an entry point for a much broader column of Turkish influence. Soon Halk Bank opened a branch in Serbia, and several other Turkish factories followed suit (Teklas, Soylemez, Aster Tekstil, Kardem Orme, Eurotay, May Denim, Feka Automotiv). Over a few short years, Turkish investments in Serbia grew significantly, and trade volumes with Turkey almost tripled (Nova Ekonomija). Such developments have had a material impact on the quality of mutual relations, upgrading them from the thawing to the honeymoon stage.

Conclusion

This article set out to study the relationship between regime type and foreign policy by scrutinizing Serbia's bilateral relationship with Turkey. This focus has provided a wider lens of observation of political power in hybrid regimes, as it looks beyond domestic politics. While accepting Serbia's classification as a 'hybrid regime' (Levitsky and Way 2002, 2010; Diamond 2002), the concept of 'hybridity' was employed more holistically to incorporate the entire trio of politics, economy, and society, thus identifying alternative resources of power the incumbents exploit at the intersection of foreign and domestic politics.

Between 2009 and 2018, Serbian–Turkish economic relations followed a dynamic path. The economic appeal of Serbia to Turkey is primarily due to its geographic and political proximity to the EU. The economic cooperation intensified after 2014, which is most visible in the tripling of the value of mutual trade. While the overall Turkish investments in Serbia have certainly grown during the period under analysis, a comparative perspective indicates that they struggled to keep pace with FDI from other countries. Turkey entered the list of the top 20 foreign investors in Serbia in 2011, reaching the 15th position in 2012, before dropping to 19th in 2018.

The empirical investigation indicates that bilateral cooperation is largely managed beyond state institutions and formal processes. On the one hand, the study of the Jeanci factory illustrates the regime's political and economic hybridity; on the other, it reveals the operation of power within the system. The outwardly capitalist setting allowed foreign investors to independently enter the Serbian market and express interest in investments. However, the investors were primarily interested in brownfield investment. While the administrative procedures for launching FDI seemed transparent and straight-forward, completing a project required informal mechanisms linked to the Serbian political leadership. The blurred formal and informal rules created dependency upon the central power base, which allowed diffusion of political power throughout the whole system, from the central down to the municipal level. The examination of Serbian-Turkish economic relations illustrated the great extent of *personalization* of political power in Serbia, as Vučić plays an essential role in brokering Turkish investments. The second finding is that the political, economic, and social hybridity enable the incumbent to have *pre-eminent control over the economy* (i.e., the approval and supervision of FDI).

The analysis of FDI here has also expanded our understanding of hybridity in the authoritarian regimes of the Western Balkans. Its emergence is closely related to Offe's 'triple transition' (Offe 1991), which, from the outset, resulted in a fusion of political and economic powers (Dolenec 2013). The fusion remains to the very present, fluctuating in its intensity over time. In the early post-communist stages, the state capture was visible in allocating privatization or management positions of key state companies to individuals close to the ruling elites. In the contemporary context, the fusion resurfaces with each new FDI project, as economic conditions and the need for foreign capital pulls has meant FDI has been a central part of the privatization game. These countries have not yet become fully functional market economies, as a significant share of resources is still owned by the state and managed by particularistic interests (Günay and Džihić 2016). The incumbents control access to state property through administrative hurdles and non-transparent procedures. While a *façade of rules set by formal institutions is visible to the naïve eye*, the actual passage of a project from proposal to completion depends on *non-institutional brokering with the ruling elite*. The article labels this phenomenon as 'social hybridity', as elites deliberately perpetuate the blurring of formal and informal rules (Mungiu-Pippidi 2005; Kmezić 2017; Fagan and Sircar 2015). Thus, social hybridity decreases functional control mechanisms and reinforces state capture in an environment where the division of powers is already murky (Kostovicova and Bojicić-Dželilović 2006; Dolenec 2013). Another critical aspect of social hybridity is the ability to negotiate political power at both the material and discursive levels (Smith and Swain 1998), further disjoining it from state institutions (Zakošek, 1997, Dolenec 2013). Additionally, the type of FDI in question shapes the growth model of the economy and indicates the strength of the rule of law in the state (Kaser, 2019). Small-scale brownfield investments (i.e., acquiring pre-existing industrial or other business facilities through privatization, the majority of which are largely state-owned) in manufacturing industries point out to teetering rule of law.

Turkish FDI in Serbia are welcome but of minuscule value compared to the EU's involvement. While Turkish interest in Serbia is understandable – given its proximity to the EU and anchoring capacity among the Yugoslav successor states – Vučić's commitment to this relationship is somewhat irrational, as the investments are fairly small, and Serbia's EU candidacy provides access to much larger assistance funds. Yet Vučić participates in every opening ceremony of a Turkish factory (even three times for the same factory, as he joined the laying of foundation stones of new facilities), all of which were widely televised. Such news bolster the image of Vucic as capable leader, especially in poorer municipalities. Little power is accumulated materially through such behaviour, but it is nevertheless symbolically potent in solidifying the leader's position. A clear message is also being sent to the Turkish investors and diplomats that all arrangements need to be negotiated through the top representative. The frequent visits with Erdoğan generate colourful images significant for demonstrating regional power, among the domestic electorate, and the neighbouring states. And while these reinforce the impression of power on both sides, the bilateral relationship is not economically deep-seated.

The very need for performativity reveals the volatile nature of this power, embedded in the dynamic of non-institutionalized cooperation and personalized relations between the two leaders. The present study has confirmed that Vučić is an authoritarian ruler while detailing the complex machinery he uses to concentrate his power. He is indeed a kingmaker who reduces decision-making processes to particularistic interests diffused through informal networks. And while his authoritarian rule grants him considerable power that stretches well beyond state institutions, it has not delivered much politically. The factories are not greenfield investments integrated into the Serbian economy. Nor do they offer much in the way of economic dividend, but represent more of a *political theatre*. They also point to the fragility and instability of hybrid regimes, precisely due to the personalization of political power within them.

The present study aims to expand the discussion on power-brokerage in hybrid regimes by including negotiations over inbound FDI from an economically powerful regional country that is also authoritarian. The hybridity of local economic systems, along with political and social hybridity, jointly form the crux of authoritarian tendencies in the Western Balkans. President Vučić demonstrates unforeseen agency in mitigating the multifarious hybridity at the intersection of foreign and domestic politics, positioning himself as an adept international actor and sought after regional ally. Analysing the relationship with Turkey reveals new contingencies, demonstrating both the fact and the parameters of Vučić's strength. While exploiting the hybrid configuration in foreign policy enables multifaceted mechanisms for consolidation of political power, such power is largely unstable due to the non-institutionalized nature of mutual cooperation.

Disclosure statement

No potential conflict of interest was reported by the author(s).

ORCID

Sabina Pacariz http://orcid.org/0000-0002-0007-3475

References

Alpan, B, and A.E. Ozturk. (2022). Turkey and the Balkans: bringing the Europeanisation/ De-Europeanisation nexus into question. *Southeast European and Black Sea Studies*, 22(1), pp.1-10. doi:10.1080/14683857.2022.2034385

Balkan Insight a. Available at: http://www.balkaninsight.com/en/article/davutoglu-erdogan-s-kosovo-statement-misinterpreted/2027/2 (Access date: 20.12.2018).

Balkan Insight b. Available at: https://balkaninsight.com/2011/04/26/davutoglu-i-m-not-a-neo-ottoman/ (Access date 18.March.2018).

Balkan Insight c. Available at: http://www.balkaninsight.com/en/article/davutoglu-erdogan-s-kosovo-statement-misinterpreted/2027/2 (Access date: 20.12.2018).

Bartlett, W., and I. Prica (2013). The deepening crisis in the european super-periphery. *Journal of Balkan and near Eastern Studies*, 15(4), pp. 367–82. 10.1080/19448953.2013.844587

Bartlett, W, and I. Prica (2017a). Interdependence between core and peripheries of the European economy: Secular stagnation and growth in the Western Balkans. *The European Journal of Comparative Economics*, 14(1), pp. 123–39.

Beach, D, and R.B. Pedersen, (2019). *Process-tracing methods: foundations and guidelines*, Ann Arbour: University of Michigan Press.

Bennett, A, and J.T. Checkel, (2015). Process tracing: From philosophical roots to best practices. In A. Bennett, and J.T. Checkel ed. *Process-Tracing: From Metaphor to Analytical Tool*, pp.3-38, Cambridge: Cambridge University Press .

Bieber, F., (2017). Post-Yugoslav Patterns of Democratization. In *Building Democracy in the Yugoslav Successor States: Accomplishments, Setbacks, and Challenges since 1990*, eds., Hassentab, C.B., Ramet S.P., and Listhaug, O, 38–57. Cambridge: Cambridge University Press.

Bieber, F, (2018b). The rise (and fall) of balkan stabilitocracies. *Horizons: Journal of International Relations and Sustainable Development*, (10), pp.176–85.

Bieber, F., (2020). *The rise of authoritarianism in the Western Balkans*. Cham: Palgrave Macmillan.

BiEPAG. (2017). The Crisis of Democracy in the Western Balkans. Authoritarianism and EU stabilitocracy. Available at: http://biepag.eu/wp-content/uploads/2019/03/BIEPAG-The-Crisis-of-Democracy-in-the-Western-Balkans.-Authoritarianism-and-EU-Stabilitocracy-web.pdf Accessed 04 04 2018

Blanchard, O, and R. Layard, (1991). *How to privatise* (No. dp50). Centre for Economic Performance, LSE.

Bryman, A., (2008) *Social Research Methods*, Oxford University Press, New York.

Bunce, V.J, and S.L. Wolchik. (2010). Defeating dictators: electoral change and stability in competitive authoritarian regimes. In *World Politics*, 62:43–86. 10.1017/S0043887109990207. 1

Business Registers Agency of the Republic https://www.apr.gov.rs/home.1435.html. (Accessed 22 11 2021).

Carine, U. Available at: http://www.upravacarina.rs/en/International%20Agreements/AgreementSerbiaTurkey.pdf (Access date: 07.11.2018).

Cigar, N. (1994). Serbia's orientalists and islam: making genocide intellectually respectable. *Islamic Quarterly*, 38(3), p.147.

Cigar, N, (2003). The nationalist Serbian intellectuals and Islam: defining and eliminating a Muslim community. In *The New Crusades* (pp. 314–51). New York: Columbia University Press.

Connolly, R. (2012). The determinants of the economic crisis in post-socialist europe, *Europe-Asia Studies*, 64(1). 35–67 10.1080/09668136.2012.635474

Dević, A, (2016). Ottomanism and neo-ottomanism in the travails of the 'Serbian National Corpus': Turkey as recurrent focus of serbian academia, *Die Welt Des Islams* 56, pp. 534–48. 3–4 10.1163/15700607-05634p12

Diamond, L., (2002). Thinking about Hybrid Regimes, *Journal of Democracy* 13:2. 2 10.1353/jod.2002.0025

Dolenec, D., (2013). *Democratic institutions and authoritarian rule in Southeast Europe*. Colchester: ECPR Press.

Džankić, J, S. Keil, and M. Kmezić. eds. (2019). *The Europeanisation of the Western Balkans: A Failure of EU Conditionality?* Cham. Palgrave Macmillian. 10.1007/9783. 10.1007/9783319914121.319914121.

Ekonomija, N. Available at: https://novaekonomija.rs/vesti-iz-zemlje/turske-investicije-u-srbiji-rast-u-turbulentnim-vremenima (Access date: 25.12.2021)

European Policy Centre https://www.epc.eu/en/Publications/Constitutional-changes-in-Turkey-A-presidential-system-or-the-preside~1d617c (Access date: 03.05.2020).

Evropa, S. Available at: https://www.slobodnaevropa.org/a/srbija_islamska_zajednica_zilkic_zukorlic/24374589.html Accessed 06 01 2021.

Fagan, A, and I. Sircar (2015). Judicial Independence in the Western Balkans: Is the EU's "New Approach" Changing Practices?. *Maximizing the integration capacity of the European Union: Lessons and prospects for enlargement and beyond.* Available at: http://userpage.fu-berlin.de/kfgeu/maxcap/system/files/maxcap_wp_11.pdf Accessed 27 10 2020

Fagan, A., and Wunsch, N., (2019). Fostering institutionalisation? The impact of the EU accession process on state-civil society relations in Serbia. *Acta Politica: International Journal of Political Science,* 54(4), pp.607–624.

Fazekas, M, and I.J. Tóth, (2016). From corruption to state capture: A new analytical framework with empirical applications from Hungary. *Political Research Quarterly,* 69(2), pp.320–34. 10.1177/1065912916639137

Fukuyama, F, (1989). The end of history? *The National Interest,* (16), pp.3–18.

Galijašević, D., (2011). Neoosmanizam: Turska izmedju juce i sutra, *Politeia* 2 125.

Gallagher, T., (2003). *The Balkans after the Cold War: From tyranny to tragedy,* p. 136. London and New York: Routledge.

Gordy, E, (2004). Serbia after Djindjic: War crimes, organized crime, and trust in public institutions. *Problems of Post-Communism,* 51(3), pp.10–17. 10.1080/10758216.2004.11052169

Gordy, E., (2013). *Guilt, responsibility, and denial: The past at stake in post-Milosevic Serbia.* Philadelphia: University of Pennsylvania Press.

Gould, J.A, and C. Sickner. (2008). Making market democracies? The contingent loyalties of post-privatization elites in Azerbaijan, Georgia and Serbia. *Review of International Political Economy* 15 (5): 740–69. 10.1080/09692290802408923

Grabher, K., (1994). The disembedded regional economy: The transformation of East German industrial complexes into wester enclaves. In A. Amin, and N. Thrift ed. *Globalization, institutions, and regional development in Europe.* Oxford: Oxford University Press. pp.177-195.

Grubiša, D,(2005). Political corruption in transitional Croatia: The peculiarities of a model, *Politička Misao,* 42(5). pp.55-74.

Günay, C, and V. Džihić, (2016). Decoding the authoritarian code: exercising 'legitimate' power politics through the ruling parties in Turkey, Macedonia, and Serbia. *Southeast European and Black Sea Studies,* 16(4), pp. 529–49. 10.1080/14683857.2016.1242872

Hanley, S, and M.A. Vachudova, (2018). Understanding the illiberal turn: Democratic backsliding in the Czech Republic. *East European Politics,* 34(3), pp.276–96. 10.1080/21599165.2018.1493457

Harders, C., (2011). Revolution I und II – ägypten zwischen transformation und restauration In Jünemann and Zorob ed. *Arabellions. Zur Vielfalt von Protest und Revolte im Nahen Osten und Nordafrika,* Springer, Heidelberg, pp. 19–42

Hellman, J.S., (1998). Winners take all: the politics of partial reform in postcommunist transitions, *World Politics,* 50:2. 2 10.1017/S0043887100008091

Infomedia. Available at: http://rominfomedia.rs/drasticno-smanjen-broj-stanovnika-u-leskovcu/ (Access date: 14.07.2018).

Jevtić, M., (1993). Ljudi i vreme, *Vreme* (Belgrade), 15 November 1993, 55.

Jevtić, M., (2011). Neoosmanizam versus panislamizam, *Politeia* 2, pp. 31–46.

Kaser, K., (2019). Economic Reforms and the Burdens of Transition. In Central and Southeast European Politics since 1989, eds. Hassenstab, C.B, and Ramet, S.P. pp. 79–105. Cambridge: Cambridge University Press.

Kmezić, M., (2017). *EU rule of law promotion: Judiciary reform in the Western Balkans.* London: Routledge.

Kostovicova, D, and V. Bojicić-Dželilović, (2006). Europeanizing the balkans: rethinking the postcommunist and post-conflict transition. *Ethnopolitics,* 5(3), 223–41. 10.1080/17449050600911091

Kuyumcu, R.A.M.İ, and H. Kösematoğlu, 2017. The Impacts of the Syrian Refugees on Turkey's Economy. *Journal of Turkish Social Sciences Research*, 2(1), pp.661-683.

Lauth, H.J, (1997). 'Dimensionen der demokratie und das konzept defekter und funktionierender Demokratien In G. Pickel, S. Pickel, and J. Jacobs (*Demokratie: entwicklungsformen und erscheinungsbilder im interkulturellen Vergleich* eds.), Frankfurt: Scripvaz, pp. 33–53. Cited in Merkel, W. (2004). Embedded and defective democracies. *Democratization, 11*(5), pp. 33-58.

Lavrič, M, and F. Bieber (2021) Shifts in support for authoritarianism and democracy in the Western Balkans, *Problems of Post-Communism*, 68:1, 17–26, DOI: 10.1080/10758216.2020.1757468.

Ledeneva, A., (Ed.), (2018). *Global encyclopaedia of informality, volume 1: towards understanding of social and cultural complexity*. London: UCL Press.

Levitsky, S, and L.A. Way, (2002). Elections without democracy: The rise of competitive authoritarianism. *Journal of Democracy*, 13(2), pp.51–65. 10.1353/jod.2002.0026

Levitsky, S, and L.A. Way (2010). *Competitive authoritarianism: hybrid regimes after the cold war*. Cambridge University Press, New York.

Lipton, D, J. Sachs, S. Fischer, S, and J. Kornai, (1990). Creating a market economy in Eastern Europe: The case of Poland. *Brookings Papers on Economic Activity*, 1990(1), pp.75–147. 10.2307/2534526

Merkel, W., (2004). Embedded and defective democracies. *Democratization*, 11(5), pp. 33–58. 10.1080/13510340412331304598

Mungiu-Pippidi, A., (2005). Deconstructing balkan particularism: the ambiguous social capital of Southeastern Europe. *Journal of Southeast European and Black Sea Studies*, 5(1), pp. 49–68. 10.1080/1468385042000328367

Mungiu-Pippidi, A., (2012). When Europeanization Meets Transformation. *Democracy and Authoritarianism in the Postcommunist World*, 1(1), pp.59–81.

N1. Available at: http://rs.n1info.com/a50041/Biznis/Otvorena-nova-fabrika-u-Krupnju.html (Access date 15.November.2018).

New York Times. Available at: https://www.nytimes.com/2017/04/02/world/europe/serbia-aleksandar-vucic-president-elections.html Accessed 12 09 2018.

Nova Srpska politička misao. Available at: http://www.nspm.rs/hronika/aleksandar-vucic-priredio-redzepu-tajipu-erdoganu-svecani-docek-ispred-palate-srbija.html?alphabet=l (Access date: 12.05.2020)

Obradović-Wochnik, J., (2013). The `silent dilemma` of transitional justice: Silencing and coming to terms with the past in Serbia. *International Journal of Transitional Justice*, 7(2), pp. 328–347.

Offe, C., (1991). Capitalism by democratic design?: Democratic theory facing the triple Transition in East Central Europe. *Social Research: An International Quarterly*, 71(3), pp. 865–92.

Offe, C., (1993). Capitalism by Democratic Design? Democratic Theory Facing the Triple Transition in East Central Europe. *Social Research: An International Quarterly*, 71(3), pp. 865–892.

Ozturk, A.E., (2021). *Religion, identity, and power: turkey and the balkans in the twenty-first century*. Edinburgh: Edinburgh University Press.

Pavlaković, V., (2005). Serbia transformed? political dynamics in the Milošević era and after. pp.13-54. In S.P. Ramet, and V. Pavlaković ed. *Serbia since 1989*. Seattle: University of Washington Press.

Pavlović, D, (2004). *Serbia During and After Milošević* Jefferson Institute, Belgrade.

Pavlović, D., (2016) Extractive Institutions in the Western Balkans. pp.127-141. In Vujačić, I., and Vranić, B. (eds.), *Urušavanje ili slom demokratije? II DEo: Slabljenje institucija u evropskom kontekstu*. Beograd: Fakultet političkih nauka Univerziteta u Beogradu.

Pavlović, D., (2019). When do neoliberal economic reforms cause democratic decline? evidence from the post-communist Southeast Europe. *Post-Communist Economies* 31 (5): 671–97. 10.1080/14631377.2019.1607436

Pickles, J, and Smith, (1998), Introduction: Theorising transition and the political economy f transformation. pp. 1-22. In J. Pickles, and A. Smith ed. *Theorizing transition: The political economy of post-communist transformations.* London and New York: Routledge.

Predsednik. Available at: https://www.predsednik.rs/en/president/biography (Access date: 13.07.2018).

Ramet, S.P., (2013). Trajectories of Post-Communist Transformation: Myths and Rival Theories About Change in Central and Southeastern Europe. *Perceptions: Journal of International Affairs* 18(2), pp.57–89.

Ramet, S.P., (2017). The challenge of democratization: An introduction. In *Building Democracy in the Yugoslav Successor States: Accomplishments, Setbacks, and Challenges since 1990*, eds., Hassentab, C.B., Ramet S.P., and Listhaug, O, 3–37. Cambridge: Cambridge University Press.

Ramet, S.P, and F.P. Wagner, (2019) Post-socialist models of rule. In S.P. Ramet and C. B. Hassenstab,ed. *Central and Southeast European Politics since 1989.Cambridge* University Press, Cambridge, pp.9–36.

Schimmelfennig, F, S. Engert, and H. Knobel, (2005). The Impact of EU Political Conditionality. In F. Schimmelfennig, and U. Sedelmeier ed. *The Europeanization of Central and Eastern Europe*, Ithaca: Cornell University Press.

Sedelmeier, U., (2019). The European Union and Democratization in Central and Southeastern Europe since 1989. In *Building Democracy in the Yugoslav Successor States: Accomplishments, Setbacks, and Challenges since 1990*, eds., Hassentab, C.B., Ramet, S.P., and Listhaug, O, pp. 539–562. Cambridge: Cambridge University Press.

Smith, A, and A. Swain, (1998). Regulating and Institutionalising capitalisms: The micro-foundations of transformation in Eastern and Central Europe. pp. 25-53. In J. Pickles, and A. Smith. ed. *Theorising transition: the political economy of post-communist transformations*, Routledge, London, and New York.

Subotić, J, 2010. Explaining difficult states. The problems of Europeanization in Serbia. *East European Politics and Societies: And Cultures*, 24(4), pp.595–616. 10.1177/0888325410368847

Subotić, J, (2011). *Hijacked justice: Dealing with the past in the Balkans*. Ithaca: Cornell University Press.

Subotić, J., (2011). *Hijacked justice. Dealing with the past in the Balkans*. Ithaca: Cornell University Press.

Subotić, J., (2017) 'Building democracy in Serbia: One step forward, three steps back'. In S. P. Ramet, C.B. Hassentab, and O. Listhaug ed. *Building Democracy in the Yugoslav Successor States: Accomplishments, Setbacks, and Challenges since 1990*. Cambridge University Press, Cambridge DOI: 10.1017/9781316848289.003, pp. 38–57.

Tanasković, D., (1992). Turci brane Sarajevo. In *Epoha*, 22 June 1992.

Tanasković, D., (1993). Interview in *Vojska* (Belgrade), 23 September 1993, p.10. Cited in Cigar, N (1994). Serbia's Orientalists and Islam: Making genocide intellectually respectable. *Islamic Quarterly*, 38(3).

Tanasković, D, (2011). *Neoosmanizam: Povratak Turske na Balkan*. Službeni glasnik, Belgrade

Vachudova, M., (2010). Democratization in Postcommunist Europe. In V. Bunce, M. McFaul, and K. Stoner-Weiss ed., *Democracy and authoritarianism in the post-communist world*, Cambridge University Press, Cambridge, pp. 82–104.

Vachudova, M.A., (2014). EU Leverage and national interests in the balkans: the puzzles of enlargement ten years on. *JCMS: Journal of Common Market Studies*, 52(1), pp. 122–38. doi: 10.1111/jcms.12081.

Vachudova, M.A, (2019). From competition to polarization in central europe: how populists change party systems and the European Union. *Polity*, 51(4), pp.689–706. 10.1086/705704

Waldner, D., (2012). Process Tracing and Causal Mechanisms. pp.65-84. In Kincaid, H. (ed.) *The Oxford handbook of philosophy of social science*. New York: Oxford University Press. Accessed 16 10 2020 doi:10.1093/oxfordhb/9780195392753.013.0004, .

Wittkowski, A., (2000) South-Eastern Europe and the European Union—promoting stability through integration?, *South-East Europe Review*, 1, pp. 79–96.

Zakošek, N., (1997). Pravna država i demokracija u postsocijalizmu. *Politička misao: časopis za politologiju*, 34(4), pp.78–85.

Zysman, J, and A. Schwartz, (1998). Enlarging Europe: The industrial foundations of a new political reality, In J. Zysman (ed.), *Enlarging Europe: The industrial foundations of a new political reality*, University of California Press, Berkeley, CA and Los Angeles, pp. 1–24. Cited in Kaser, K. (2019). Economic Reforms and the Burdens of Transition. pp.79-105. In Ramet, S. P. and C.B. Hassenstab, *Central and Southeast European Politics since 1989*. Cambridge: Cambridge University Press. .

Appendix – List of Interviewees

Position	Date	Code
Serbian high-ranking diplomat	02.03.2018	Interview SRB2018_1
President of the Serbian–Turkish Business Association	04.03.2018	Interview SRB2018_2
Turkish high-ranking diplomat	07.03.2018 15.05.2018	Interview TUR2018_1
Deputy director in a Serbian state institution involved in the flood protection projects sponsored by TIKA	17.02.2018	Interview SRB2018_4
Turkish investor	17.02.2018	Interview TUR2018_2
Serbian entrepreneur involved in the flood protection projects	17.02.2018	Interview SRB2018_5
Director of Serbian state company responsible for implementation of the flood projects	20.02.2018	Interview SRB2018_7
Journalist in Turkish media agency	22.02.2018	Interview SRB2018_16
High-ranking representative of Halk Bank	26.02.2018	Interview TUR2018_3
Turkish high-ranking diplomat	03.03.2018	Interview TUR2018_4
High-ranking representative of Beko company in Serbia (Turkish investor)	26.02.2018	Interview TUR2018_5
Turkish high-ranking diplomat	01.03.2018	Interview TUR2018_6
High-ranking representative of Halk Bank in Serbia	05.10.2018	Interview TUR2018_7
High-ranking representative of LC Waikiki Serbia (Turkish investor)	11.10.2018	Interview TUR2018_10
Turkish high-ranking diplomat	14.10.2018	Interview TUR2018_11
Turkish high-ranking diplomat	19.10.2018	Interview TUR2018_12
Serbian high-ranking diplomat	23.10.2018	Interview SRB2018_20
Turkish high-ranking diplomat	03.11.2018	Interview TUR2018_13
Turkish high-ranking diplomat responsible for the Turkish economic relations	09.11.2018	Interview TUR2018_15
High-ranking representative of Jeanci Factory (Turkish investor)	19.11.2018	Interview TUR2018_16
High-ranking representative of Teklas (Turkish investor)	26.12.2018	Interview TUR2018_17
Public servant in the Serbian Chamber of Commerce, responsible for cooperation with Turkey	27.12.2018	Interview SRB2018_21
Turkish high-ranking diplomat	28.09.2019	Interview TUR2019_01

Measuring Turkey's contemporary influence in Bosnia and Herzegovina: myth and reality

Adnan Huskić and Hamdi Fırat Büyük

ABSTRACT
Turkey and Bosnia and Herzegovina share deep historical, political, and cultural ties. Bilateral relations between the two have undergone several transformations in parallel with domestic and international political developments and in light of shifts in Turkey's role in the international arena. After decades of negligent and isolationist policies, Ankara finally offered Bosnia a place in Turkish foreign policy following the end of the Cold War, as it came to occupy a position of significant importance for Turkey under the rule of political Islamist Justice and Development Party (AKP). However, Turkey's influence has been debated in positive and negative ways at the same time often creating a contradiction between reality and discourse. This article aims to evaluate Turkey's influence in Bosnia through interviews with experts on political, economic, cultural, media and religious ties between the two in order to portray the potentials and limits of Turkish foreign policy towards Bosnia.

Introduction

The nature of Turkish influence and presence in Bosnia and Herzegovina (hereinafter referred to as BiH or Bosnia) is quite unique. For one, Turkey is a North Atlantic Treaty Organisation (NATO) member state that is openly supportive of BiH's deeply problematic bid to join the alliance (Preljevic 2017). Also, despite the obvious stalling of their own European Union (EU) accession process, Turkey remains very supportive of BiH's EU accession. On the other side, Turkey represents an emerging regional hegemon; this has become very clear with their distinct departure from a Kemalist, secular, and western-oriented republican Turkey towards the more Islamist, nationalist, and competitive authoritarianism of the past decade. Now labelled as the 'New Turkey,' it rejects its previously dogmatic Western orientation, and embraces its Ottoman past, building and structuring its foreign policy accordingly (Aydıntaşbaş 2019). BiH plays a relatively important role in this narrative, given the numeric strength of ethnic Bosniaks in Turkey, and the strength of identity linkages with Turkey.

When it comes to Turkey's influence in Bosnia and the Balkans, myths and realities often conflict and are debated by public, academics and politicians. The first group who are close to Turkish and Bosniak ruling political elites exaggerates and glorifies Turkish influence and offer the country and its leader as regional hegemon especially in relation to the region's Muslims. The second group who questions Turkey's current role in the West, however, underestimates and harshly criticizes Turkey's policies mostly due to Turkey's new approach based on Islam and deteriorating relations with the West as well as its poor democratic record at home. The latter also often describe Turkey as a foreign, external or illiberal actor in the Balkans alongside with Russia, China and Gulf countries even though Turkey is a Balkan country and historically part of culture, identity and tradition of the region. This paper aims to determine and measure what Turkey's contemporary influence is in BiH and how it was developed and perceived in the country. In attempting to fill a gap in the knowledge on the subject, the aim of this paper is to provide evidence-based understanding of the nature of exogenous influence. The research will provide a comprehensive overview of Turkish influence in BiH by mapping key societal segments: the political, economic, cultural, and religious. It will also provide an understanding of the perception and public support that Turkey might enjoy in BiH. In this regard, 29 interviews with Turkish, Bosnian, regional and international experts, academics, civil society representatives and practitioners as well as journalists, clerics and officials from international institutions were conducted in addition to the desk research. At the first part of the interviews, the research aimed to score exercise for interviewees to assess Turkish influence which achieved using different tools. Second, interviewees attended in-depth and semi-structured interviews to reveal Turkey's footprint in BiH decision-making in several domains. The interviews provided important qualitative data and opinions of interviewees for a more in-depth interpretation of the desk research findings.

Two phases of contemporary Turkish–Bosnian relations

Turkey's relationship with BiH cannot be analysed outside of its historical context. While modern Kemalist Turkey tried to create distance between its imperial past and its pro-Western orientation, the new Turkish foreign policy adopted by the Justice and Development Party (AKP) embraces and tries to build upon this past (Rasidagic and Hesova 2020). Turkey is a former imperial power, whose dominion included BiH and much of the Balkans for nearly five centuries. During the Ottoman era BiH underwent a process of Islamization that was unusually widespread, giving rise to many controversial (and) mythical interpretations of the origins of Bosnian Muslims and their religion prior to the arrival of the Ottomans. The Ottoman Empire undoubtedly left a lasting mark in BiH which contributes to the contemporary image of Turkey. Turkey's hesitance to engage more actively in BiH, until recently, had its roots in the Kemalist rejection of religion, and consequently Turkey's desire not to be seen as yet another Muslim country, as well as Turkey's strategic orientation towards EU and the NATO, i.e. the West. Fundamental changes in Turkish foreign policy behaviour, which came with the rise to power of the AKP and Recep Tayyip Erdoğan, consisted of at least two distinct phases. The first phase of more active involvement followed the adoption of a foreign policy vision for a New Turkey in a new world order, as laid out by Ahmet Davutoğlu, where the

Balkans and BiH played a relatively significant role. The second, and more recent phase, was characterized by rather inconsistent and erratic foreign policy actions of Erdoğan. During this period Turkish soft power spread throughout the Balkans; Sarajevo and BiH served as the base camp. This proactive Turkish role in BiH was naturally not seen favourably by all domestic actors, given the prevalence of identity politics in BiH's political discourse. Politicians from Republika Srpska and their Serbian peers, and intellectuals and journalists, attached the label of Neo-Ottomanism to Turkish foreign policy assertiveness in the region (Tanasković 2011). For both Davutoğlu and Erdoğan the Ottoman period and the 'Ottoman cultural circle' indeed play a role, and form a basis of modern Turkey's re-engagement in the Balkans, and are embraced as such, rather than rejected as before. However, they deny that the new policy could and should be seen as neo-Ottomanism (Fisher Onar 2009). This approach is also described as Ottoman romanticism by the Turkish Historian Halil Inalcik (Yavuz 2020).

As Erdoğan began his final ascent towards becoming an unchallenged power figure in Turkey, Turkish politics established stronger and more exclusive ties with the Bosniak political elite, or rather a part of it: a single party's political leadership with a political platform similar to that of the AKP. This approach drew criticism of Turkey's role in Balkans by other predominantly Bosniak political parties, as well as civic-minded intellectuals and journalists. The absence of stronger economic links has been a relatively controversial aspect of Turkish-BiH relations. Frequently, Turkey has been portrayed as paying lip service to Bosnia and Bosniaks, whereas Turkish investments and preferential trade deals went in fact to other countries, most notably Serbia (Karabeg 2017). An objective assessment of BiH's capacity to attract Foreign Direct Investments (FDIs) inevitably leads to the conclusion that it is due to country's systemic deficiencies (legal complexity, incompetent and oversized public administration, weak rule of law and widespread corruption) and the privatization of relations by the part of Bosniak political elite, that a stronger Turkish economic footprint has not been established.

> We should not forget that the majority of Turkish Bosniaks do not favour Erdoğan's Islamist policies. Around 55 per cent of Turkish Bosniaks vote for social-democratic Republican People's Party (CHP), 15-20 per cent vote for the other opposition parties and the rest vote for AKP and others. Turkish Bosniaks are usually secular, liberal and open minded. (STAV 2020a)

Turkey's interest in BiH is not a recent phenomenon; a relatively numerous and influential Bosniak diaspora in Turkey partly accounts for this interest. However, several interviewees emphasized that Turks of Bosniak origin, for the most part, do not favour Erdoğan's Islamist policies, and sit, politically, in the republican, secular and liberal camp.

An alternative to the EU?

Turkey has performed well in soft power domains (culture, education, religion and media); however, its influence in foreign policy, internal politics and economy has been rather limited. There has been some appeal to Erdoğan's style of rule (authoritarian strongman) among BiH and regional political elites that appear to be strongly drawn to it

(Pargan 2017). Reciprocally, BiH is instrumental in Erdoğan's drive to strengthen his Islamist credentials and the political agenda at home, elevating Turkey to the status of regional power.

Despite the rhetoric of Turkish decision makers, contributing to a democratic consolidation of the region and BiH, as well as the region's EU membership processes, is not a priority in Turkey's current agenda. Personal relations between strongmen represent a cornerstone of Turkish foreign policy in the region. Arriving at agreements in a non-transparent manner is the usual strategy for Erdoğan, which makes authoritarian leaders of Central European (CE) or Western Balkan (WB) states preferable interlocutors to democratic governments in the West. It is for this reason that Turkey provides implicit support to authoritarian regimes, as authoritarianism opens up more manoeuvring space. Critics of Turkey's activism in the Balkans and Turkish foreign policy in general accuse Ankara to undermine the EU's interest in the region. This is not only because of Turkey's own policy choices but also because the EU's inaction for a new enlargement towards the Western Balkans that has come to a stopping point. As Denis Macshane stated for Carnegie Europe that in the last twenty years has talked but did not take a real step to make small Western Balkan states full members (Carnegie Europe 2021). EU officials and leaders of European countries have come and gone but made no difference regarding a new enlargement. At the same time, the EU had to deal with its own issues including Brexit, economic crisis and later the refugee crisis that fuelled a debate on the EU's own future. Under these circumstances, it is often accepted that the winners of this power vacuum in the Western Balkans are Russia's Vladimir Putin, China's Xi Jinping and Turkish President Recep Tayyip Erdoğan whose country's membership process is practically deceased due to democratic backsliding in the country as well as never ending international disagreements with the West. Same critics say that these actors have infiltrated and gained influence in the Western Balkans to undermine EU cohesion and coherence.

However, in this research, interviewees agree that Turkey has neither offered an alternative to the region's EU membership bid, nor has it cooperated with Russia to undermine the Western agenda in the Balkans and BiH to perpetuate a specific anti-Western agenda. Turkey's political, economic, and administrative capacity are limited, and at this time do not allow for such a role. Turkey has supported BiH's Western agenda but also followed a new independent policy while the national political context in Turkey has been highly de-Europeanized (Demirtaş 2015). Furthermore, it has not shied away from instrumentalising Bosniaks on occasions as part of its anti-Western propaganda for gaining more votes in Turkish elections, as it was seen with the example of Erdogan's election rally in 2018 in Sarajevo which President Erdogan's similar activities were banned by European governments in their countries.

Turkey's political influence – real and perceived

Turkey's political influence in BiH has become the subject of relatively high scholarly and practitioner attention ever since changes in Turkey's foreign policy, and a re-engagement in the region, came about as a result of changes on the domestic front in Turkey. In these analyses Turkey is often bundled with other non-Western actors, each of which is unique in terms of their presence, methods employed, and foreign policy aims in the region and

BiH. Turkey's specific position in this regard stems from the fact that, compared to other exogenous actors whose influence is analysed, Turkey is a NATO member, and is still, albeit vaguely, committed to its EU candidature. These elements place Turkey's foreign policy and agenda in broad concordance with the general course set by Western international actors in BiH. However, the recent transformation of the Turkish state and Erdoğan's consolidation and centralization of power have led to an increasingly negative human and civil rights record, and a general democratic backsliding, which has put Turkey increasingly at odds with the West, raising questions about the nature and impact of Turkish influence in BiH. There have been at least two important phases of contemporary Turkish-BiH relations. The first began with the arrival of Ahmet Davutoğlu in the position of minister of foreign affairs in 2009, and was signified by his personal efforts and multilateral diplomacy. During this period Turkey used its diplomatic and economic power to broker deals between BiH and Serbia as part of tri-lateral initiatives. With Davutoğlu out of picture, multilateralism in the Balkans was replaced by direct links with political strongmen. This second period was marked by Erdoğan's rise to a position of unchallenged power in Turkey. While there certainly are more nuanced shades of Turkish foreign policy towards BiH and the region, these two phases are of special importance for our analysis, with particular emphasis placed on the post-2016 Erdoğan phase.

Turkish interest in BiH is not a novel phenomenon; historically, the presence of a large Bosniak diaspora in Turkey partly accounts for their interest in BiH and Sandžak[1] in particular. Throughout the last centuries, starting with the Ottoman period, and intensifying during the Ottoman withdrawal from the Balkans and the Balkan Wars, people from the Western Balkans and the wider Balkan area (which today make up at least 25% of Turkish population) have been participating in moulding Turkish policy on all levels; they have been among those making decisions, on equal terms with Anatolian Turks (Büyük 2019).

The starting point in this analysis was an obvious discrepancy between the Turkish footprint in the economy, religious affairs, and culture in BiH, and the general perception of the political influence it wields. BiH's economy has achieved a significant level of convergence with the EU and the immediate region, which leaves very little room for alternatives. FDI figures confirm this, placing Turkey at relatively modest place 11th place, dwarfed by the EU and neighbouring states (Figure 1).

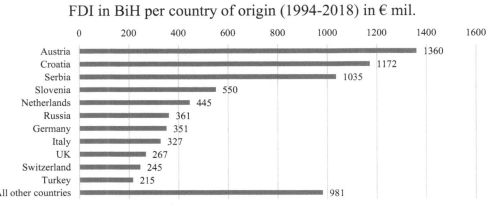

Figure 1. Source: Authors based on data from Central Bank of Bosnia And Herzegovina (CBBiH).

In terms of trade relations, Turkey has been outperformed by EU countries, which make up the bulk of foreign trade for BiH, followed by Central European Free Trade Area (CEFTA) countries (Figure 2).

However, repeated public polls paint a markedly different picture of Turkey, and where it stands, in terms of the importance ascribed to it by the general population. Turkey is seen favourably mostly among the Bosniaks, though there are signs of growing support among two other ethnic groups, albeit still at a very low level. Since mid-2000, Turkey became significantly more visible in BiH, primarily as a result of the waning Western presence and weakening normative influence, rather than anything else. This period was characterized by significant global changes that affected both BiH and Turkey. Turkey witnessed the renaissance of a traditionalist and Islamist AKP, which gradually became the dominant political force, and Erdoğan as an undisputed leadership figure. Turkey's initial approach to BiH started during the period when Ahmet Davutoğlu held the position of minister of foreign affairs. It was during this time that Turkey displayed assertive, yet coherent and predictable foreign policy behaviour, engaging in the region as a constructive broker. During this period Turkey used its economic and diplomatic leverage with Serbia and Croatia, and its trustworthiness in the eyes of Bosniaks, to engage in several tri-lateral meetings that sought to alleviate tensions and resolve disputes in the BiH-Serbia-Croatia triangle. This approach yielded some successes, but it eventually died out, due to domestic changes in Turkey, and the emergence of unfavourable regional dynamics. Some interviewees argued that relations between BiH and Turkey, while cordial, have for decades been driven mainly by interests. This conclusion might be not so easy to detect, given the amount of 'romantic rhetoric' from both sides that is very much pushed forward, which makes this hard to perceive. Here we are not speaking about relations between two states and two national politics, but rather about the domestic political considerations of the two political leaders, Erdoğan and Izetbegović. Our study leads to the hypothesis that for Erdoğan personally, the Balkans are part of a broader context, while he is mainly concerned with maintaining his power, in anticipation of the 2023 elections, if not earlier. Many of his recent, relatively erratic, foreign policy moves are currently being rationalized in the Turkish Ministry of Foreign Affairs

	Country	Exports in 2019			Imports in 2019
1	Germany	1,691,763,841.00 KM	1	Croatia	3,518,230,616.00 KM
2	Croatia	1,452,695,892.00 KM	2	Serbia	2,784,912,679.00 KM
3	Serbia	1,393,285,005.00 KM	3	Slovenia	1,785,250,540.00 KM
4	Italy	1,312,806,999.00 KM	4	Germany	1,783,055,500.00 KM
5	Austria	1,098,048,667.00 KM	5	Italy	1,685,366,730.00 KM
6	Slovenia	1,027,700,876.00 KM	6	Austria	1,058,044,896.00 KM
7	Montenegro	448,691,797.00 KM	7	Turkey	828,485,013.00 KM
8	Turkey	296,190,313.00 KM	8	Hungary	752,545,921.00 KM
9	Hungary	276,092,390.00 KM	9	USA	559,573,524.00 KM
10	France	264,590,803.00 KM	10	Netherlands	556,495,931.00 KM

Figure 2. Source: Authors based on data from Central Bank of Bosnia And Herzegovina (CBBiH).

(MFA) to that end. Erdoğan's goal is assuredly to establish himself as the pre-eminent Muslim political leader, which explains in part his recent interest in Africa, the Middle East and Eurasia (Öztürk 2018). He emphasizes the anti-colonial aspect of his identity, which goes down well with numerous audiences worldwide.

Increasing importance of personal relations

The dominant channels of Turkish influence in BiH are today based on personal relations between Erdoğan and Izetbegović (Büyük and Öztürk 2019). While this approach is hardly completely novel, as Turkey has traditionally operated via 'personal proxies' in BiH (A. Izetbegović, H. Silajdžić, B. Izetbegović), it is now the dominant *modus operandi* for exercising influence. However, Turkey does not shy away from pressuring BiH authorities, even those outside the Party of Democratic Action (SDA) or non-Bosniak circles, when necessary. Turkish diplomats aggressively lobbied BiH MPs, who were part of the delegation to the Council of Europe Parliamentary Assemby (CoE PA), to vote against a resolution condemning Turkey, managing to persuade MPs from the main Bosniak party of SDA, the largest Serb party, Alliance of Independent Social Democrats (SNSD) and the main Croatian political party Croatian Democratic Union (HDZ), who sided with Turks on this occasion. Intense, and undiplomatic, pressures on political figures in BiH became particularly visible following the 2016 coup, and the post-coup purges in Turkey, which included a crackdown on members and institutions allegedly belonging to Fethullah Gülen's network (Slobodna Evropa 2019). To this end Turkey put significant pressure on the SDA, explicitly targeting institutions and individuals working for them, and particularly those of Turkish origin. However, in October 2016, Bosna Sema was sold to US-based Global Investment LLC, and renamed Global Education. The news outlet Faktor, close to the Turkish government, dubbed this 'Gülen selling, Gülen buying' deal, detailing apparent connections of an academic leading the process with Gulen Network in the U.S. Bosna Sema Schools was later sold to a British educational fund, Richmond Park Schools, which again reportedly has ties with the Gülen network (Huskić 2019).

The SDA failed to deliver on its promise of a crackdown on individuals related to Gülen's network, due to administrative fragmentation, and broad consensus requirements that prevent any external actor from assuming or exercising full and direct control despite the proxy's capacity. A smear campaign by prominent SDA members previously close to Gülen's network was carried out, predominantly by media close to the SDA, and particularly those financed by Turkish money. This campaign of vilification portrayed Gülen's network in an extremely negative light, as an organization that corrupts youth, and as an unnecessary and foreign element. Even non-Bosniak officials from state institutions responded to Turkish warnings by increasing their monitoring over Bosna Sema institutions, and by advising parents not to enrol their children there (Huskić 2019).

Turkey has established firm control over the SDA, via its relationship with Izetbegović, to such an extent that it does not shy away from issuing direct orders protecting the interests of Erdoğan and the AKP. Most recently, the Turkish Embassy in Sarajevo explicitly forbade SDA officials from meeting with Ekrem İmamoğlu, the newly elected Mayor of Istanbul following the opposition parties' joint efforts in 2019 local elections in which President Erdogan lost almost all major Turkish cities and towns, who paid a visit to Sarajevo in his first international act since coming to office. The arrest of Fatih Keskin, Dean of Una Sana College (part of the so-called Gülen's network) showed the cross-party influence that Erdoğan commands. Keskin's lawyers feared that the secrecy surrounding his arrest, and the obscure charges, as well as his hasty transfer to Sarajevo, might indicate a possibility that he was intended to be illegally extradited to Turkey in a Kosovo-like operation.[2] The case received widespread media attention, leading to Keskin's eventual release. Some observers believe that absent the ability to apprehend and extradite the people that Erdoğan demanded, the SDA has resorted to spectacular and widely publicized arrests, knowing that these would fail, in an attempt to instil fear and the sense of insecurity among the remaining members of Fethullah Gülen's network in BiH, and emphasizing that BiH had become an increasingly Gülenist-unfriendly country.

A narrow but important section of Bosniak elites and populace still remain emotionally tied to Turkey. There is a strong opposition to Turkish ties with Moscow, as it emboldens the Serb factor, (Subašić 2019) hence the rise in positive sentiments towards Turkey among the Bosnian Serb population. Interviewees noted that on the cultural level, secular elites are opposed to Turkey's overt religious influence. At the same time, they adore the Turkish film industry and literature, and promote Turkish secular writers, thus protesting against the marriage of religion and politics model of the AKP administration. Privately, sections of Bosniak elites and academia, and even diplomats, have sympathy for the Gülen movement due to its perceived moderation, and abhor the crude, authoritarian and increasingly undemocratic *modus operandi* of the Erdoğan administration.

Bosnian power fragmentation

> Turkey's influence in politics is very limited because of power sharing setup in Bosnia. For instance, Turkey is more influential in North Macedonia and Albania in this sense. Turkey's political influence on Bosniaks is further limited because Turkey focuses solely on SDA and Izetbegović and in fact, SDA does not represent all Bosniaks.(STAV 2020b)

Questionnaires and interviews, conducted for the purpose of an assessment of Turkish smart power in the domestic and foreign policy domains, show that almost all respondents in the research agree that the crucial barrier to stronger Turkish influence is the administrative fragmentation and power-sharing character of BiH. Despite having a potent proxy in the SDA and Izetbegović, Turkey has not been able to see its interests served as desired. At the same time, the potential to influence decision-making is assessed as relatively high, though it remains largely unutilized. Most respondents agree that Turkey wields a measure of potential influence here, and that the SDA could be instrumental in that sense.

Regarding government's composition, most respondents believe that Turkey does not exercise this form of influence. There is one known instance when Turkey tried to influence the BiH government's composition, of an individual appointment in 2019, when Erdoğan met with Aleksandar Vučić and Bosnian leaders for the opening ceremony of a Turkish-sponsored motorway project between Belgrade and Sarajevo. This influence is limited to the SDA, and should the need arise Turkey would be able to use this leverage and influence individual appointments. According to some respondents, Turkey also occasionally acts to prevent appointments, rather than actively promote particular appointees.

Regarding Turkey's ability to influence government course of action, their position towards Turkey and to ensure the accommodation of Turkish interests and foreign policy goals and agenda a similar decision-making fragmentation problem on the BiH side, and the multiplicity of actors, acts to inhibit direct control. However, there are examples of direct influence on MPs from BiH, as mentioned above, to vote against a resolution that condemned Turkey in the CoE PA. As mentioned above, Turkey strongly pushed the SDA to move against the Gülen Movement's institutions and individuals after 2016, but, according to some respondents, the SDA's inability to deliver in this sense (Bosna Sema managed to avoid SDA's hostile takeover) led to Erdoğan's disappointment with Izetbegović. This partial instrumentalization of the SDA and Bosniaks, especially with regard to Alija Izetbegović and Srebrenica, shows the limits to which the partnership between AKP and SDA can go. The reconstruction of Alija Izetbegović's birthplace in Bosanski Šamac, and the frequent positive mentions of Alija Izetbegović, are seen favourably among conservative Bosniaks; however, making the TV series about Izetbegović's life seemed a bit too much, even for his supporters. A similar situation occurred in 2017, when Erdoğan used the Srebrenica Genocide to criticize the Netherlands for their government's decision to ban his rallies, an act that was met with outright criticism by some BiH observers (Avdić 2017).

Economic relations: plenty of room for improvement

While Turkey's political influence grew rapidly on Bosnian political groups, the Muslim Bosniaks in particular, the economic relations have failed to reach to a similar level. Turkey prides itself for being an economic powerhouse, and more recently a net donor of international aid; indeed, emphasizing Turkey's economic success was a hallmark of Erdoğan's rule. Erdoğan's recent erratic and conflictual behaviour has placed severe strains on the stability of the Turkish currency and its economy. For Turkey, BiH and the Balkans are not a focus of economic activity. Some importance is attributed to the region, but BiH remains marginal in these considerations (Figure 3). In economic terms, BiH is geographically placed between Turkey and the EU, and its trading ties depend on these countries (legal framework, transport infrastructure, etc.). Frequent mentions of BiH in Erdoğan's political speeches has failed to translate into a stronger economic footprint, which is one of the main criticisms of Turkey's presence in BiH. Turkey's stronger economic ties with Serbia are frequently cited in support of the claim that Turkey mostly pays lip service to BiH and Bosniaks, while doing business elsewhere.

The low levels of economic cooperation are partly offset by relatively generous aid, channelled through the Turkish Cooperation and Coordination Agency (TIKA), and the religious office – Diyanet. Due to its demonstrably unfriendly investments and business environment BiH has failed to attract greater Turkish investments, while Bosniak political elites remain satisfied with Turkish aid and political support, which they use

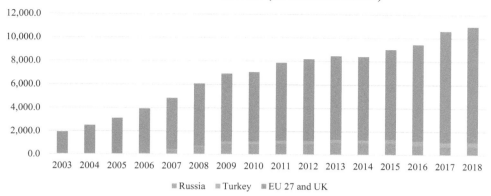

Figure 3. Source: Authors based on data from Central Bank of BiH (CBBiH).

as domestic leverage. Turkey invests elsewhere in the region, while BiH receives the bulk of Turkish international aid, which seem to compensate for the lack of more significant Turkish investments (Deutsche Welle 2018). The data from the OECD suggest that BiH is the biggest recipient of Turkish foreign aid in Europe (Figure 4).

Turkish investments in the Western Balkans are mainly located outside of BiH, with very few in the country, and Turkish investors have never made any significant breakthrough, unlike German and Austrian investors (Figure 5, Figure 6 and Figure 7). Turkish FDI in factories like Sisecam Lukavac and Hayat Natron Maglaj represent different kinds of investment, with no alignment with Ankara's official rhetoric. People resent the aggressive Turkish push to sell its products here, but this is significantly mitigated by an opening up of Turkish markets for BiH meat, flour, and other products.

> Economic relations have never been perfect between Turkey and Bosnia. Turkey does large projects in other Balkan countries as they offer subsidies and incentives unlike Bosnia. Turkey lags behind other countries mostly because Bosnian market is ultimately not profitable. (Authors Interview 2020c)

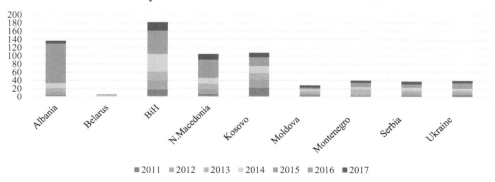

Figure 4. Source: Authors based on OECD data.

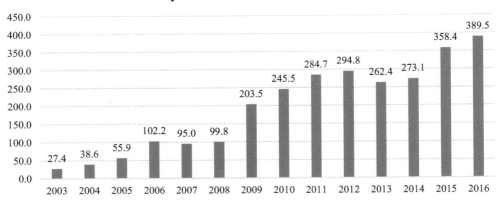

Figure 5. Source: Authors based on data from Central Bank of BiH (CBBiH).

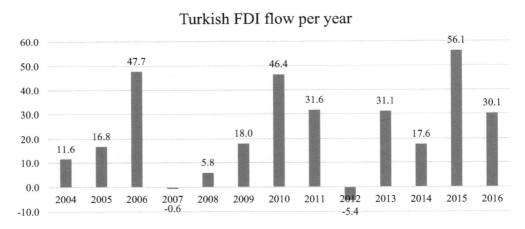

Figure 6. Source: Authors based on data from Central Bank of BiH (CBBiH).

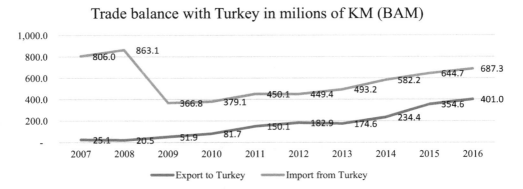

Figure 7. Source: Authors based on data from Central Bank of BiH (CBBiH).

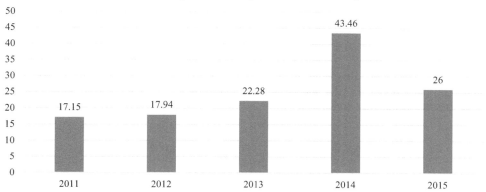

Figure 8. Source: Authors based on data from TIKA – Annual Reports.

On the other side, Turkish state agencies like TIKA or the Yunus Emre Institute (YEE) have compensated for what real businesses originating from Turkey have failed to achieve. Some respondents believe that there is a significant level of public dissatisfaction due to Turkey's disinterest in getting more involved economically. In its more than 24 years in BiH TIKA implemented 900 projects and activities, valued at $82 million (Anadolu Agency 2020) (Figure 8). TIKA has undertaken projects in various sectors such as education, health, development of administrative capacities, etc. TIKA also often works in favour of the Izetbegović family. Prior to the presidential elections, TIKA renovated the BiH Presidential building, which had been partially burned down during social unrest in 2014, and donated several public buses and trams in cooperation with Turkish municipalities. Most donations were accepted by Bakir Izetbegović in large ceremonies, with coverage by Turkey-sponsored media houses. TIKA also funded the construction of the Haematology Clinic in Sarajevo, whose General Manager is Sebija Izetbegović, the wife of Bakir Izetbegović. She faced strong criticism at the time, for her managerial style and lack of qualifications, and while the construction of Haematology Clinic partly offset that criticism, it also serves as a prime example of the nature of relations between two countries. TIKA also provides aid in the areas of agriculture, and the protection of cultural heritage, especially dating from the Ottoman period. Since 2016, there are no publicly available data regarding the financial aspects of Turkey's aid to BiH. Bosnia's first foreign private bank, Ziraat Bank Bosnia, on the other hand, failed to support businesses in the country (Figure 9 and Figure 10). Furthermore, it's sunk credits that were given to names close to AKP and SDA triggered debates even in Turkish parliament (İleri Haber 2021).

An assessment of Turkish smart power in the area of the economy points once again to the administrative fragmentation, and the power-sharing character of BiH, as the main inhibitors to stronger Turkish influence. Secondly, the relatively small economic footprint, and interest in Turkey for BiH's economy, partly explains the results of the assessment.

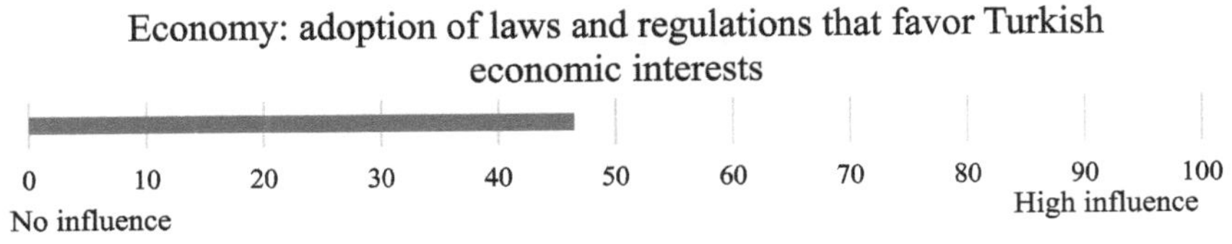

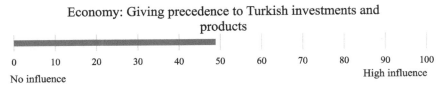

Figure 9. Assessment of Turkey's ability to influence decision-makers in BiH in economic field in relations to the adoption to laws and regulations that favour Turkish economic interests. Source: Authors based on elite interviews.

```
Economy: Giving precedence to Turkish investments and
                        products
├────┼────┼────┼────┼────┼────┼────┼────┼────┼────┤
0    10   20   30   40   50   60   70   80   90   100
No influence                                 High influence
```

Figure 10. Assessment of Turkey's ability to influence decision-makers in BiH in economic field in terms of green-belting and/or giving precedence to Turkish investments and products. Source: Authors based on elite interviews.

Turkey's growing media influence in BiH

In the sphere of the media, Turkey's presence has increased since the mid-2000s, and subsequently intensified during the Erdoğan era. Since the demise of the Gülen Movement, which in the past held formidable influence in various domains, the AKP has struggled to recapture its former partner's influence. One of Turkey's first incursions into the media domain in BiH took place as part of the expansion of the Gülen network, with the short-lived *Novo vrijeme* daily and its later news portal. As the AKP and Erdogan rose to power, and the conflict between him and Gulen intensified, Turkey invested directly in BiH's media via the Simurg Media company, under which the daily *Faktor* and the weekly *Stav* are published. Both outlets are known for their pro-Erdoğan stance, and as SDA (more precisely, Izetbegović) mouthpieces, and Turkish Airlines provides free copies on their flights from Sarajevo. In addition, the Turkish Anadolu Agency (AA) has operated its Bosnian-Croatian-Serbian language centre in Sarajevo since 2012. It is one of 13 regional centres in the world, and the only one in the Balkans besides Skopje. Sarajevo, Skopje and Brussels are the only three AA regional centres in Europe. In addition to AA, Turkish Radio Television (TRT), the Turkish public broadcaster, has its regional office in Sarajevo with a sizable staff. All these media outlets are also known to have been supportive of the SDA and Izetbegović, publishing frequent interviews, news and analysis. In addition to direct control of media in BiH, Turkey has, on a regular basis, organized study visits, and free holidays to Turkey, for editors and reporters from newsrooms and local media organizations in an attempt to promote Turkey as an advanced society, and to soften and offset the criticism of these media, some of which have written critically on Turkish policy from the BiH perspective.

Our analysis of reporting in the major BiH media focused on the narrative and terminology, framing and priming, to the extent that time allowed. Overall, the media that are not owned by, or affiliated with, Turkey present neutral to positive narratives on Turkey, while *STAV* and *Faktor* unquestionably operate as the AKP's and Erdoğan's apparatus focusing on topics such as Turkey's 'brotherly' support to Bosnia (STAV 2020a) and President Erdogan's quest for a new global order (STAV 2020b). Some media assume in general a critical stance, focusing on Erdoğan's rising authoritarianism, his crackdown on journalists, deteriorating civic and human rights, etc. These latter outlets are media which are generally critical of the BiH government, and pro-Western in their stance. Most media, regardless of their editorial policy, perpetuate the use of two terms that are generally associated as pro-Erdoğan and pro-AKP. The use of the term FETO, (Fethullahçı Terör Örgütü/Fetullahist Terrorist Organization), to denote the Gülen network, is widespread. Articles mention 'FETO' or extend this to pleonasms such as 'organizacija FETO', 'teroristička mreža FETO' or 'teroristička organizacija FETO', with the last of these terms being used by Bakir Izetbegović too. The second term that has entered the journalistic vernacular in BiH is 'AK partija' instead of AKP. This draws on a rather subtle semantic difference in the Turkish language where 'ak' denotes 'white', 'clean', or 'unblemished', and while irrelevant in the BiH context, when used by Bosnians in Turkey it carries a certain symbolism, and shows a pro-AKP stance.

> Balkan Muslims in general are suspicious of Erdoğan's Islamist policies opting rather for an established Balkan way of religious life. Turkey's Islamist policies are generally not welcomed by Balkan Muslims apart from a small number of Bosniaks who depend on Turkey for support. Bosniaks and Balkan Muslims are becoming increasingly less supportive of Erdoğan. (Authors' Interview 2020d)

In August 2017, the Turkish Embassy in Sarajevo organized a press conference announcing the intention of Turkish state television TRT and production company Sancak Medya to make a TV series about the life of Alija Izetbegović, the late first President of Bosnia and Herzegovina, and prominent Bosniak political figure, but also one of founders of the SDA. Some interviewees confirmed to us that the popularity of Alija Izetbegović in Turkey apparently surpasses his popularity in BiH.

Culture and education

Cultural and educational activities have become one of the key areas for Turkey in order to increase its influence in BiH. Turkey has worked hard to win hearts and minds in BiH by funding high-profile cultural events, and by transforming BiH culture to align with Turkish customs (an example being mass circumcision with the distribution of Turkish flags afterwards), which is both an indoctrination at a very early age and an appropriation of religious customs to increase sympathies for Turkey. Some localities in Turkey have organized mass Iftars, which although attended by Rijaset officials, do not seem to represent an endorsement and are criticized as a Turkification of Bosnian Muslims.

The Turkish cultural centre Yunus Emre Institute (Yunus Emre Enstitüsü [YEE]) maintains offices in three cities in BiH – Sarajevo, Mostar and Fojnica. The YEE website indicates that only BiH and Kosovo have three such national centres, which testifies to the importance of the cultural/religious element in the spreading of Turkish influence. The YEE centres were founded in 2007 by decree by Erdoğan as a mechanism of Turkish soft power. The YEE took over the Turkology project from TIKA, which had been running since 1999. Under the broad umbrella of promoting Turkish culture and language, the YEE has provided support for the teaching of Turkish in schools. 'The project started with only 10 teachers in 2011, rising to 70 in 2017, providing some 8,200 students in 150 schools with Turkish language lessons' (Huskić 2019). The YEE marked the anniversary of the failed coup of 15 July with a commemorative race in Sarajevo, under the title the 'Race in Honour of Democracy'. The same anniversary was commemorated in the historical Sarajevo landmark *Vijećnica* with a photo exhibition.

For the time that Erdoğan and Gülen were politically aligned, the spread of Gülen's influence in BiH ran without any inhibitions, and in parallel to that of the Turkish official line. Gülen affiliates had been present in BiH since 1997 under the name of *Bosna Sema* which operated some 15 educational institutions in Sarajevo, Bihać, Zenica, Tuzla and Mostar. The first schools run by Turks were opened by the Gülen Network during the Bosnian War and were welcomed by Bosniaks. After the war, the number of schools multiplied, in several BiH towns, and *Bosna Sema* received generous support from successive Turkish governments and their local Bosniak counterparts. As a matter of the fact, the International Burch University's campus in Sarajevo was opened by Turkish President Abdullah Gul in 2010. While the Gülen-Erdogan partnership was working well at home, Gülen schools benefitted from this abroad, and it was often accepted that schools were called Turkish and not Gülen.

In addition to schools and universities, the Gülen movement established the *Izvor nade* foundation (Source of hope) and printed for some time the now defunct media *Novo vrijeme* [New Time], whose name alludes to the largest Gülenist newspaper in Turkey called *Zaman* [Time]. The Turkish government's purges, which took place after the coup, reached BiH through both diplomatic networks and private channels. The Turkish authorities signalled to SDA officials in government structures that they expected them to act to annul the presence and influence of what Turkish authorities now deemed to be FETO (Fethullahist Terror Organization). The schools have faced many political and financial hardships, because of high pressure from the Turkish government and BiH politicians, but the schools have managed to survive and are working at full capacity.

After the alliance between Erdogan and Gülen broke down, and especially after the Turkish government declared Gülen Network as a terrorist organization, Ankara moved to replace Gülen's educational institutions with a newly established *Maarif Foundation* wherever possible. The Foundation opened schools all over the Balkans, including a university in Tirana. The *Maarif Foundation* currently has several hundred students in a high school, primary school and a nursery school in Sarajevo, the majority of which are Bosniaks, and children of Turkish officials living in Sarajevo. *Maarif* schools became popular in a short time, with the support of Turkish and BiH governments, and the relatively low tuition fees compared to other private schools in BiH. In addition to *Maarif Schools*, there are *Maarif Colleges* (a nursery, primary and high school) run by the *Sedef Foundation*, the founder of the International University of Sarajevo (IUS). The IUS was opened by the Sedef Foundation, offering university education mainly to the Turkish *Imam Hatip School* (Theological High School) graduates, as they were not eligible to enrol in secular faculties in Turkey. However, it later turned into a Turkish soft power institution with generous support from the Turkish government and started offering scholarships to BiH students. Several top AKP names sit on its board, including Sevgi Kurtulmuş who is wife of Numan Kurtulmuş, Vice President of President Erdogan's ruling AKP. Sedef Foundation's board has also representatives of several Turkish islamist NGOs such as Ensar and TURGEV Foundations that are close to President Erdogan's political and family circles (Sedef Foundation 2021).

Importance of Turkey graduates for bilateral relations

In addition to Turkey's educational activities in BiH, thousands of BiH students have studied in Turkey with Turkish state and private scholarships. The AKP institutionalized the scholarship system under the Turkish Directorate of Turks Abroad and Kin Societies (YTB) and named it *Turkish Scholarships*. According to YTB figures, 9,555 students from Balkan countries graduated from Turkish universities in 2019, with another 1375 students still currently enrolled in Turkish universities; of these, 532 graduates and 135 current students are from BiH. However, these numbers do not include students who studied in Turkey before the current *Turkey Scholarships* programme, military students, high-school students and students who benefited from different scholarship programmes provided by the Turkish state or private institutions. According to estimates, the total number of BiH students is around 3,000. These graduates represent the main source of human resources for many Turkish or Turkey-related institutions in BiH. These graduates have been considered as Turkey's ambassadors in their respective countries, and the appointment of the new BiH Ambassador to Turkey has bought a new meaning to this statement; as an example of the role Turkish graduates play in Turkey–BiH relations, Adis Alagić, the new BiH Ambassador to Ankara, is a 35 year old former advisor to a Bosniak Member of BiH Presidency and a graduate of the *Turkey Scholarships* program. He is also a founder of Turkish Graduates' Association in BiH (TUMED).

The perception of Turkey in BiH's public domain has been the subject of several studies. The most reliable is the regional study undertaken by the International Republican Institute (IRI) as part of their regular regional annual survey. According to this survey, from 2020 Turkey was perceived as the second-largest donor to BiH by 18% respondents, after the EU with 27% and ahead of Russia with 11%. Sixty-five per cent of all respondents hold a favourable opinion of Turkey, which clearly stretches beyond ethnicity in BiH (Figure 11 and Figure 12). Only Germany is ranked higher than Turkey, whereas Russia, China and the US lag behind. The perception of Turkey's economic footprint and overestimated, with 40% considering it the most important economic partner, with only Germany ahead with 51% (International Republican Institute 2020).

Non-Governmental Organizations (NGOs) sponsored by Turkey ought to be perceived of as an extension of Turkey. Turkish NGOs, religious groups and lobbying institutions have all opened offices in Sarajevo, along with other Turkish institutions. Semerkand, Anadolu Youth Association (AGD), Humanitarian Relief Foundation (IHH), Turkish Red Crescent and the Union of International Democrats (UID) are among those who have opened branches in Sarajevo. The UID, Erdogan's lobbying institution in Western Europe, gained prominence after it organized Erdogan's election rally in Sarajevo in 2018, after he was banned from organizing such an event in Western Europe. All those institutions draw their staff from the ranks of Turkophile Bosniaks who were educated in Turkey and in Turkish institutions, such as the International University of Sarajevo (IUS). The same can be said for the human capital of all Turkish state and private institutions that operate in BiH.

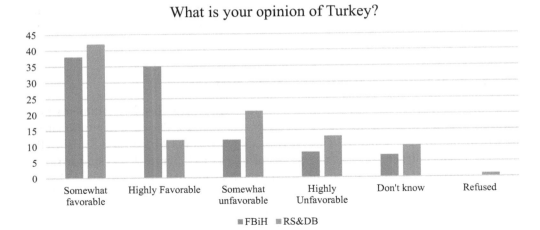

Figure 11. Source: IRI Bosnia And Herzegovina: Understanding Perceptions of Violent Extremism and Foreign Influence.

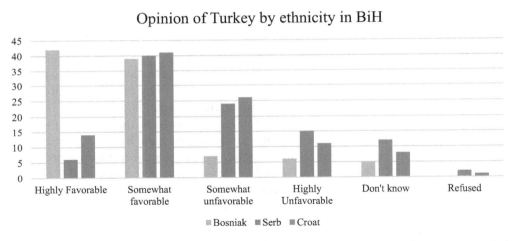

Figure 12. Source: IRI Bosnia And Herzegovina: Understanding Perceptions of Violent Extremism and Foreign Influence.

Even though these appear to proceed without a direct involvement of the Islamic Community (IC) in BiH, mass public events organized by Turkey, but wholly uncommon for BiH, have not been subject to open criticism by BiH's IC. It seems that the IC refrains from criticism of Turkey in such situations for the pragmatic reasons discussed above which could explain the IC being conspicuously absent from the list of organizers.

Turkey has dismantled its own civil society, and there are relatively poor connections between Turkish and BiH civil society institutions. There are some Turkish GONGOs who may have some connections with BiH Civil Society Organizations (CSOs), but on the ground they have had a poor impact on policymaking. The majority of civil society in BiH is critical of Turkey and Erdoğan, because of the undemocratic and autocratic rule in

Turkey. However, there are government funded NGOs and SDA affiliated NGOs that have advanced Turkish interests, such as the SDA youth branch, the Foundation of Alija Izetbegovic (mainly financed by Muzafer Cilek, the honorary council of BiH in Bursa and the wealthy owner of Cilek Company), BIGMEV (founded by Cilek, the new BiH Ambassador to Turkey was a coordinator there for many years), IHH Bosnia, and the International Union of Democrats Bosnia (who organized Erdogan's rally in Sarajevo).

Religious relations: friendly but equal

Religion is one of the main areas which President Erdoğan's political Islamist government focused in foreign policy front portraying Turkey and its leader Erdogan as the protector of Muslims around the world (Öztürk 2016). Bosnia and the Balkans have become an important laboratory for these Islamist foreign policy formulations, yet Turkey faced several challenges. Unlike all other religious institutions across the Balkans and Europe, the Turkish Religious Authority (Diyanet) is a full state institution, and the chief cleric is appointed by the head of the government. This system was designed by Mustafa Kemal Ataturk, the founder of modern-day Turkey, abolished the monarchy and caliphate to create in its place a secular and modern republic. The Diyanet was designed as an instrument to preserve the new republic's strict division of politics and religion, that had traditionally been united in the Ottoman state (Öztürk 2016). The system worked well until the rise of the AKP, and the elevation of religion and religious institutions. Until that time, they had only exercised a minimal role in Turkish politics, under pressure from secularist and Kemalist ruling political and bureaucratic elites. Both religion, and the Diyanet as an organization, gained unprecedented importance under the politically Islamist Erdoğan governments. The system, which was designed to ensure the separation of religion from politics, was now used under Erdoğan's government as a policy instrument in its domestic and international politics, including engaging with other Muslim communities and institutions (Öztürk and Gözaydin 2018).

When the AKP's proactive foreign policy endorsed the former glory of the Ottoman Empire, and when Ahmet Davutoğlu formalized the country's soft power approach and associated institutions, the Diyanet was given a special place. In a short time, the Diyanet has become the main institution to establish relations, and further enhance Turkey's influence on Muslim communities worldwide, and on their religious institutions. To attain these ends, generous aids, donations, scholarships for students, training programmes and restorations and renovation projects of local Islamic monuments were instrumental, with clear effects on the countries in the region. The total value of donations disbursed by the Diyanet, or the numbers of student and clerics who attended Diyanet programs, are not made public in Turkey. However, an increased volume of programmes and projects, as well as the Diyanet's budget, which has risen sharply over the last few years, signifies its new and important role in domestic and foreign politics. The Diyanet's annual budget in 2020 is nearly € 1.5 billion, surpassing the budgets of several ministries.

Relations between the Diyanet and the BiH Islamic Community (Rijaset) have flourished during this period. The Rijaset has enjoyed quite generous support in aid and donations, as well as numerous renovations projects funded by the Diyanet. BiH's Rijaset gives its relations with the Diyanet high visibility, painting an image of a traditional and historic partnership between the two, highlighting their common Ottoman past, culture and religious practices. For the majority of local, Turkish and international interviewees, Turkey's role is still more welcome compared to other foreign Islamic influences such as Iran, the Gulf States and Salafis, which unlike Turkey do not share similar religious practices with BiH. However, BiH's Rijaset jealously guarded its independence, and has remained free from the Diyanet's direct influence when it comes to issues such as fatwas, the appointment of senior clerics, and elections for the Grand Mufti (Figure 13). The Rijaset therefore attempts to balance an outright resistance to any direct influence from the Diyanet, while enjoying its generous support.

Another important element in the relations between the Diyanet and the Rijaset is the issue of superiority. The Diyanet has sought to establish itself as an umbrella institution that brings all Muslims together, especially those living in the former Ottoman territories, in line with Erdoğan's desire to be seen as the pre-eminent Muslim political leader globally. Embracing cultural elements of Neo-Ottomanist and Islamist policies is instrumental in this sense. Interviewees familiar with its inner workings argue that the Rijaset, however, rejects any subordinate role, underlining that the Diyanet and Rijaset are equal partners who cooperate on many issues. It is worth noting is that the Rijaset has similar ambitions, though on a smaller scale, in seeking to establish itself as an umbrella institution for Balkan Muslims, building on its historically central role for Balkan Muslims during the Yugoslav era. The Diyanet has failed to appreciate the structure, mentality, and policy-making procedures in the Rijaset as well as BiH clerics, which is part of general lack of detailed understanding of BiH and the Balkans within Turkish society and decision-makers. The Rijaset has a centuries old tradition as an independent institution which brings clerics, intellectuals and community members together, and regulates the religious affairs of Muslims relatively independently from the government. This particularity escapes many observers, including the Diyanet, as it tends to see Muslim politicians and the SDA as one and the same with the Rijaset, as is the case in Turkey, expecting them to act harmoniously when it comes to Turkey or the Diyanet. Despite the obvious overlap between the SDA and the Rijaset,[3] they still operate as separate organizations.

> Bosnian Rijaset did not allow Turkish Diyanet to open its branch in Bosnia because they did not want their clear and direct influence in the country. Albania, North Macedonia and Bulgaria allowed for this and we can see that they regret their decision due to Diyanet's active role in foreign policy during Erdoğan era. Bosnian Rijaset's system is very different from Turkey's Diyanet. There is a 500 years old tradition in Rijaset and they reject Diyanet's increased influence. However, they pragmatically accept Turkey's financial support. (Authors' Interview 2020e)

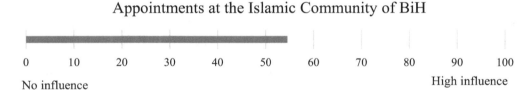

Figure 13. Assessment of Turkey's ability to influence decision-makers in BiH regarding the appointments at the Islamic Community of BiH. Source: Authors based on elite interviews.

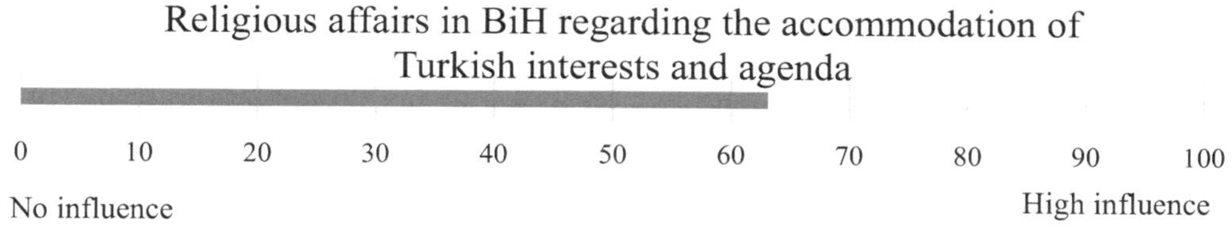

Religious affairs in BiH regarding the accommodation of Turkish interests and agenda

0	10	20	30	40	50	60	70	80	90	100

No influence   High influence

Figure 14. Assessment of Turkey's ability to influence decision-makers in BiH regarding the position towards Turkey by the Islamic Community in BiH. Source: Authors based on elite interviews.

Questionnaires and interviews conducted for the purpose of an assessment of Turkish religious influence show that, over the last few years, the methods used by Turkish foreign policy practitioners were crude, and hence unappealing to the public. The Islamic authority's bureaucracy has complained in private about the damage Turkey is doing to the Rijaset, so the Islamic authorities have maintained symbolic relations, but are not buying into the Turkish political model, and have resisted it, politely affirming the independent structure of the Rijaset (Figure 14). However, at the same time, the Rijaset has, pragmatically, kept relations alive and enjoys the financial support of the Diyanet.

Bosniak conservative politicians, and Rijaset representatives, have used the principles of Ankara's policy towards BiH and the region, as discussed above, for their own purposes and interests. They know it is good to have mosques, Turkish baths, bridges, tombs, etc., rebuilt, which will attract tourists and create jobs. The Rijaset has been following such an Islamic international policy for decades, using available Iranian, Saudi and Turkish resources to rebuild its own infrastructure (Karčić 2010).

Conclusion

Turkey's influence and footprint in BiH have been growing over the past two decades, mainly as a result of domestic changes in Turkey and in BiH. Its influence has changed in nature, from being an ambitious, constructive, regional broker to forging personal links with strongmen. Turkish influence today is mainly channelled via the SDA, and our findings indicate that even within the SDA there is no overwhelming support for these kinds of linkages. The personal appropriation of relations by Izetbegović is not looked upon favourably by the other mainly Bosniak parties either. The rationale behind Turkey's involvement in BiH is based mainly on the domestic political considerations of Erdoğan and the AKP and trying to have a leverage in Ankara's relationship with other actors, the EU in particular. As such, it is prone to volatility, and hence difficult to predict. A strengthening of opposition to Erdoğan, as evident in the results of local elections in Turkey, is likely to increase pressure in BiH as a means of compensating for Erdoğan's loss of credibility domestically. The cultural and religious segments are particularly important here, as is the affirmation of Erdoğan's leadership in the Muslim world.

The continuing democratic backsliding in Turkey, and the strengthening of authoritarian tendencies provides a desirable model for prospective authoritarians in the region, and in BiH. Relations between strongmen are being increasingly strengthened, leading to further and accelerated democratic regression in BiH and the region. While Erdogan's good relations with regional power figures such as Serbia's Vučić, Albania's Rama and Bosnia's Izetbegović and even Bosnian Serb leader Dodik may have eased some barriers for Turkish investments including the Turkey sponsored motorway between Belgrade and Sarajevo, these same relations have not so far alleviated problems between ethnic groups, nor have they reduced tensions. On the contrary, despite these linkages, tensions have seemed to rise. Consequently, the restoration of a democratic culture in Turkey is likely to have positive effect on relations in the region, as it will reduce obscure personal dealings, and replace these with more transparent and accountable relations.

As part of its current approach, Turkey is engaged in a cultural transformation of Bosnian Muslims, which is deployed with the reluctant support of the Rijaset. While not endorsing such activities, the Rijaset accepts Turkish aid and assistance, but seeks to preserve its historic independence. Turkish influence in BiH is currently completely subverted to the interests of Erdoğan and the AKP; diverse agents, from Turkish politics and diplomacy, to media and religious organizations originating from Turkey, all perpetuate these narratives and interests. Turkey's economic leverage is bound to decrease in BiH, and there are two reasons for this. First, Turkey's economy itself is in a very serious crisis, and secondly BiH is not a profitable investment market. Indeed, Turkish investors who came to BiH for emotional or political reasons left soon after for Serbia, because Serbia provides guidance and incentives for Turkish investors.

A rapprochement between Vučić and Erdoğan is likely to increase Turkey's influence in BiH, since Milorad Dodik refrains from openly criticizing Turkey, probably because of Vučić, as evident in his recent moves (N1 2021). That provides another partner for Turkey, in addition to Bosniaks. However, Bosniak society and politicians strongly disapprove of Turkey's engagement with Serbia because they feel betrayed when Turkey opens factories and invests in Serbia. The Russia–Turkey rapprochement has had a very limited effect on Turkey–BiH relations. Turkey and Russia have proved capable of cooperating in certain domains, like Syria, where they both see a common interest. In BiH and the Balkans, they support different groups and with different interests. Still, good Russia–Turkey and Serbia–Turkey relations indirectly soften the political rhetoric among Bosnian Serb politicians with regard to Turkey, and vice versa.

> Democracy should be restored in Turkey for a better foreign policy. If authoritarianism and political polarisation due to harsh Islamist policies of the government continues, Turkey will eventually lose Bosnia and Bosniaks. Bosnia is doing well with the West in its own way and this does not stop them from improving relations with Turkey. However, if Turkey continue to follow current radical path and if Bosnia is forced to choose between the two, it will definitely choose the West and the EU. (Authors' Interview 2020f)

As interviewees noted that Turkey's domestic problems, poor human rights record, rising authoritarianism, and souring relations with the West create confusion for BiH politicians and society about Turkey's role and future. Erdoğan's pressure on BiH politicians to hand over the members of the Gülenist Movement he alleges are terrorists, the rigid language of Erdoğan-sponsored media and NGOs, and the proactive role of ardent Erdoğan supporters has resulted in a significant polarization in BiH and within Bosniaks. These two factors have increased negative narratives about Turkey and Erdoğan. Erdoğan's future is uncertain; he was defeated in last year's local elections against a united opposition, and he is challenged by former colleagues such as Davutoğlu and his former economy minister Ali Babacan. In the absence of Erdoğan, Turkey's engagement with BiH will continue, but it will certainly change in character and shape. Erdoğan's selective and Islamist policies, and the strong reliance on the SDA and Izetbegović are likely to change should the AKP lose at the state level in the same way they did to the new secular government in Istanbul, Ankara and Izmir.

The peak of Turkish influence in the Balkans coincided with its period of promising democracy, a flourishing economy and good relations with the EU and the West. According to the majority of interviewees, Turkey could become a reliable partner if it were to return to democratic values and its support for BiH and the Balkan countries in field of Euro-Atlantic cooperation. Despite its concerted efforts, Turkey's influence has been limited due to the structural complexity of the BiH polity, and the narrow and limited channel through which Erdoğan's Turkey operates.

Notes

1. The Sandzak region, which lies in southwest Serbia and northern Montenegro, has no political status at present but does have a strong historic and ethnic identity, mainly because the majority of the roughly half-million people there are Muslim Bosniaks. Centuries ago, when the Ottomans ruled the Balkans, it was one of seven so-called 'Sanjaks', or Ottoman provinces, of the Bosna Eyalet, or State of Bosnia, and was called the 'Sanjak of Novi Pazar' after its largest town. It was also mentioned and identified in the Congress of Berlin in 1878, where the great powers redefined a reduced Ottoman Empire in Europe.
2. In March 2018 the Kosovo Intelligence Agency and the Kosovo Police extradited to Turkey six alleged members of Fethullah Gulen's movement, allegedly without the consent of the office of the Prime Minister of Kosovo for which the heads of both the intel agency and Kosovo Police were promptly sacked.
3. For an elaboration of the nature of the coalition which developed between religious communities in Bosnia and Herzegovina and the emerging ethno-national political parties in early 1990s see Abazović 'Za naciju i Boga: Sociološko određenje religijskog nacionalizma'.

Acknowledgments

Authors acknowledge the contribution of Roman Shutov and Ana Marinič for this paper regarding methodology and interviews as well as desk analysis of Turkish perception of Bosnia and Herzegovina and media footprint of Turkey in Bosnia and Herzegovina.

Disclosure statement

Authors chose not to disclose the identity of interviewees due to high political polarisation in Turkey and for the sake of more open and vivid political debate.

References

Anadolu Agency. 2020. TİKA Bosna Hersek'te 24 yıla 900 proje sığdırdı'. *Anadolu Agency.* Accessed January 9 2020. https://www.aa.com.tr/tr/dunya/tika-bosna-hersekte-24-yila-900-proje-sigdirdi/1697363

Avdić, S., 2017. Evropa, Turska i Mi: Lako je tuđim (našim) genocidom Evropu mlatiti!. *Slobodna Bosna*, March 14. Accessed 15 November 2021. https://www.slobodna-bosna.ba/vijest/48129/evropa_turska_i_mi_lako_je_tudjim_nasim_genocidom_evropu_mlatiti.html

Aydıntaşbaş, A. 2019. From myth to reality: How to understand Turkey's role in the Western Balkans. *European Council on Foreign Relations.* Accessed 15 November 2021. https://ecfr.eu/publication/from_myth_to_reality_how_to_understand_turkeys_role_in_the_western_balkans

Büyük, H.F., 2019. Diaspora politics: Turkey's new Balkan ambassadors. *Balkan Insight*, March 19. Accessed 10 November 2021. https://balkaninsight.com/2019/03/19/diaspora-politics-turkeys-new-balkan-ambassadors

Büyük, H.F, and A.E. Öztürk. 2019. The role of leadership networks in Turkey–Balkan relations in the AKP era. *Turkish Policy Quarterly* 18: 119–127.

Carnegie Europe. 2021. Has the EU Lost the Western Balkans?. October 14. Accessed 30 November 2021. https://carnegieeurope.eu/strategiceurope/85563

Demirtaş, B. 2015. Turkish foreign policy towards the Balkans: A europeanized foreign policy in a de-europeanized national context?. *Journal of Balkan and near Eastern Studies* 17 (2): 123–140. doi:10.1080/19448953.2014.994283.

Deutsche Welle. 2018. Turkey's economic woes power Balkan reboot. September 27. Accessed 5 October 2021. https://www.dw.com/en/turkeys-economic-woes-power-balkan-reboot/a-45561659

Fisher Onar, N. 2009. Democratic depth: The missing ingridient in Turkey's domestic/foreign policy nexus?. In *Another Empire? A decade of Turkey's foreign policy under the justice and development party*, edited by K. Öktem, A. Kadioglu, and M. Karli, 61–75. Istanbul: Bilgi University Press.

Huskić, A. 2019. Bosnia and Herzegovina: Abandoned by the West, embraced by the East. In *The Western Balkans in the world: Linkages and relations with non-western countries*, edited by, F. Bieber, and N. Tzifakis, 83–107. London: Routledge.

İleri Haber. 2021. Ziraat'in Bosna Hersek iştirakiyle ilgili çarpıcı iddialar!. September 9. Accessed 15 November 2021. https://ilerihaber.org/icerik/tarikat-baglariyla-ortulen-usulsuzlukler-damada-bagli-paralel-yonetim-ziraatin-bosna-hersek-istirakiyle-ilgili-carpici-iddialar-129708.html

International Republican Institute. 2020. Western Balkans Regional Poll. Retrieved 10 August 2021. https://www.iri.org/sites/default/files/final_wb_poll_for_publishing_6.9.2020.pdf

Karabeg, O. 2017. Zašto Turska više ulaže u Srbiju nego u Bosnu i Hercegovinu?. *Radio Free Europe*, August 27. Accessed 15 November 2021. https://www.slobodnaevropa.org/a/most-turska-bih-erdogan-izetbegovic/28698411.html

Karčić, H. 2010. Globalisation and Islam in Bosnia: Foreign Influences and their Effects. *Totalitarian Movements and Political Religion* 11, no. 2: 151–66. doi:10.1080/14690764.2010.511467.

N1. 2021. Erdogan dolazi u Sarajevo, Dodik zbog toga prekida bojkot Predsjedništva BiH?. August 23. Accessed 15 November 2021. https://hr.n1info.com/regija/erdogan-dolazi-u-sarajevo-dodik-zbog-toga-prekida-bojkot-predsjednistva-bih/

Öztürk, A.E. 2016. Turkey's Diyanet under AKP rule: From protector to imposer of state ideology?. *Southeast European and Black Sea Studies* 16, no. 4: 619–35. doi:10.1080/14683857.2016.1233663.

Öztürk, A.E. 2018. Transformation of the Turkish Diyanet both at home and abroad: Three stages. *European Journal of Turkish Studies*, no. 27. doi:10.4000/ejts.5944.

Öztürk, A.E. and İ. Gözaydın. 2018. A frame for Turkey's foreign policy via the Diyanet in the Balkans. *Journal of Muslims in Europe* 7, no. 17: 331–50. doi:10.1163/22117954-12341370.

Pargan, B., 2017. Erdogan a role model for 'strongmen' in the Balkans?. *Deutche Welle*, April 21. Accessed 8 August 2021. https://www.dw.com/en/erdogan-a-role-model-for-strongmen-in-the-balkans/a-38540867

Preljevic, H. 2017. Unsatisfied? The rocky path to NATO membership – Bosnia And Herzegovina: A new approach in understanding the challenges. *Croatian International Relations Review* 23, no. 80: 33–59. doi:10.1515/cirr-2017-0020.

Rasidagic, E.K. and Z. Hesova. 2020. Development of Turkish foreign policy towards the Western Balkans with focus on Bosnia and Herzegovina. *Croatian International Relations Review* 26, no. 86: 96–129. doi:10.37173/cirr.26.86.4.

Sedef Foundation. 2021. Vakıf Yönetim Kurulu. Accessed 10 October 2021. https://www.sedef.ba/tr/content/saraybosna-egitimi-destekleme-ve-gelistirme-vakfi

Slobodna Evropa. 2019. Erdogan i Dodik o 'gulenovcima' u BiH. July 9. Accessed 7 November 2021. https://www.slobodnaevropa.org/a/30045462.html

STAV. 2020a. Erdoğan Za Stav: "Od Nezavisnosti Turska Bosnu I Hercegovinu Nije Ostavila Samu, Niti Će Je Ikada Ostaviti". December 16. Accessed 2 December 30 2021. https://arhiv.stav.ba/erdogan-za-stav-od-nezavisnosti-turska-bosnu-i-hercegovinu-nije-ostavila-samu-niti-ce-je-ikada-ostaviti/

STAV. 2020b. Erdogan: Trenutni Globalni Sistem Ne Reaguje Na Krize Koje Se Događaju Širom Svijeta. November 9. Accessed December 30 2021. https://arhiv.stav.ba/erdogan-trenutni-globalni-sistem-ne-reaguje-na-krize-koje-se-dogadjaju-sirom-svijeta/

Subašić, E. 2019. Nova geostrategija Balkana: Igra li Turska za Rusija?. *Aljazeera Balkans*, September 29. Accessed 4 August 2021. http://balkans.aljazeera.net/vijesti/nova-geostrategija-balkana-igra-li-turska-za-rusiju

Tanasković, D. 2011. *Neoosmanizam - povratak Turske na Balkan*. Belgrade: Sluzbeni glasnik.

Yavuz, H. 2020. *Nostalgia for the empire: The politics of Neo-Ottomanism*. London: Oxford University Press.

Relations between Turkey and Kosovo: factors and dynamics

Afrim Hoti, Bardhok Bashota and Bekim Sejdiu

ABSTRACT

Relations between Kosovo and Turkey are unique because of the difference in their sizes, potential and influence of these two countries in international arena, and their shared history. Studies on Turkey–Kosovo relations often fail to focus on Turkish foreign policy, which this paper attempts to remedy by analysing the political factors that shape relations between Kosovo and Turkey. This paper assesses the disappearance of the bipolar world order and up to the present. It later discusses relations between the two countries since 1990, when the issue of Kosovo took centre stage in international politics. Further, we explore the evolution of Turkey's policy towards the Balkans, including Kosovo's perceptions of its relationship with Turkey. Finally, the analysis focuses on the triangular relations between Kosovo, Brussels and Turkey.

Introduction

The geopolitical and ideological transformations with the end of the Cold War in the Balkans paved the way for the re-positioning of the major powers. The Western powers, assembled under the Euro-Atlantic structures, i.e., NATO and the EU, played a determinant role in managing the consequences of the bloody dissolution of Former Yugoslavia and putting the newly-emerging states into the path of democratic transition. Yet, the Euro-Atlantic vector was not the sole international parameter in the region. The geopolitical relevance, historical traces and socio-cultural heterogeneity of the region would necessarily pull other actors into the play. The major geopolitical rivalry and competing political interests were manifested between Russia and the Western countries throughout Yugoslavia's dissolution process. As a regional power with particular interests in the Balkans, Turkey has, for most of its part, tried to assert its pre-eminent role within the general multilateral structures and in partnership with the major NATO and EU countries.

Is it possible today to paint the same political landscape when it comes to the positioning of Turkey and the EU in the region? This article addresses this question by analysing Turkey's policy towards Kosovo and the EU factor that permeates this relation. This article argues that Balkans is one of the major terrains where Turkey has been trying to play its version of near abroad policy, and Kosovo assumes a vital place within this milieu. Within this gambit, Turkey's attempts to exercise its influence in Kosovo has to be seen within the broader foreign policy agenda towards the Balkans. However, we argue that Turkey can maintain its pivotal role in the Balkans in tandem, not a competition with the EU and within the wider Euro-Atlantic umbrella.

This article consists of four parts. Initially, we provide a short retrospective on Turkey's approach towards the dissolution of communist Yugoslavia during the 1990s, with a particular focus on Kosovo. The second part of the analysis explores the metamorphosis of the Turkish foreign policy in Erdogan's era and, within this context, Ankara's relations with Kosovo. Our analysis provides a general overview of the factors and dynamics that underpin relations between Kosovo and Turkey. In the third part, relations between them are explored in light of Turkey's growing activism in Kosovo and how this is perceived in Kosovo. The fourth part of the analysis examines the EU factor in the relation between Turkey and Kosovo. In this way, we elaborate on the importance of the EU dimension in relations between Turkey and Kosovo.

Turkey's policy towards Kosovo in the course of the dissolution of Yugoslavia

The Kosovo problem was the first episode in the dissolution of communist Yugoslavia. This problem surfaced in 1989 when Milosevic forcefully removed Kosovo's legal status as a federal unit, which it enjoyed under the Yugoslav Constitution of 1974. This aggressive constitutional manoeuvre stirred widespread protests and strikes in Kosovo, which were bloodily suppressed by the special police units acting under the direct orders from Belgrade. From 1989 to 1998, an severe oppression was established by Belgrade in Kosovo, whereby Albanians who constitute over 90% of the population were fired from every public institution, including schools and hospitals. This policy was implemented under the brutal police measures, which were confronted by non-violent civil resistance organized by the Kosovo Albanians under the umbrella of the so-called 'parallel state' (Clark 2000; Vickers 1998, 277; Judah 2008, 64–74).

The international community had largely ignored the situation in Kosovo during the first half of the 1990s, focusing almost exclusively on dealing with the war in Croatia, and Bosnia and Herzegovina. Furthermore, the Kosovo problem was seen as a human rights issue, whereas its profoundly political dimension, namely its legal status against the backdrop of Yugoslavia's dissolution, was almost entirely neglected (Clark 2000; Campbell 2000; Mertus 1999). Even as a human rights problem, the Kosovo issue was constantly marginalized in the international agenda, even though Serbian repression remained a permanent feature of the daily life of the Kosovo Albanians.[1]

During this period, Turkey's approach towards former Yugoslavia and Kosovo was formulated within the general policy of major Euro-Atlantic countries. It is important to note that the Turkish President, Turgut Özal, was among the first world leaders to receive the pacifist Kosovo leader, Ibrahim Rugova, in 1991. However, although Ozal stated his support for a political solution to the Kosovo problem, he declared that Turkey would reject the recognition of the independence of Kosovo in case of its proclamation (Ogulturk 2012, 241–242; Shipoli 2018, 179–180). Turkish authorities sympathized with the Kosovo Albanians oppressed under Milosevic's regime, yet Ankara refrained from assuming an active role – as opposed to Bosnia, where Turkey adopted an open and active policy in support of the Bosniaks. In Ankara's lenses, the Kosovo issue was much more complex, particularly its hypothetical parallel with the Kurdish problem in Southeastern Turkey (Ogulturk 2012, 240).

The ending of the Bosnian war with the Dayton Agreement in 1995 and the sidelining of the Kosovo issue from the international agenda persuaded Albanians in Kosovo to abandon the non-violent political strategy they were pursuing against Belgrade's repressive policy. From 1997 on, and particularly during 1998, the armed clashes erupted between an emerging Albanian guerilla force called the Kosovo Liberation Army (KLA) and the police and military forces of Serbia. The unfolding events heralded the familiar scenario seen in Bosnia and Herzegovina, with the Belgrade regime pursuing the systematic campaign of attacking Albanian civilian targets and pursuing the policy of 'scorched earth' after every major clash with the KLA (Schuman 2004, 54; Morrison 2018, 95). Once again, another episode of Yugoslavia's dismemberment assumed a central place in the international political agenda.[2]

From the outset of the war in Kosovo, Ankara's role was crippled because Turkey was not part of the major international political mechanisms dealing with the crisis, particularly the Contact Group and the Security Council. Furthermore, the official Belgrade's strategy of drawing unfounded parallels between Kosovo and every possible separatist tendency for security problems in different countries around the world, including Turkey's Kurdish issue, initially clouded Ankara's view towards the Kosovo issue. This fact notwithstanding, the Turkish government followed the unfolding of the crisis closely. The conflict in Kosovo and former Yugoslavia coincided with the more assertive Turkish foreign policy in the immediate aftermath of the Cold War. Özal's idea of Turkey as a regional power, stretching its influence from the Adriatic to the Chinese Wall, was the most typical manifestation of new foreign policy activism in Ankara (Makovski 1999). This ambition was to be tested sharply in Bosnia and Kosovo. On the other hand, Turkish public opinion and political elite paid utmost importance to the traces of the Ottoman historical heritage in the Balkans and particularly in Kosovo, where there was also a Turkish minority living. 'Turkey did not want to see the traces of its history to be erased in Bosnia and Kosovo,' the Foreign Minister Ismail Cem lamented in 1999 (Cem 1999). Furthermore, Ankara perceived the Balkans as an important geostrategic location and a gateway to the European Union. Last but not least, Ankara was keen on keeping NATO as involved as possible in the Balkans.

Such intertwined nature of the situation produced mixed reactions from Ankara. At the beginning of the war in Kosovo, Turkey retained a relatively passive position and formulated its policy within the framework of NATO and the UN (See more: Altuna 2003, 117–120). In March 1998, the then Turkish Foreign Minister Ismail Cem paid a visit to Belgrade to offer a three-point plan to Milosevic: first, to immediately stop the fighting in Kosovo; secondly, to give educational rights to Albanians, as agreed in 1996; and finally, to give back to the Albanians the rights of the 1974 constitution (Uzgel 2001). The Turkish position in Kosovo evolved tremendously as the crisis endured, and the brutality of Serbian forces ramped. On the one hand, the public pressure in Turkey started to mount as a 'second Bosnia' unfolded. On the other hand, the fears about a possible re-emergence of the 'religious axes' in the post-Cold War Balkans became more visible in the Turkish perceptions. These concerns were expressed openly by the Turkish top political figures, such as the Turkish Premier Ecevit, who declared that 'the

Serbia-Orthodox union, the foreign policy based on the Serb-Orthodox axis', was considered the driving force towards the polarization 'that might be far more dangerous than the ideological polarization' (Hale 2000; Abazi 2008, 4).

As the expulsion of Albanians from Kosovo by the Serbian state intensified, a possible refugee flow to Turkey became an additional issue of concern. The Turkish President Suleyman Demirel declared that 'the people who have been subject to cruelty in Kosovo are our brethren' (Hale 2000, 264–265). He urged the international community to take lessons from Bosnia and expressed Turkey's readiness to participate actively in the possible UN peacekeeping force (Demirtas-Coskun 2006, 275).

As early as 13 October 1998, the Turkish Foreign Ministry stated that NATO was preparing for possible action in Kosovo and that Turkey, in accordance with the already-approved law by the Grand National Assembly, would participate in such an operation (Gazete 1998, 2). On 24 March 1999, in response to the commencement of the NATO operation against the Federal Republic of Yugoslavia, the Turkish Foreign Ministry stated:

> ... being [a] country which attributes importance to the maintenance of peace and stability in Balkans and having historic human and cultural ties with the region, Turkey has made great efforts to the resolution of the conflict through the peaceful settlement. However, it has been observed that the Serbian regime has not shown willingness to work towards fulfilling the expectations of the international community, and the whole Kosovo population [...]. The attitude of the FRY has made the phased military operation inevitable. Being a NATO member, Turkey gives a full support to the North Atlantic Council (Altuna 2003, 132).

During the NATO bombing campaign, Turkey actively participated in the operation, initially in the monitoring flights and then directly taking part in the bombing campaign. It provided a detachment of F-16 fighters based in Italy. Turkey also offered its airbases of Balikesir, Bandirma and Corlu for NATO aircraft, should the bombings intensify.

Turkey's engagement in Kosovo increased dramatically with the ending of the war and the deployment of the international administration over Kosovo. The international presence in Kosovo had two components. The first was the military component consisting of NATO and states, which cooperated with NATO in the framework of 'International Security Force' (KFOR). The second was the civil component, known as the 'United Nations Interim Administration Mission in Kosovo' (UNMIK). Turkey participated actively in both dimensions of international administration over Kosovo, which lasted from 1999 until 2008.

Turkey's relations with Kosovo since 2008: the key determinants

Since the Justice and Development Party (*Adalet ve Kalkınma Partisi* – the AKP) came to power in Turkey in 2002, the new political elite in Ankara felt that the conjunction of the new international landscape, economic progress of the country and the re-invention of Ottoman historical heritage favoured the repositioning of Turkey. Many authors have emphasized that this 'Neo-Ottoman inclination' of Turkish foreign policy has its roots in Turgut Ozal's vision of rediscovering Turkey's imperial legacy and a new consensus at home among the country's multiple identities (Taspinar, 2012: 128). Within this new vision, Turkey was no longer the Eastern tail of the West but the epicentre of a new setting emerging on its outskirts (Sejdiu 2018, 107; Vracic 201616, 7). Within this paradigm, Turkey was not anymore to be seen as one of the key NATO allies in a sensitive region(s) but, as Demirtas-Coskun points out, Ankara promoted itself as *primus inter pares* based on its geography and history rather than on democratic credentials or human development level (Demirtas-Coskun 2006, 135). Turkey strived to be an indispensable bridge-builder between different countries, regions, and cultures (Mamedov 2020, 195; Sejdiu 2018, 107). The most symptomatic articulation of this paradigmatic shift was the doctrines of 'zero problems with neighbors' and 'strategic depth,' masterminded by Professor Davutoglu – who served as a foreign policy advisor to the Prime-Minister Erdogan, Foreign Minister and Prime Minister. Thus, Turkey became a more assertive international actor, and it introduced new foreign policy instruments – including cultural diplomacy – but also displayed inconsistencies and euphoria.[3]

Kosovo has been one of the testing grounds for the new trajectories of Turkey's new foreign policy. The relations between Kosovo and Turkey are underpinned by a combination of factors of geopolitical, historical, economic, and socio-cultural nature (Rey 2018, 18). Before elaborating on these factors, it is essential to note that 17 February 2008 is the 'D-day' for relations between Kosovo and Turkey. Although the complex nature of the relation between Kosovo and Turkey cannot be reduced to a single episode, Turkey's swift recognition of Kosovo's independence rightfully deserves particular attention as it reveals the general parameters within which Ankara formulates its foreign policy approach towards the Balkans and Kosovo.

Independence of Kosovo and Turkey: geopolitical dimension and the re-arrangement of national balances

On 17 February 2008 Kosovo declared independence from Serbia. Turkey became among the very first countries to recognize it. Kosovar officials have reiterated their gratitude to Turkey for being one of the first countries to recognize Kosovo's independence and support the recognition process and the overall state-building progress in Kosovo (Sejdiu 2018, 106).

Turkey's move to swiftly recognize Kosovo's independence in February 2008 was based on a sober calculation of the new constellations in the Balkans. With the independence of Kosovo, the Albanian factor has strengthened its position in the region. Just one year after the independence of Kosovo, specifically in 2009, Albania joined NATO, while the political influence of the Albanians in Northern Macedonia has increased rapidly after 2001. Turkey is an experienced reader of the ethno-national parameters and geopolitical map of the Balkans. Hence, Ankara understood very well the central role that the Albanian factor was assuming within the sensitive regional geopolitical setting.

This reading of the national equilibriums in the Balkans and the position of the Albanians in this setting plays an important role in Ankara's Balkans policy and, by default, its approach towards Kosovo. The architect of the new Turkish foreign policy, Ahmet Davutoglu, has expressed this viewpoint constantly. He would repeat this stance even after leaving governmental functions, as he did in 2017 in an interview with the leading Kosovo daily 'Koha Ditore' when he stated candidly that there could not be peace and stability in the Balkans without Albanians who live in seven countries (Ditore 2017).

There are three additional, but not less important, factors that have influenced Turkey's position towards Kosovo's declaration of independence. First, Turkey's increased involvement in Kosovo signalled a regional power and a trustworthy ally of the key NATO and EU member states. It is sufficient to see the list of recognitions that Kosovo got in the first week following February 17[h], 2008, to confirm this fact. Kosovo was recognized by the overwhelming majority of the NATO and EU countries within a few weeks after it declared its independence (Ministry of Foreign Affairs and Diaspora of Kosovo, 2021). The goal of Turkey to assume a pre-eminent role within the multilateral actions towards Kosovo was expressed very succinctly by the Turkish President Demirel amid the NATO intervention in 1999. Arguing in favour of Turkey's active role in the US-led military campaign against Milosevic, President Demirel had stated that 'the crisis in Kosovo presented Turkey with the opportunity to show that it was a first-class NATO member' (Hale 2000, 264–265). By the same logic, in 2008, Turkey could hardly afford to be left behind the key NATO and EU countries in taking a position on such a vital geopolitical development in the Balkans, such as the recognition of the independence of Kosovo and building relations with the newly-born country in the centre of the Balkans.

The second factor that has traditionally refrained Ankara from taking a more active role in Kosovo was the imaginary parallel with the Kurdish problem in Turkey. Indeed, it was the fear that Russia, Serbia or other countries might draw a parallel between Kosovo and the Kurdish problem in Southeastern Turkey that influenced Ankara's position towards Kosovo during the first half of the 1990s (Nachmani 2003, 134). However, this time, for all the reasons mentioned above, Ankara avoided the trap in which Spain and some other countries fell. Kosovo issue arose out of the dissolution of a Yugoslav communist federation, to which Kosovo was a constitutive part. The Kosovo conflict was brought to the point of NATO's military intervention, international administration, and independence as an outcome of Serbia's brutal campaign aiming to ethnically cleanse Kosovo of the Albanian majority. None of these factors is present in the Basque region and Catalonia, Transylvania, Crimea.

The third factor is related to historical paradigms and, in connection to that, the presence in Turkey of a huge number of Albanian-origin citizens and the presence in Kosovo of a vibrant Turkish ethnic minority served as a strong impetus for Turkey to forge strong relations with Kosovo. One of the preferred anecdotes of Erdogan was that they were concerned that Erdogan could have made a decision to recognize Kosovo's independence even before its declaration, due to the pressure of his personal friends in Turkey, many of whom have Albanian ethnic background (Sejdiu 2018, 106). More Kosovo origin citizens are living in Turkey than there are Kosovars in Kosovo; the Turkish Foreign Minister Ahmet Davutoglu stated in a press conference with his Kosovar counterpart, Skender Hyseni, in Ankara, in 2009. At the same conference, Davutoglu also argued that Kosovo holds a central place in the Balkans, and this is why for Turkey, it is essential to have strong relations with Kosovo (Ihlas Haber Ajansı 2009).

An exaggerated and unbalanced bilateral economic cooperation

The role of the economic factors in relations between Turkey and Kosovo is important, although this factor is often exaggerated. This overemphasizing the importance of Turkish investments in Kosovo is related to some significant investments of the Turkish companies in critical sectors in Kosovo and the debate about the potential involvement of personal interests of individual political leaders on both sides. Thus, the Turkish-American consortium Bechtel-Enka has won public tenders of more than a billion Euros for constructing the two largest highway projects in Kosovo. This bidding process was heavily criticized for the lack of transparency, so were the privatization of the electricity distribution company (Kosovo Electricity Distribution Supply-KEDS) by the Turkish company Calik Holding and the concession of the Airport of Prishtina given to the Turkish-French Consortium, Limak- Aéroports de Lyon. All these bidding processes were criticized by the media and civil society for the lack of transparency and unfair prices (Sejdiu 2018, 109).

However, economic relations between countries should be analysed by facts and factors that are more objectively defined. To start with, Kosovo is a small market with limited economic potential. As such, with the exception of mining and energy, where Kosovo has vast natural resources (particularly reserves of lignite), its economic profile can hardly make it a strategic destination of big international investors. Kosovo is an important trade partner for Turkey, and both countries have endeavoured to boost economic ties. They have concluded several agreements in this regard, such as the Agreement for Economic Cooperation, Agreement on the Elimination of Double Taxation , and Free Trade Agreement. Furthermore, around 300 Turkish companies are registered in Kosovo, of which eleven are considered big companies (Embassy of the Republic of Kosovo in Ankara,).[4] Turkey was constantly ranked among Kosovo's five largest trade partners, although the trade balance has been disproportionate. Thus, according to the Kosovo Agency of Statistics, in 2019, for example, Turkey was the second-biggest exporter to Kosovo, while it ranked 12th in the imports of Kosovo goods and services (Kosovo Agency of Statistics 2021:5).

The value of Turkish investments in Kosovo for the period 2009–2019 is estimated to be around 450 million Euro (Radio Free Europe 2020). Beyond the specific bilateral context, for Pristina, Turkey holds t potential to serve as a bridge for Kosovo's economic relations with the Middle East and parts of Asia and Africa. This is an additional factor that makes Turkey a strategically important country for Kosovo in economic terms. The Istanbul Airports and Turkish Airlines are commonly used by the Kosovar businessmen, workers and others for their overseas transports. The visa-free regime between Kosovo and Turkey and the good flight connections of Istanbul with Pristina are an advantage for Kosovar institutions, companies and citizens and is another great advantage for Kosovo business people and citizens alike.

Cultural diplomacy as Ankara's new foreign policy tool

Ankara utilized its new foreign policy weapon extensively in Kosovo, namely 'cultural diplomacy.' Cultural diplomacy became the central instrument of Turkey's strive for exercising its version of 'soft power' in what is perceived as the former Ottoman geo-cultural space. In a broader theoretical outlook, the concept of soft power is a theoretical product of the liberal school of international relations theories. The authorship of the concept is attributed to Nye (2004), who distinguished between 'hard' and 'soft' manifestations of political power in the international arena. In his view, power is expressed in a 'soft manner' when a country has the ability to reach the desired objectives through cooperation and attraction, rather than through coercion and imposition – the latter being an expression of 'hard power' (Nye 2004). Many authors, such as Ahmet Erdi Ozturk, have observed that Ankara sought to explore religiously – coloured soft power in the Balkans in order to assert its influence and prestige (Ozturk 2021). Ozturk explains that 'soft power is based mostly on identities, lifestyles, belief systems and any other normative capacity to exercise influence on others' (Ozturk 2021, 158).

Cultural diplomacy was conceived by AKP as a diplomatic tool to lure the ethno-social groups, political forces and individual leaders who shared ottoman nostalgia and religious piety. The topic of cultural diplomacy and its intersection with the concept of soft power in Turkey's policy towards Kosovo warrants more space than this paper can provide.

It is sufficient here to highlight that, in the practical realm, the concept of cultural diplomacy as formulated by Ankara consists of three components: first, reference to historical and religious factors as a tool for projecting soft power in an imaginary Ottoman geography (Demirtas 2015, 10; Sejdiu 2018, 145–149). Second is the usage of non-conventional institutional mechanisms for pursuing foreign policy goals, such as the Turkish Cooperation and Coordination Agency (TIKA), Yunus Emre cultural centres; the Religious Directorate (Diyanet); the media outlets (Anadolu Agency 2018); scholarships for international students. The third is the polishing of foreign policy discourse with heavy religious colours and emotional historical narratives.

The discourse that Ankara uses to speak about its 'small brothers' in the Balkans is imbued with religious tones and historical folklore. In his famous 'balcony speeches', after every electoral victory of the AKP, Erdogan never forgot to mention countries and cities of the Balkans where traces of the Ottoman past are more vivid. His messages, such as that after the victory of the AKP in local elections in 2014 when he cherished 'the brothers in Bosnia, Macedonia and Kosovo for celebrating his electoral victory,' have been full of galvanizing tones (Daily News 2014). A year earlier, during his visit to Kosovo, the former Speaker of the Turkish Grand National Assembly, Cemil Cicek, stated that relations between Kosovo and Turkey are 'spiritual' (Püttmann 2020, 2; Bechev 2012, 138). Almost in choir, the Turkish officials have attributed a fundamental role to the cultural element, primarily defined along religious lines and perception of common historical heritage, to describe Turkey's relation with Kosovo and the Balkans in general. Nobody went further in trying to pack the relations between Kosovo and Turkey into the religious paradigm than the Deputy Prime Minister of Turkey, Numan Kurtulmus. During a visit to Kosovo in 2016, Kurtulmus, almost resembling an imam, stated recklessly that "Kosovo is a European country which has absorbed Islamic culture in its roots. As such, Kosovo is the most important point of the Islamic geography in the West (Shekulli 2016).

Relations with Turkey, cultural diplomacy and EU dimension: Kosovo's perspective

The official position of Kosovo on relations with Turkey is expressed through the official documents and speeches, as well as by the public discourse in general. Following the official page of the Embassy of the Republic of Kosovo to Turkey, 'Republic of Kosovo and Republic of Turkey share the same vision for democratic stability, good neighbourly relations and the Euro-Atlantic integration of the region' (Embassy of Republic of Kosovo in Ankara). This is how the official Prishtina articulates Kosovo's regional vision and relations with Turkey. The Ministry of Foreign Affairs of Turkey expresses in a similar tone its official policy towards Kosovo: 'Turkey attributes utmost importance to the stability, territorial integrity and development of Kosovo, as well as its integration in the European and Euro-Atlantic structures and consolidation of friendly and con-structive relations with her neighbours in the region' (Republic of Turkey, Ministry of Foreign Affairs, 2015).

However, the views of Prishtina and Ankara are conflicting when it comes to the importance of the historical and religious factors in shaping the relations between the two countries. Unlike Ankara, Prishtina does not attach significance to historical legacy and religious elements in its relations with Turkey. For Kosovo, Turkey's geopolitical value is measured by its current potential rather than its historical grandeur. Size and population, geography, economic development, strong army, NATO membership and the loud voice in many other international platforms are attributes that make Turkey an important player in international politics. In Kosovo's perspective, there is no role for religion in this equation. Quite the contrary, tendencies to give to the relations between Kosovo and Turkey a religious denomination are met with concern and rejection in Kosovo and among Albanians in the Balkans (Kosovo 2.0 2016).

The Albanian ethno-national identity is unique and, as such, very different from the other ethnic nations of the Balkans. This is not adequately understood in Turkey and elsewhere. One of the unique features of the Albanian national movement, which developed in the second half of the nineteenth and beginning of the twentieth century, was the side-lining of religion from the national identity. Unlike other nations of the Western Balkans, religion did not play a pivotal role in the Albanian nation forming movement in the Balkans, but quite the opposite. It could not have been different, as Albanians in the Balkans have heterogeneous religious identities, namely Islam, Orthodoxy, Roman Catholicism and Bektashi (Blumi and Krasniqi 2014, 475–516; Unesco 2011). ' ... [do] not look to church or mosque, the Alabanian's religion is Albanianism,' reads a powerful verse in the poem 'Oh Albania, Poor Albania' of Pashko Vasa, in the mid-nineteenth century. Vasa, a Catholic from Northern Albania who served in important functions in the Ottoman Administration (including the post of the Governor of Lebanon), was one of the prominent poets and intellectual pioneers of the Albanian National Awakening movement in the nineteenth century. His message to the Albanians was to mobilize around ethnicity and language, which meant putting aside the religious affiliation that risked tearing apart the dream for a coherent national identity (see Duijzings 1999). Albanian national conscience attaches paramount impor-tance to the subjective feeling of common ancestry from the Illyrian tribes and objective unifying elements of distinctive folk tradition and language. For the

Albanian historical narrative, the detachment of Albanians from the occidental back-yard, first by the Ottoman Empire for five centuries and then by the communist ideology for another half a century, was a tremendous historical misfortune (Sejdiu 2018, 110). Therefore, it was not surprising that Ankara's request to re-examine the history textbooks about Ottoman Empire met with vehement rejection from most Kosovo and Albanian intellectuals who perceived this as an attack on Albanian historical memory (Sejdiu 2018, 113). Today, Kosovo, Albania and Albanians in the Balkans consider integration in the Euro-Atlantic structures not only in political and economic terms but also in socio-cultural dimensions, as a paramount national aspiration. Hence, trying to place Kosovo in any geo-cultural map, pained with religious colours, is flawed in the conceptual ground and can be very damaging for Kosovo's international cohesion and international position. Nor does any tendency to treat Kosovo as a satellite contributes to the relations between the two countries. Indeed, if Kosovo is to play a satellite, then it will navigate into the Euro-Atlantic – primarily American – orbit.

Kosovo has a strategic interest to have strong relations with a Euro-Atlantic Turkey. Thus, for Kosovo, Brussels is a pivotal parameter in relations between Kosovo and Turkey. Two episodes have demonstrated the profoundly detrimental effect for relations between Turkey and Kosovo if the latter would be sandwiched between Turkey on the one side, and the US and EU, on the other. The first case has to do with the secret operation that the Kosovar authorities carried out in 2018 for handing over to Turkey six Turkish nationals who Ankara accused of being members of the Fethullah Gulen's network (a Pennsylvania-based cleric accused by Turkey of staging the attempted coup of July 2016). The deportation of six alleged members of the Gulen Movement lacked transparency in terms of the legal procedures and international standards that apply in such situations. This prompted a harsh reaction in Kosovo and abroad, and the Prime Minister at the end of March 2018, dismissed the Interior Minister and the Chief of Intelligence for not informing him about the action. After the decision of the Prime Minister of Kosovo, Turkish President Erdogan has angrily lamented that 'he would make the Kosovo Prime Minister pay' (Welle 2018; Radio Free Europe 2018). Allegedly, the action of clandestine deportation of six alleged Gulenists was orchestrated by the President of Kosovo, who was perceived as a close personal ally of President Erdogan. An ad-hoc Parliamentary investigative commission in Kosovo drafted a report, which found 31 legal violations in the process of deportation of the six alleged Gulenists (Radio Free Europe 2019). Furthermore, criminal court proceedings have been initiated against the Director of the Kosovo Intelligence Agency and two officers of the Kosovo Police for alleged mishandling of this operation.

In connection to this event, the EU spokesperson stated that 'the arrest and subsequent deportation of six Turkish nationals legally residing in Kosovo raise questions about the respect of the due process of law. The rule of law is a fundamental principle of the European Union' (Radio Free Europe 2018aa). Brussels was concerned with this development, as the deportation of alleged Gulenists was perceived as a blow to the rule of law system in which the EU has been investing so heavily with the EULEX mission (Shipoli 2018, 186).

The second episode, which developed an open crack in relations between Turkey and Kosovo, was related to the decision of Prishtina to open its embassy in Jerusalem. This came after some agreements were reached between Kosovo and Serbia in the White House and the presence of President Trump in September 2020. These agreements, among many other issues, facilitated recognition of Kosovo's independence by Israel and the opening of the embassies in Jerusalem by Kosovo and Serbia, respectively (The Guardian 2021). Despite fierce reactions and requests from Ankara to Pristina not to proceed with opening the Embassy in Jerusalem, Kosovo opened the Embassy in Jerusalem in March 2021 (Daily Sabah 2021).

Turkish policies in the Balkans and Kosovo: EU perspective

EU and Turkey are prominent actors in many other strategic issues and areas, such as the refugee crisis, conflicts in the Middle East, Afghanistan, Russia, etc. The Balkans is one piece of the big puzzle of cooperation or rivalry between them. The EU views on Turkish policy towards the Western Balkans, including Kosovo, have been largely influenced by the policies of Erdogan's AKP. Koppa argues that the approach of AKP on the issue of the EU perspective for the Western Balkans, including Kosovo, embraces the stamp of three periods. During the first period (2002–2009), AKP has adopted mainly pro-EU and pro-Western discourse. In the second period, 'Davutoglu era' (2009–2016), Ankara's approach towards the Balkans was driven by the tendency to return to the glorious Ottoman past; third period, or the era of 'Sultan Erdogan' (2016 onwards), the Turkish policy is characterized by pragmatism and authoritarianism based on historical references (Koppa 2020, 3–6). In other words, the AKP's discourse towards the Balkans and Kosovo has initially been coordinative; it evolved into competitive and then into a distrustful – not to say a rival discourse.

With coming to power in 2002–2003, Erdogan and the AKP engaged robustly to meet the criteria for EU membership, particularly on putting the security sector under civilian control. When the EU proclaimed in the Thessaloniki Summit in 2003 that the countries of the Western Balkans have a European perspective, Turkey declared its unwavering support for their full integration in the Euro-Atlantic structures (Shipoli 2018, 181–182; Aydıntasbas 2019). Shipoli succinctly observes that during the UN administration, it was very reasonable for Kosovo to build intensive relations with Turkey and benefit from its institutional experience and political and economic potential, including the experience in meeting the EU criteria (Shipoli 2018, 182). On the other hand, by constructive engagement with the Balkan countries, particularly with Kosovo, Turkey strengthened its credentials in the eyes of the EU and attributed to itself the role of a crucial actor in promoting peace and stability in the region (Ergil, 20,018: 157). EU, on its part, has appraised Turkey's efforts in the region. Thus, in 2005 and 2010, the EU Commission stated that:

"Turkey has continued to promote stability and security in neighbouring areas such as the Balkans, [. . .] as a country with close political, economic, historical and cultural ties with the region [. . .] Bilateral relations with other enlargement countries and neighbouring EU Member States have been developing positively (European Commission 2005, 2010).

However, the partner role with the EU started to be questioned by the new activism in the Turkish foreign policy under the vision of Davutoglu. Turkey became increasingly assertive and competitive in the Balkans, particularly Kosovo (Koc and Onsoy 2018, 360). EU also contributed, at least indirectly, to the unilateral path of Turkey. The financial crisis of 2008–2009 and the evaporation of the enthusiasm for enlargement towards the Balkans transmitted pessimism in the region (Ekinci 2009). Turkey was there to fill the gap. One strategic step Turkey took was its decision to lift the visa regime with Kosovo in 2009. This has been an important step for citizens of Kosovo, which continues to be the only country in the region with no visa liberalization with the EU. This isolation is imposed on Kosovo by the refusal of some countries, mainly France and the Netherlands, to allow visa liberalization for Kosovo, notwithstanding the fact that in 2018 the EU Commission concluded that Kosovo had fulfilled the criteria for visa liberalization (Schengenvisa News 2018; European Western Balkans 2021). Obviously, this fact discredits the EU and boosts the image of Erdogan and Turkey in Kosovo (Ozkanca 2016, 36, 43).

The EU has generally been cautious in expressing publicly any anxiety over Turkey's increased assertiveness in Kosovo and the region – with few exemptions as was the case of reaction from Brussels about the deportation of Gulenists. However, the European leaders have occasionally expressed in public what many think in private. French President Macron stated in the EU Parliament in 2018 that the Balkans was an area where the EU was rivalled by Russia and Turkey. This stirred a reaction from Ankara, with the Spokesperson of the Ministry of Foreign Affairs stating that 'being a Balkan country as well, Turkey's aim and priority in the region today, as it has been in the past, was the maintenance and strengthening of peace, stability and sustainable development' (Anadolu Agency 2018). Austria's Foreign Minister Sebastian Kurz went even further, when he bluntly stated his discomfort with the 'cultural diplomacy' of Turkey and Saudi Arabia, when he declared that 'in Sarajevo and Pristina, for example, women are paid to wear the full veil in public [...] we cannot look on and do nothing' (Handelsblatt 2017). In a similar tone, Herbert Raymond McMaster, former national security advisor to US President Donald Trump, warned that Turkey was spreading extreme Islamist ideologies worldwide. In his observation, Turkey was actively involved everywhere, from West Africa to Southeast Asia, and particularly in the Balkans (Voice of America 2019).

Beyond the public eyes, EU representatives and Western diplomats have been nervous about the growing Turkish assertiveness and unilateralism in Kosovo. What state officials and diplomats were not willing to say was expressed by various politicians, academics and other pundits. Given the growing uneasiness in Brussels and other Western capitals with Turkey's activism in the region at the expense of the EU, some former high-ranking Turkish officials have declared that 'The EU needs to adjust itself to this reality that Turkey's influence is not something that they can prevent' (Politico 2018).

Some observers had pointed out that the EU scepticism towards Turkey's discourse towards the Balkans started when an authoritarian one-man-rule-based system was installed in Ankara. They even invented the term 'Erdoganism' or 'Sultanism' to describe this peculiar political culture and model that was unfolding in Turkey (Tziarras 2018, 1–4; Bartlett and Prelec 2020, 241–243). In this depiction, 'Erdoganism' connotes a political philosophy and governing style which embodies political Islam, Turkish nationalism and

Anti–Westernism, but which derives its legitimacy through the democratic electoral process (Ergil 2018, 169; Yilmaz and Bashirov 2018, 1818–1819). Some authors, such as Ergil and Koppa, have opined that for the AKP followers, being Anti-Western is a political and religious necessity (Ergil 2018, 171). This Anti-Western sentiment was further nurtured by the belief of President Erdogan and his followers that Western circles were involved in the coup d'état attempt in July 2016, and this led to tensions in relations with the USA, Germany, the Netherlands (Ergil 2018, 175; Koppa 2020, 5).

Against this backdrop, notwithstanding the fact that Turkey has reiterated its benign intentions in the Balkan region, there are serious doubts among the EU politicians and public opinion, who perceive Ankara's policy as an attempt to provide an alternative address and a political model for the Balkans (Aydıntasbas 2019). For the EU and USA, this fact is in itself worrisome, as the Turkish political model under Erdogan sets the ground for illiberal democracy in Europe and, as such, is in contradiction with the reform agenda along liberal-democratic lines that the EU and the US have been promoting in the region (Stratfor Report 2009). In relation to Kosovo, the concerns about the possible transplant of this illiberal political model are even more significant as this may undermine the enormous EU and US investments in the rule of law and democratization in the country (Shasha 2020, 93–98).

Even though Turkey's active role may be interpreted as a challenge, or even an obstacle in the Europeanization of the Balkans, including Kosovo, there is no argument that Turkey has an open tendency to incite de-Europeanization in the region (Alpan and Ozturk 2022). As some authors have succinctly argued, it is more plausible to say that Turkey has benefited from the 'Europeanisation fatigue' in the region whereby the EU has shown more interest to preserve the *status quo*, rather than a continuation of reforms that have started earlier in Kosovo and other Balkan countries (see, Zweers 2019; Bechev 2012).

Conclusion

The essential conclusion of this analysis is that the interaction of geopolitical and economic considerations with historical factors shapes the relations between Kosovo and Turkey. This conjunction progressively pushed Turkey to abandon the initial hesitation to get more actively and resolutely involved in Kosovo during the 1990s. The NATO intervention to stop the repetition of the second Bosnia in Kosovo, and the declaration of Kosovo's independence on 17 February 2008, marked the two pivotal moments that highlight the evolution of Turkish policy towards Kosovo. Turkey's relations with Kosovo entered a new phase on 17 February 2008, when it became one of the first countries to recognize the independence of Kosovo. Since 2008, relations between Turkey and Kosovo have been shaped by complex factors and circumstances. Historical parameters have a visible imprint on this relation, with the major trace being the presence in Turkey of a large number of citizens with Albanian origin and the existence in Kosovo of many traces of Ottoman history. The swift recognition of Kosovo's independence by Turkey is a milestone momentum in the history of relations between the two countries and Turks and Albanians in general. This episode has demonstrated that Turkey is a vigilant reader of national constellations in the Balkans and, in this milieu, the importance of the Albanian factor.

However, the post-independence period for Kosovo has been characterized by the resurfacing of divergences between Ankara and Pristina when it comes to the importance of religious factors and historical narratives in shaping the relations between the two countries. Kosovo considers Turkey as a strategic partner, but whose relevance is associated with its Euro-Atlantic orientation and political and economic potential. Hence, any rivalry of Ankara with the EU and the West, in general, would have a negative repercussion for Turkey's relations with Kosovo. If Kosovo becomes a battleground for such a major rivalry, this can have very detrimental effects on Kosovo. Being irritant in clashes between big powers or blocks is something that small countries try to avoid. Moreover, Kosovo's Euro-Atlantic orientation has no alternative in political, security, and socio-cultural dimensions. Hence, Kosovo rejects attributing any significance to 'cultural diplomacy,' i.e., using religion as a base for construing Kosovo–Turkey relations. This has to do also with the very peculiar identity traits of Albanians and their unique national awakening movement of the nine-teenth and twentieth century. In this context, while Turkey has all legitimate rights to maintain its historical traces in the region, moreover being itself a Balkan country, Ankara has not appropriately understood the sensitivity of bringing religion and competing for historical narratives into its policy towards the Balkans and Kosovo, in particular.

The EU-Turkey congruence in the Balkans could happen only as a joint invest-ment. Turkey is a Balkan country with huge potential and legitimate interests. On the other hand, the inconsistencies in the EU policies towards the region, particu-larly Kosovo, have created scepticism and a vacuum. The limited space of this article prevented us from providing the views from the opposite angle, namely the short-comings of the EU policy towards the Balkans and Kosovo. Be that as it may, Brussels, as the capital of Euro-Atlantic structures, is a pivotal parameter in relations between Kosovo and Turkey – albeit not the only one. Ankara and Pristina use quite different lenses to measure this vector's importance in their relations. Hence, the perception of rivalry between Turkey and the EU has negative consequences for its relations with Kosovo. This analysis has demonstrated that the fear that Turkey would try to project itself unilaterally as a critical player in the region and trans-plant the model of illiberal democracy has caused anxiety in the Western capitals. As a general corollary, demonstrated in 1999 with the NATO's military intervention to stop the mass atrocities in Kosovo and again in 2008, with the declaration of Kosovo's independence, Turkey can play a pre-eminent role in the Balkans only within the multilateral Euro-Atlantic umbrella.

Notes

1. A report issued by Amnesty International in 1994, for example, informed that 'the police use violence with impunity on a daily basis'. The Report continued by stating that 'thousands of ethnic Albanians have witnessed police violence or experienced it at first hand.' Further Amnesty International reported that 'Police officers express their ethnic hatred towards their victims. A particularly savage instance involved a police officer slashing a Serbian symbol on the chest of an 18-year old ethnic Albanian'. Other incidents

mentioned in this report involved 'killing of six-year-old boy by the police and severe beating of a 90-year-old man, in one of their daily raids on Kosovar Albanian homes' (quoted in Bellamy 2002, 51).

2. On 24 September 1997, for the first time after the eruption of the armed conflict, the Contact Group voiced its concern about the situation in Kosovo and issued an appeal for negotiations.

3. One typical example of inconsistencies are radical oscillations in the relations between Turkey and Syria in the course of one decade (see Taspinar 2012, 137).

4. Among the big Turkish companies present in Kosovo are considered: Enka, Calik Holding, Limak, Newco Balkan, TEB Bank, National Trade Bank, Is Bank, Zirat Bank.

Acknowledgement

Afrim Hoti benefited from funding offered by the Jean Monnet Network, 'Linking the Europe at Periphery (LEAP)', supported by the European Commission (Project number: 612019-EPP-1-2019-1-TR-EPPJMO-NETWORK).

Disclosure statement

No potential conflict of interest was reported by the author(s).

References

Abazi, E. 2008. Kosovo Independence: An Albanian perspective. *Fondation for Political, Economic and Social Research, Policy Brief*. April. http://setadc.org/wp-content/uploads/2015/05/SETA_Policy_Brief_No_11_Enika_Abazi.pdf (accessed June 13, 2021).

Alpan, B., and A.E. Ozturk. 2022. Turkey and the Balkans: Bringing the Europeanisation/De-europeanisation nexus into question. *Southeast European and Black Sea Studies* 22, no. 1. forthcoming.

Altuna, E. 2003. The Kosovo crisis and Turkey. PhD diss., Bilkent University, Ankara. September

Anadolu Agency. 2018. "Turkish foreign ministry responds to macron on Balkans" Turkish foreign ministry responds to macron on Balkans (aa.com.tr). (accessed July 30, 2021).

Aydıntasbas, A. 2019. From myth to reality: How to understand Turkey's role in the western Balkans. *Policy Brief*. March 13. https://ecfr.eu/publication/from_myth_to_reality_how_to_understand_turkeys_role_in_the_western_balkans/ (accessed July 25, 2021).

Bartlett, W., and T. Prelec. 2020. UAE Sultanism meets illiberal democracy. In *The western Balkans in the World: linkages and relations with non-western Countries*, F. Bieber, and N. Tzifakis. ed., London: Routledge 241–259 .

Bechev, D. 2012. Turkey in Ballkans: Teaking a broder view. *Insight Turkey* 14, no. 1: 131–46.

Bellamy, A.J. 2002. *Kosovo and International Society*. London: Palgrave Macmillan.

Blumi, I., and G. Krasniqi. 2014. Albanians' Islam(s). In *The oxford handbook of European Islam*, J. Cesari. ed., Oxford: Oxford University Press 475–516 .

Campbell, G. 2000. *The road to Kosovo: A Balkan Diary*. USA: Westview Press.

Cem, I. 1999. Russian envoy comment on NATO operations, Kosovo, anatolia', quoted in Migdalovitz, C., Kosovo: Greek and Turkish perspectives. *CRS Report for Congress*. 25 March, 1999 https://www.hsdl.org/?view&did=451446 (accessed March 3, 2016).

Clark, H. 2000. *Civil Resistance in Kosovo*. London: Pluto Press.

Daily News 2014. Turkish PM Erdoğan's post-election 'balcony speech' http://www.hurriyetdailynews.com/full-text-turkish-pm-erdogans-post-election-balcony-speech.aspx?pageID=238&nID=64341&NewsCatID=338 (accessed August 5, 2021).

Daily Sabah. 2021. "Kosovo rejects Turkey's call on Jerusalem embassy, says its 'done deal" Daily Sabah. (accessed June 19, 2021).

Demirtas, B. 2015. Turkish foreign policy towards the Balkans: A Europeanised foreign policy in a de-europeanised national context? *Journal of Balkan and near Eastern Studies* 20, no. 10: 1–17. doi:10.1080/XXXXXXXX.2015.XXXX.

Demirtas-Coskun, B. 2006. *Turkey, Germany and the wars in Yugoslavia: A search for reconstruction of State identities*. Berlin: Logos Verlag.

Ditore, K. 2017. Albanians key to Balkan peace. https://www.koha.mk/ekskluzive-davutoglu-per-gazeten-koha-shqiptaret-kyc-per-paqen-ne-ballkan/ (accessed June 18, 2021).

Duijzings, G.H.J. 1999. Religion and the politics of identity in Kosovo. *University of Amsterdam*. https://pure.uva.nl/ws/files/1513644/108604_UBA003000255_012.pdf (accessed June 17, 2021).

Ekinci, D. 2009. Turkey and the Balkans in the post-cold war era: Diplomatic/Political, economic and military Relations. PhD diss., Bilkent University, Ankara. Department of International Relations.

Embassy of Republic of Kosovo in Ankara at. http://www.ambasada-ks.net/tr/?page=1,75 (accessed August 2, 2021).

Ergil, D. 2018. Turkey's power and influence on Kosovo in phillips In *Threats and challenges to Kosovo's sovereignty*, L. David. ed., Prishtina-New York: Columbia University 118–134 .

European Commission. 2005. Turkey 2005 progress report. *Brusseles*. November 9. https://www.ab.gov.tr/files/AB_Iliskileri/Tur_En_Realitons/Progress/Turkey_Progress_Report_2005.pdf (accessed June 1, 2021).

European Commission. 2010. Turkey 2010 progress report. Brussels. November 9. https://ec. europa.eu/neighbourhood-enlargement/sites/near/files/pdf/key_documents/2010/package/tr_rapport_2010_en.pdf (accessed June 15, 2021).

European Western Balkans. What is holding Kosovo's visa liberalisation back? https://european westernbalkans.com/2018/12/26/holding-kosovos-visa-liberalisation-back/ (accessed July 7, 2021).

Gazete, R. 1998. Kosova Kriziyle İlgili Olarak Oluşturulabilecek "Çokuluslu Müşterek Güç"e Katılmak Üzere Türk Silahlı Kuvvetlerinin Yurtdışına Gönderilmesine, Anayasanın 92 nci Maddesine Göre İzin Verilmesine Dair. https://www.resmigazete.gov.tr/arsiv/23492.pdf (accessed June 28, 2021).

The Guardian. 2021. Kosovo opens embassy in Jerusalem after Israel recognises its Independence. https://www.theguardian.com/world/2021/mar/14/kosovo-opens-embassy-in-jerusalem-after-israel-recognises-its-independence (accessed August 5, 2021).

Haber Ajansı, I. 2009. "Balkanlar'ın refah alanı haline gelmesini istiyoruz" https://www.iha.com. tr/haber-balkanlarin-refah-alani-haline-gelmesini-istiyoruz-86335/ (accessed August 3, 2021).

Hale, W. 2000. *Turkish foreign Policy: 1774 – 2000*. London: Frank Cass Publisher.

Handelsblatt. 2017. "EU, Russia and Turkey struggle for Balkan Influence" Balkan Rivalries: EU, Russia and Turkey struggle for Balkan influence (Handelsblatt.com). (accessed August 10, 2021).

Judah, T. 2008. *Kosovo: What everyone needs to know*. New York: Oxford University Press.

Koc, Z.E., and M. Onsoy. 2018. An evaluation of Turkey's western Ballkans policy under the AKP and prospects for the post- Davutoğlu era. *SUTAD Bahar* 43: 355–67.E- 2458-9071

Koppa, M.E. 2020. Turkey, Gulf States and Iran in western Balkans: More than the islamic factor? *Journal of Contemporary European Studies* 29, no. 2: 251–63. doi:10.1080/14782804.2020.1754769.

Kosovo 2.0. 2016. Signs of strain in Kosovo-Turkey relations. https://kosovotwopointzero.com/en/signs-of-strain-in-kosovo-turkey-relations/ (accessed July 29, 2021).

Kosovo Agency of Statistics. 2021 https://mint.rks-gov.net/desk/inc/media/DE72B5E5-2827-4C52-94A2-EC9F7B08597B.pdf (accessed June 17, 2021).

Makovski, A. 1999. The new activism in Turkish foreign policy. *Sais Review* 19, no. 1: 92–113.

Mamedov, I. 2020. The Balkan policy of Turkey in connection with the Kosovo crisis 1998-1999. *Istorija 20. Veka* 1: 185–202. https://www.ceeol.com/search/article-detail?id=83784610.29362/ist20veka.2020.1.mam.185-202 Accessed 18 June 2021

Mertus, J.A. 1999. *Kosovo: How myths and truths started a war*. Berkley: University of California Press.

Ministry of foreign affairs and diaspora of Kosovo. 2021. *Republic of Kosovo*. https://www.mfa-ks. net/al/politika/484/lista-e-njohjeve/48 (accessed June 14, 2021).

Morrison, K. 2018. *Nationalism, identity and statehood in Post-Yugoslav*. London & New York, NY: Bloomsbury Academic.

Nachmani, A. 2003. *Turkey facing new millennium: Coping with intertwined conflicts*. Manchester: Manchester University Pres.

Nye, J.S. 2004. *Power in the global information age: From realism to globalization*. London: Routledge.

Ogulturk, M.C. 2012. Turkey's Balkan policy after the Cold War in the context of the Independence process of Kosovo. PhD diss., Yeditepe University, Graduate Institute of Social Science.

Ozkanca, O.D. 2016. Turkey and the European Union: Strategic partners or competitors in the western Balkans? *Journal of Regional Security* 11, no. 1: 33–54.

Ozturk, E.A. 2021. *Religion, Identity and Power: Turkey and the Balkans in the Twenty-First Century*. Edinburgh: Edinburgh University Press.

Politico. 2018. "Turkey's Balkan comeback" Turkey's Balkan comeback – POLITICO Turkey's Balkan comeback – POLITICO. (accessed June 25, 2021).

Püttmann, F. 2020. Imagining islam in Kosovo-The social construction of the Kosovar Muslim subject among European political actors. *Southeast European and Black Sea Studies* 20, no. 2: 307–25. doi:10.1080/14683857.2020.1778984.

Radio Free Europe. 2018. Kosovo's haradinaj rejects erdogan's criticism of firings over deported turks. https://www.rferl.org/a/kosovo-haradinaj-rejects-turkey-erdogan-criticism-firings-over-deported-turks/29141270.html (accessed August 2, 2021).

Radio Free Europe. 2018a. EU Criticizes Kosovo, Turkey over deportation of six erdogan political foes. https://www.rferl.org/a/eu-criticizes-kosovo-turky-over-deportation-six-erdogan-political-foes/29144413.html (accessed August 4, 2021).

Radio Free Europe. 2019. Commission of inquiry: Expulsion of 6 Turkish citizens constitutes 31 constitutional and legal violations. (evropaelire.org) (accessed August 11, 2021).

Radio Free Europe. 2020. "Turkish millions on Kosovo market" Turkish millions on Kosovo market (evropaelire.org). (accessed July 20, 2021).

Republic of Turkey, ministry of foreign affairs. 2015. https://www.mfa.gov.tr/relations-between-turkey-and-kosovo_.en.mfa (accessed June 22, 2021).

Rey, J.D. 2018. Kosovo. In *The influence of external actors in the western Balkans. A map of geopolitical players* Hänse, L. and Florian Feyerabend (eds.) , 17–20. Berlin: Konrad Adenauer Stiftung.

Schengenvisa News. 2018. EU commissioner avramopulos says Kosovo fulfilled all visa liberalization criteria. https://www.schengenvisainfo.com/news/eu-commissioner-avramopoulos-says-kosovo-fulfilled-all-visa-liberalization-criteria/ (accessed August 5, 2021).

Schuman, M.A. 2004. *Nations in Transition: Serbia and montenegro*. New York: Facts on File.

Sejdiu, B. 2018. Rethinking the relations between Kosovo and Turkey: Between facts and emotions in Phillips In *Threats and challenges to Kosovo's sovereignty*, L. David. ed., Columbia University 103–107 .

Shasha, D., 2020. The strategic role of external actors in the western balkans: Kosovo's perspective. Austrian Institute for European and Security Studies, Study. https://www.aies.at/download/2021/Role_of_External_Actors_in_WBDeutscherExecutiveSummary_1.pdf (accessed July 30, 2021).

Shekulli. 2016. Zv/kryeministri Kurtulmush: Kosovën E Shohim si shtet me të cilin kemi lidhje shpirtërore. http://shekulliagency.com/bota/zvkryeministri-kurtulmush-kosoven-e-shohim-si-shtet-me-te-cilin-kemi-lidhje-shpirterore/ (accessed June 16, 2021).

Shipoli, E. 2018. Kosovo and Turkey: On the path to Euro-Atlantic integrations In *Threats and challenges to Kosovo's sovereignty*, D.L. Phillips. ed., Columbia University 135–147 .

Stratfor Report. 2009. "EU: rapidly expanding into the Balkans" EU: Rapidly expanding into the Balkans (stratfor.com). (August 10, 2021).

Taspinar, O., 2012. *Turkey's Strategic Vision and Syria. The Washington Quarterly*. summer

Tziarras, Z. 2018. Erdoganist authoritarianism and the 'new' Turkey. *Southeast European and Black Sea Studies* 18, no. 4: 593–98. doi:10.1080/14683857.2018.1540408.

Unesco. 2011. Island of peace: Documentary on religious coexistence in Albania. http://www.unesco.org/new/en/member-states/single-view/news/island_of_peace_documentary_on_religious_coexistence_in_alb/ (accessed June 30, 2021).

Uzgel, I. 2001. Balkanlarla Iliskiler.In *Turk Dis Politikasi: Kurtulus Savasindan Bugune Olgular*. B. Oran. ed., Belgeler, Yorumlar. Ankara: Iletisim 10–637 .

Vickers, M. 1998. *Between serbs and albanian: A history of Kosovo*. New York: Columbia University Press.

Voice of America. 2019. US official accuses Turkey https://www.voanews.com/usa/us-official-accuses-turkey-pushing-extreme-islamistideology (accessed November 9, 2021).

Vracic, A. 2016. *Turkey's role in the western Balkans*. Berlin: Stiftung Wissenschaft und Politik.

Welle, D. 2018. "Kosovo PM Ramush Haradinaj orders probe into Turkey extraditions. https://www.dw.com/en/kosovo-pm-ramush-haradinaj-orders-probe-into-turkey-extraditions/a-43208889 (accessed July 28, 2021).

Yilmaz, I., and G. Bashirov. 2018. The AKP after 15 years: Emergence of erdoganism in Turkey. *Third World Quarterly* 39, no. 9: 1812–30. doi:10.1080/01436597.2018.1447371.

Zweers, W. 2019. Between effective engagement and damaging politicisation: Prospects for a credible EU enlargement policy to the western Balkans. *Policy Brief* May. https://www.clingendael.org/sites/default/files/2019-05/PB_Western_Balkans_May19.pdf Accessed 15 August 2021

Assessing a decade of Romania-Turkey strategic partnership in an era of ambivalence and 'De-Europeanisation'

Aurel Lazăr and Miruna Butnaru-Troncotă

ABSTRACT

The redefinition of Turkey's national identity under the rule of President Erdoğan's Justice and Development Party (AKP) influenced its foreign policy. For many years, Turkey maintained an ambivalent position towards the EU, and as a NATO ally and only by the end of 2020 it disclosed an openly anti-Western position. In this context, there is a rich literature studying Turkey's actions to reassert its influence in the Western Balkans, but there is less scholarly attention on Turkey's relations with Romania – its Black Sea neighbour and NATO ally. Building on recent literature on Turkey's regional strategies and tendencies of 'De-Europeanisation', we scrutinized the country's bilateral relations with Romania between 2008 and 2020. The analysis relies on mainly qualitative data and offers a chronological account of the main diplomatic interactions between the two governments, placed in the context of significant regional events. The article concludes that, compared to the Balkans, there are the same ambivalent tendencies in Turkey-Romania relations. It shows that Turkey acted as a relevant economic partner and security ally for Romania at the Black Sea, while distancing more and more from the EU and asserting a more active role as a regional player in the Middle East and in the Balkans.

Introduction

Back in 2011, after a renewed electoral victory of the Justice and Development Party (*Adalet ve Kalkınma Partisi* – AKP), Turkey's foreign policy priority was to join the European Union (EU). The last decade, however, brought decisive changes to Turkey's foreign policy due to domestic factors and regional events, as well dynamics inside the EU. In the years following the Arab Spring, Turkey started to adopt new foreign policy practices in its neighbourhood (more visible in the Western Balkan countries with a Muslim population), while its EU accession negotiations ground to a halt. By 2021, not only has the EU membership ceased to be a priority for Turkey anymore, but the EU-Turkey relations have even deteriorated to their 'lowest point' in decades.

There is a vast literature offering different analytical perspectives on Turkey's 'U turn' and why it is important for the relationship with its neighbours. Beyond the domestic factors, regional dynamics are very relevant in understanding a state's foreign policy changes. Constructivist authors, in connection to the Copenhagen School's Regional Security Complex Theory (RSCT), explained how identity and self-perceptions shaped Turkey's foreign policy shifts over the last fifteen years and how this influenced its patterns of cooperation and conflict with its neighbours (Diez 2005). According to the RSCT, Turkey sits at the intersection of multiple security complexes, very different from each other, without genuinely being part of any of them, which makes it act as an 'insulator state' (Buzan and Wæver 2003). Scholars argued that the initial role attributed to Turkey within the RSCT framework as an 'insulator' between the different regions has altered, and over the years, it transformed into 'a conductor', transmitting varying security dynamics between different RSCs and taking a more active regional position (Barrinha 2014). Moreover, they showed that more prominently after the Arab Spring, Turkey's leadership has become increasingly belligerent, disclosing an EU-related narrative marked by resentment, and accusing the EU of 'double standards', referring not only to the long-frozen accession negotiations but also to issues such as the failure of the EU to grant Turkey a visa-free regime, as stipulated in the Ankara Agreement. In this context, Turkey-EU relations were described as reaching a historic low point (Bahgat 2021). In May 2021, members of the European Parliament even called for the EU-Turkey formal suspension while insisting that any positive agenda with Turkey should be made conditional upon democratic reform, accusing Ankara of confrontational and hostile foreign policy. Thus, we believe that a re-assessment of Turkey's regional role reflected in its bilateral relations with its EU-member neighbours and NATO partners such as Bulgaria, Greece, or Romania is necessary.

Turkey's actions to reassert its influence in the Western Balkans and its attempt to compete with the EU for regional influence has attracted increasing scholarly attention (Dursun-Özkanca 2019). Numerous analyses further focus on Turkey's special relationship with neighbouring Bulgaria, partly due to a strong Turkish minority in the latter (Öztürk 2021). The same applies to academic analyses on Greco-Turkish maritime disputes, couched in competing narratives of national sovereignty over the delimitation of maritime boundaries in the Eastern Mediterranean (Alpan 2014). But Turkey's relations with Romania, its most important trading neighbour and NATO ally, remain under-researched. Romania is absent from academic inquiries that focus on Turkey's regional assertiveness. The relevance of this analytic focus resides in the fact that Romania is a neighbouring country with unique historical ties to Ankara. Moreover, in 2021 Romania and Turkey celebrated a decade of intensified cooperation since they signed a Strategic Agreement. In this context, we believe it is relevant to re-evaluate Turkey's foreign policy towards Romania – an EU and NATO member that shares with Turkey the same RSC and to scrutinize its evolution over the last decade. Romania and Turkey share common interests in the Black Sea. As such, the conduct of their bilateral relations towards enhanced cooperation can influence regional security dynamics, especially in handling common threats posed by the Russian Federation and the existing 'frozen conflicts' in the area.

Recent studies confirm that Turkey acts as an 'ambivalent actor' in the Balkans and that this is part of Turkey's 'ethno-nationalist religion-oriented foreign policy' (Öztürk 2021). For the last decade, scholars discussed how Turkey used its soft power to consolidate its influence in the Western Balkans. In this context, we aim to analyse the instruments used by Turkey in the case of its other neighbouring strategic partner – Romania. Diplomatically, within NATO and the EU, Romania's good relationship with Turkey is considered an asset for cooperation in the Black Sea region. In order to validate this assumption, we aimed to understand how the relations between the two countries developed over the last decade, placed within a regional and an EU-related context.

While in recent years, Turkey has visibly stepped up its economic, cultural, political and diplomatic relations with the Western Balkans. One crucial question is whether it attempted to do the same with Romania. How did the Europeanization/De-Europeanization ambivalent tendencies in the shifting Turkish foreign policy unfold in the case of Turkey-Romania relations? How did other evolutions inside the EU and at the Romanian domestic level influence the bilateral relations? To tackle these questions, we will analyse the main changes in Turkey's foreign policy between 2008 and 2020, as reflected in its bilateral relations with Romania. We focused on Turkey's main foreign policy instruments in Romania for the last decade. The paper is organized as follows: In the first part, we bridge two sets of scholarly contributions explaining Turkey's shifts in foreign policy and define the main analytical framework for analysing Turkey-Romania relations. Next, we create a timeline of the main regional and domestic events that determined changes in Turkey's foreign policy and highlight the main features of Romania-Turkey relations placed in the overall context of 'De-Europeanisation'. In the last section, the conclusions point towards the same ambivalent tendencies that are observable in Turkey-Romania relations over the last decade and beyond, with Turkey being a relevant economic partner and security ally at the Black Sea, while distancing more and more from the EU and asserting a more active role as a regional player in the Middle East and in the Balkans.

Turkey's shifting regional identity

Scholars agree that Turkey is a difficult case to study as a regional actor, as it is laced at the intersection of very different regions. Thus, in terms of foreign policy analysis, Turkey was most commonly treated as 'an outlier', an exceptional case in international relations theory and Europeanization/De-Europeanization literature. We further aim to illustrate how the two strands of literature complement each other, offering the basis of the analytical framework to understand Turkey's relations with Romania better. Buzan and Wæver (2003) defined the regional role played by Turkey within the Regional Security Complex Theory (RSCT) as an 'insulator state'. This concept establishes a location occupied by one or more units where larger regional security dynamics stand back-to-back. In their view, insulators occupy the borders between regions that are zones of weak interaction. Because Turkey is not capable of clearly presenting itself as a pole in any Regional Security Complex (RSC), Buzan and Wæver (2003) considered that it seemed likely for Turkey to remain an 'insulator state' between the Middle East and European RSCs. The authors also noted that Turkey is not able to bring the different complexes together into one coherent strategic arena (Buzan and Wæver 2003, 41). They showed that Turkey could only become a great power or superpower if it first became a regional power. For this to happen, Turkey must intensify its security relations with the RSCs around its borders. Next, it needs to start playing a regional role while asserting a specific foreign policy identity, which materialized in the case of Turkey's regional behaviour beginning with 2002, when AKP came to power. There is consensus in the literature that Turkey has become much more active on the international stage by endorsing a more aggressive foreign policy posture and a more assertive stance regarding international security issues. Given these transformations, a growing number of authors argued that Turkey's role as an 'insulator state' should be reconsidered.

Scholars argued that even if RSCT may have been accurate in portraying Turkey's regional position by the 2000s, the new political strategies formulated by Ankara have had a considerable regional impact, and this concept does not fit the realities on the ground (Barrinha 2014). Even though in the early 2000s, when Turkey's foreign policy activism and aggressiveness were not very explicit, Diez (2005) was one of the first authors to challenge the 'insulator state' status attributed to Turkey by Buzan and Wæver. He considers that since the Helsinki European Council in 1999, it is much more likely that Turkey can no longer be seen as being outside the European RSC. Diez also pointed out that, unless the EU rejects Turkey's candidacy or Ankara suspends its EU accession process, which started to materialize more visibly by 2020, Turkey would remain a member of the European RSC. Moreover, Kaliber (2009) emphasized that, as an analytical tool, the term 'insulator' is not well equipped to examine Turkey's intense security interactions with its regional neighbours. In his opinion, the term is liable to simplistic and historical generalizations since it implies rigidity and stasis rather than dynamism and perpetual change. Kaliber used RSCT to analyse Turkey's regional security dynamics but rejected the necessity for RSCs to be fixed geographical entities, allowing a more flexible interpretation of Turkey's position on the periphery of Europe (2009). Considering its transformation from an insulator state to an emerging power or a game-changer, Amour (2020) argues that, given its regional activism in recent years, Turkey can be attributed the status of regional power. We believe this observation is worth testing Turkey's foreign policy towards one of its strategic partners at the Black Sea – Romania. Their bilateral relationship needs to be explored in connection to the tense regional context marked by Turkey's inclination to assert its political and military power, which has deteriorated its relations with the EU and NATO.

Moreover, trying to depict the main features of Turkey's new regional identity, scholars also discussed how Turkey used its soft power to consolidate its influence in the Western Balkans, where it acts as an 'ambivalent actor' and that this is part of its 'ethno-nationalist religion-oriented foreign policy' (Öztürk 2021). Other authors claim that Turkey's regional activism and the transition from the status of 'insulator state' to a regional power are meant to determine the international community, especially the West, to recognize and legitimize the regional influence of the Turkish state. Schmidt (2020) mentioned Turkey as one of the regional powers whose goal is to achieve supremacy, emphasizing its religious ties to the neighbouring regions, more visibly the Western Balkans, through Islam. To conclude on this point, the authors agree that these foreign policy changes marked Turkey's regional behaviour and led to the end of its 'insulator status' and to the manifestation of a more robust regional power identity as projected in its relation with the Western Balkans. We believe that there is a need to bridge these observations based on RSCT with the debates on 'De-Europeanisation' in EU studies, as they are complementary in assessing Turkey's main tendencies in its regional policy.

Turkey's ongoing 'De-Europeanisation'

Another strand of literature focused on the same timeframe (connected to AKP's consolidation in power from 2002 to the present) argued that while Turkey decided to be more engaged in its neighbouring regions, it also started to distance itself from the EU integration prospect known as 'De-Europeanisation'. Among the numerous scholarly debates around Turkey's distancing from the West, a particular focus was placed on the country's ambivalent EU membership prospects, which were already long-disputed not only on political and economic, but also on cultural, religious, and societal grounds (Aydın-Düzgit 2012). Since 2005, Turkey's EU membership has remained a distant prospect beyond the numerous ups and downs of the process. In the first part of the last decade, the literature on Europeanization included the case of Turkey together with other candidate countries from the Western Balkans (Aydın-Düzgit 2012; Börzel and Soyaltın 2012). Yet, during recent years, the scholarly focus has shifted to its opposite – the process of 'De-Europeanisation' and Turkey was one of the case studies most often invoked in relation to this new concept.

'De-Europeanisation' is one of the newest concepts in EU studies, pointing towards the reversibility of EU-induced reforms, resistance and contestation over EU norms, values and institutions (Alpan and Ozturk 2022). The concept has been explored in several consistent empirical studies, not only referring to the negative impact on the EU outside its borders (in relation to candidate countries, aspiring to a future membership), but also to EU member states. A recent Special Issue dedicated to this very topic confirms that 'foreign policy in the European Union is being De-Europeanised' (Müller et al. 2021). It is defined as 'a progressive re-nationalisation of foreign policy, whereby member states seek to protect national prerogatives and policy preferences, thus reduce consultation and coordination at the EU level' (Tonra 2018). So, as the EU itself is confronted with 'De-Europeanisation' tendencies, so do some candidate countries, particularly those with the most distant membership perspective. Since 2005, Turkey's EU accession has been an element of discord among EU member states (Kaliber 2013). At the same time, EU accession became an element used in domestic politics in Turkey, particularly by the AKP's Prime Minister, now President Erdogan. Scholars showed that since 1999, when it received the EU candidate country status at the Helsinki Summit, Turkey has been experiencing a controversial path of Europeanization that evolved in distinct stages: from progressing Europeanization (the 2000s) to selective Europeanization (2005–2007) and recently moved towards 'De-Europeanisation' (that started in 2011, and from 2016 to present it accelerated).

Putting together the main contributions on the topic, we observed a specific periodization for Turkey's 'De-Europeanisation' that coincides with the period when it started to affirm a more active regional identity and when it ceased to be an 'insulator'. Over the past decade, the focus of research has been on the limits of the EU's transformative power to bring change in the Balkans and Turkey and connect to a concern with domestic actors in the process of enlargement conditionality (Börzel and Soyaltin 2012). These scholarly debates intensified after 2016 and led to the emergence of a new conceptual framework identified as 'De-Europeanisation', which was illustrated most coherently with the visible deterioration of EU-Turkey relations.

Building on these two strands of literature that tackle Turkey's new regional role and its 'De-Europeanisation' tendencies, we further analyse whether Turkey has projected any components of its new foreign policy identity, which it already projected on the Western Balkans, in Romania – one of its strategic partners, NATO ally and EU member with a clear security agenda in the Black Sea region. As such, we will analyse Romania-Turkey bilateral relations between 2008 and 2020, focusing on two main elements: (1) the dominant features of the Strategic Partnership between the two countries and the way they manifested in bilateral actions that allow us to observe whether they share the same Regional Security Complex; and (2) if and how Turkey's 'De-Europeanisation' together with other domestic factors in both countries in relation with the EU/ NATO had impacted their bilateral relationship.

Methodological note

We aimed to provide a chronological analysis of Romania-Turkey bilateral relations over the last decade, starting shortly before the two countries signed the Strategic Partnership and until 2020. We included in the analysis other relevant domestic factors in both countries and notes on the regional context and the most critical milestones in Turkey's transformation towards 'De-Europeanisation' and its attempts to project a new regional power perspective. The data used are mainly qualitative and include the analysis of official documents and statements of leading foreign policy decision-makers from Bucharest and Ankara (that were accessible online in Romanian and English language) that we have interpreted in the framework of a more affirmative Turkish regional policy. To point out the main events that fostered the contacts between the two states and the extent of the relationship, we investigated all relevant bilateral contacts made public by the Romanian and Turkish Ministries of Foreign Affairs, and we organized them based on frequency (total bilateral contacts per year) as well as their content (Table A3 in Appendices). The main sources used were the 'Press Releases' section of the ministries' official pages, searching keywords as 'Bucharest', 'Romania', (for the Turkish Ministry's website) 'Turkey' 'Ankara' for the Romanian one. We coded the content of each official meeting under the following categories: *business, culture, energy, economic, experience exchange, general (other topics than the categories), security, European matters and the trilateral Ro-Tu-Pol (Romania- Turkey-Poland)*. We analysed all references on bilateral talks and negotiations between the two countries that we ordered chronologically in connection with the periodization identified in the specialized literature. We also included regional events that impacted both the Romania-Turkish bilateral relation and the domestic political scene in the two countries in the context of the EU/ NATO regional dynamics and with regard to another relevant regional player – Russia. Although the total number of meetings between Turkish and Romanian diplomatic representatives has not been constant over the last ten years, this does not necessarily give a complete picture of the state of relations between Bucharest and Ankara. To overcome this limitation, we added a short analysis of the statements made by official representatives from the two countries with the occasion of signing the Strategic Partnership (in 2011) and the occasion of the 10th anniversary of the partnership (in 2021). The findings were organized in three main stages, based on the main features and centred around events that marked the bilateral relationship as follows: (1) 2008–2013; (2) 2014–2016 and (3) 2017–2020.

An overview of Turkey-Romania relations (2008–2020) – the main findings

There are many reasons why Turkey and Romania relations have a 'special' status, particularly when compared to other European countries in Turkey's neighbourhood. First, the two states have long and strong historical relations, sharing the same geographical area at the Black Sea. But the relations were marked in the past by conflict, numerous tensions and power asymmetry, as for many hundreds of years, some of the Romanian historical provinces (Moldova, Wallachia, Dobrudja) were controlled by the Ottoman Empire. Soon after Romania's independence in 1878, relations with the Ottoman Empire started to improve. In 1933, Romania and Turkey signed the Treaty of Friendship, Non-aggression, Arbitration and Conciliation. One year later, the two countries were among the signatories of the Balkan Entente. While during the Cold War period, the bilateral relationship was marked by platitude, with positive developments beginning only by the early 2000s. Second, in the terms of the Copenhagen School criteria, Romania and Turkey are part of the same European RSC, and they share security interests, which constitutes a significant driver for enhanced cooperation that already materialized in the Strategic Partnership the two countries signed in 2011. Beyond the bilateral aspects, the two countries interacts at the multilateral level. Turkey supported Romania's accession to the EU and NATO, while Romania supported Turkey's aspirations of EU membership. This is also illustrated in common memberships of Turkey and Romania in the main regional cooperation organizations, which have also stimulated their cooperation (Table A1 in Appendices).

Over the last decade, Turkey and the Balkans have reached their peak of mutually beneficial relations, economic enlargement, and 'pro-active' utilization of the transnational state apparatus on the part of Turkey (Öztürk 2021, 102). The overall findings point towards an ambivalent relationship between Turkey and Romania over the last decade, partially confirming the tendencies observed in the case of Turkey's activism in the Balkans. The data confirm that Turkey used its new foreign policy practices in relation to Romania only to a lesser extent. Moreover, our findings show that despite the intensified economic and cultural relations connected to Romania's small but active Turkish minority and beyond, the two countries have numerous contrasting views on the geopolitics of the Black Sea basin, which remained a source of tension over the last decade. We have identified a visible intensification of relations between Romania and Turkey starting with 2012 (following the signing of the Strategic Partnership in 2011) that continued until 2014 (See Table A3 in Appendices). Next, we observe a certain decrease in contacts to less than half than in the first two years. A similar pattern could also be observed between 2018 and 2020. During the period analysed in our study, the frequency of meetings where European matters were discussed remained constant. Despite the accentuated 'De-Europeanisation' at the domestic level, it is interesting to note that EU-related issues were not absent from Turkey's bilateral relationship with Romania.

One general feature that we observed was that over the last decade, Romania supported Turkey's accession to the EU, and it often refrained from criticizing Ankara's aggressive and ambitious foreign policy stance. Nevertheless, there were several regional incidents where Romania clearly positioned itself in opposition with Turkey, such as the 2008 Russo-Georgian war; the annexation of Crimea; the creation of the Black Sea Flotilla; the activities carried out in Romania by the Gülenist 'Lumina Educational Institutions' and during Ankara's assertive posturing in the Eastern Mediterranean.

Another feature that we identified is that the security and economic topics were predominant in the official meetings, and this is also supported by statistical data that confirm the constant rise in trade relations between Romania and Turkey over the last decade. This proves that the economic and security aspects are the main pillars of the bilateral relationship, which contrasts with Turkey's primary policy instruments in the Western Balkans that include cultural and religious elements together with the economic and security ones.

Another identified feature is Turkey's shifting foreign policy focus and its anti-Western tendencies, most visible after 2016. Ever since, Turkey maintained an ambivalent position towards the EU and as a NATO ally, and this was only partially visible in its bilateral relations with Romania. Let us analyse in detail all these features.

2008–2013 – the climax of cooperation

Between 2008 and 2013, the Romanian-Turkish bilateral relations have improved significantly in several fields such as political, economic, environmental and societal, culminating in the signing of the Strategic Partnership in 2011 – the highlight event of this period. However, three years prior, the two states had contrasting reactions to NATO's actions in the Russia-Georgia war of 2008, which, nevertheless, has not directly affected the bilateral relations between Turkey and Romania. The Russo-Georgian War posed an immediate challenge to Ankara's regional interests and placed its leaders in a difficult diplomatic position. This was the first moment when Turkey showed signs of shifting its focus away from its role as a NATO member towards that of regional power and positioned itself as a pragmatic international player, acting first and foremost based on its national interest (Torbakov 2008). This also coincides with what Tonra defined as 'the re-nationalisation' of foreign policy (2018) that became a feature visible in other states' behaviour, too, not just Turkey.

Despite the differences during the Russo-Georgian war of 2008, the relationship between Bucharest and Ankara recorded positive developments, especially in the political field. In 2008, in the context of the official visit paid in Bucharest by Köksal Toptan, then-Speaker of the Turkish Grand National Assembly, Romanian officials expressed their readiness to provide technical support for Turkey's accession to the EU. The two sides also tackled economic and environmental matters, with the focus on intensification of trade and cooperation between Romanian and Turkish businessmen and advancing initiatives designed to foster Romanian-Turkish companies' access to Caucasus and North Africa markets. The Turkish officials expressed their readiness in supporting Romania's role in the Southern Gas Corridor developments, in reducing pollution in the Black Sea and in building a highway around the Black Sea (Damian and Dinu 2017, 2).

Starting with 2009, Romania and Turkey's cooperation also intensified in the cultural field. In October 2009, Babeş-Bolyai University of Cluj Napoca inaugurated the Institute of Turkish and Central Asian Studies. Two years later, the Turkish 'Yunus Emre' Foundation inaugurated two cultural centres in Bucharest and Constanţa, with the scope of intensifying the mutual cultural cooperation and promoting Turkish values and history in Romania.

The climax of cooperation between Romania and Turkey was reached in December 2011, when the two countries' constant efforts and commitment to enhance their mutual relations determined them to upgrade the profile of their relationship and sign a Strategic Partnership. The declaration of the agreement was signed in Ankara by the then presidents of Romania (Traian Băsescu) and Turkey (Abdullah Gül). The document emphasized the special nature of Romanian-Turkish relations and created a framework for the further enhancement of cooperation in politics, economy, security, culture and education. During the negotiations, Traian Băsescu reaffirmed Romania's support of Turkey's EU accession process and praised the evolution between the two countries in the trade sector, stressing that in the first nine months of 2011, bilateral economic exchanges volumes exceeded 3.5 billion US dollars (Romanian MFA 2011–2020). On his part, Abdullah Gul underscored that the relations between Romania and Turkey are excellent, especially from the economic viewpoint, mentioning that the two countries aim to reach a trading volume worth 10 billion US dollars annually (Dąborowski 2011). Even though the Strategic Partnership tackled primarily economic and strategic matters, the two countries' officials also discussed building a mosque in Bucharest and an Orthodox church in Istanbul on a reciprocity basis. In the context of the signing of the main Romanian-Turkish strategic partnership, particular emphasis was placed on intensifying the cooperation in several fields of activity, with an emphasis on strengthening economic cooperation. Romania's President gave assurances of Romania's support for Turkey's accession to the EU and repeatedly stressed that the Turkish state and its representatives are and will remain Romania's friends. For his part, the Turkish President stressed the importance of strengthening economic cooperation between Romania and Turkey and thanked Romania for its support in Turkey's EU accession process (Romanian MFA 2011–2020). These were the guiding principles of the bilateral relationship, as expressed by the main political representatives of the two countries. It is important to underline that this partnership with Romania occurred right at a time when Turkey's role as a regional power was increasing, and the AKP's political leadership was aspiring to transform Turkey into a regional power and later into a global power (Gürzel 2014).

Although 2011 has a special significance for the relationship between Romania and Turkey, this year also marked a new stage in the relationship between Turkey and its Euro-Atlantic partners. Analysts identified the year 2011 as a critical milestone for understanding Turkey's rift with the West because 2011 witnessed not only a new round of electoral victories of AKP but also the beginning of the 'Arab Spring'. In this context, 2011 marked at the same time 'the downturn in EU-Turkey relations with the growing disenchantment by both sides' (Aydın-Düzgit and Kaliber 2016) and 'the populist transformation in Turkey's foreign policy' (Kaliber and Kaliber 2019). Scholars stressed that starting with this period, 'Turkish foreign policy has undergone a more radical recalibration characterised mainly by the re-inscription of the West as the "other" of Turkey' (Kaliber and Kaliber 2019, 2). Signs of De-Europeanization are then also continued within the Government's violent reaction towards the Gezi Park protests of 2013 (Kaliber 2014).

2014–2016 – diverging security policy views and Turkey's soft power actions in Romania

Most visibly, after the mass protests in Gezi Park of Istanbul, De-Europeanizing dynamics in Turkish foreign policy discourse have been systematically replaced by a vehement anti-Westernism visible in public speeches, statements, press releases and declarations of AKP members (Kaliber and Kaliber 2019, 2; Yilmaz 2016). Numerous authors showed that already with AKP's new elections in 2011 and mostly after the 2016 'coup d'état attempt' the EU was losing its transformative influence on Turkey (Alpan and Diez 2014; Yilmaz 2016; Cebeci 2016; Aydın-Düzgit and Kaliber 2016), with the two sides directly confronted one another. Scholars argued that 'the first decade of AKP rule, when foreign policy was thinly populist, was characterised by steady De-Europeanisation, increasing engagement with regional issues and a decentring of Turkey's Western orientation' (Kaliber and Kaliber 2019). In this context, we can see that between 2014 and 2016, Turkey's distancing from Euro-Atlantic values was also visible in the relationship between Ankara and Bucharest. This period was marked primarily by increasingly contrasting positions of Bucharest and Ankara regarding the Russian Federation`s hostile actions in the Black Sea region. After the contested annexation of Crimea by the Russian Federation in March 2014, the two states did not reach a consensus regarding the increase of NATO's profile in the Black Sea. Even though the negotiations between the two countries took place in multilateral formats, the state-to-state level also played a substantial role, especially in the context created by the 'coup d'état attempt' in Turkey taking place in 2016 and by the bilateral religious matters. However, the Romanian and Turkish officials' reactions to the Russian intervention differed greatly. Romania considered the Russian Federation's intervention in Eastern Ukraine an act of aggression and supported the US proposal to create the Black Sea Flotilla. On the other side, Turkey's policy-makers avoided declaring the Russian Federation an aggressor state. Moreover, Ankara refused to introduce sanctions against the Russian Federation as the EU and the US did. In fact, there has been enthusiasm on the Turkish side about the potential to increase exports to the Russian Federation due to Moscow`s decision to embargo food products from European countries. In this context, the then Turkish Economy Minister, Nihat Zeybekci, described the economic cooperation with the Russian Federation 'as an opportunity for Turkey to bolster its exports not only of food, but also consumer goods', and mentioned that 'Ankara should make this opportunity a strong, long-term, permanent and corporate one' (Devranoglu and Caglayan 2014).

Moreover, Turkey's foreign policy strategy on the Black Sea security architecture and its relationship with NATO have diverged from Romania's. For instance, Turkey opposed allied efforts to deter Russian actions in Ukraine and to strengthen the security of NATO's Eastern Flank. Following the failed coup attempt on 15 July 2016, Turkish foreign policy has marked the beginning of a new phase, as Ankara has adopted a more transactional, unplanned, ad hoc, opportunistic type of foreign policy, based on expediency. According to Dalacoura (2017), the foreign policy decisions taken by the

Turkish state following the failed coup attempt resulted in strained relations with the EU and NATO and intensified cooperation with the Russian Federation. The rapprochement between Turkey and the Russian Federation made the creation of the Black Sea Flotilla difficult, mainly due to the fact that Turkey has categorically opposed the US initiative.

The period 2014–2016 was marked by contradictions regarding regional dossiers and a number of issues concerning the bilateral relationship. Turkey-Romania relations were also tested in the context of the increasing assertiveness of the AKP Government that followed the so-called 'coup d'état attempt' in July 2016. To punish the alleged organizers of the coup, the Erdoğan regime decided to block the activities carried out by Fethullah Gulen supporters and affiliated organizations. Thus, Ankara requested support from its allies and partners, including Romania, who decided not to follow Ankara's requests. For instance, Bucharest has not obliged the Lumina Educational Institutions affiliated with the network allegedly controlled by the Fethullah Gulen to cease their activities in the country. This decision has not affected the activities of the educational institution and created a favourable context to extend its operations in Romania. For instance, during 2016–2020, the number of educational institutions affiliated to Lumina Educational Institutions increased in Romania from 11 to 14 (Siclitaru 2016).

Another issue that created friction between Romania and Turkey was the construction of the Great Mosque in Bucharest. Ankara made constant efforts to determine the Romanian political establishment to authorize the construction of the largest Turkish mosque in South-Eastern Europe, with a capacity of over 2000 people (Chiriac 2015). However, the Turkish side decided to cancel the project due to the constant opposition manifested by various Romanian civil society actors and intense protests. Seen in the light of Turkey's soft power instruments in the Balkans, Ankara's decision to build the Great Mosque in Bucharest was another attempt to expand its influence in the region. For the same purpose, in February 2015, the Tgovernmenternment opened a new office of the Turkish Cooperation and Coordination Agency (Türk İşbirliği ve Koordinasyon İdaresi Başkanlığı – TIKA) in Bucharest. Since then, it has been engaged in more than 120 projects in various fields such as health, humanitarian, culture, education, sports, mass media etc. (Biçer 2019).

It should be noted that Turkey uses TIKA's activities as an important foreign policy instrument, and it is especially active in countries with a sizable Turkish-Tatar community. From this point of view, TIKA's actions are relevant because there are about 50,000 Turks and Tatars living in Romania (Romania National Institute of Statistics 2011). Despite TIKA's work being public, and some of the projects being carried out in partnership with the host countries, the links of some of TIKA officials with the Turkish National Intelligence Agency raises questions about its real intentions. For example, Rahman Nurdun, former head of TİKA, currently serves as Undersecretary of the National Intelligence Agency of Turkey – MİT (Öztürk 2021). Considering these aspects, the role played over time by TİKA in the overall economy of the Romania-Turkey bilateral relationship is particularly important. The projects developed by the organization with the Turkish-Tatar minority are the primary soft power tool in Romania, if not the most important one. Although Turkey has successfully used soft power tools such as religion, culture, education etc. in most Balkan countries (Öztürk 2021), we argue that its successes in Romania have been less significant, being limited to the economic and cultural sector. Moreover, as we have seen in the case of the Great Mosque project in Bucharest, Ankara officials have taken a step back in order not to jeopardize the bilateral relationship with Romania, which did not happen in the case of a similar project in the centre of Prishtina (Kosovo), despite street protests (Bami 2020).

2017–2020 and beyond – ambivalent approaches and increased signs of 'De-Europeanisation'

The rule of law backsliding in CEE countries (Poland, Hungary and to a lesser extent Romania) that reached its peak between 2017 and 2018 has raised questions on the EU's ability to tackle instances of democratic backsliding effectively not only in legal terms but also from a political point of view, which affected its credibility in foreign and security policy. Romania was one of these 'Eastern Europe discontents', directly criticizing the European Commission. At the same time, it was witnessing political instability, massive anti-government street protests and a conflict between the President and the Prime Minister, who were diverging even on foreign policy topics. In the end, Romania reversed its controversial decisions in the field of judiciary already by the summer of 2019, coming back to terms in relation with the EU. Still, Hungary and Poland continued to preserve a callous line against the EU. These tendencies match the prospect of a 're-nationalisation' and 'De-Europeanisation' tendencies occurring even among EU member states. This should also be included in the bigger picture of the regional and EU context of the bilateral relations.

It is relevant to point out that, much like Turkey, Romania too were experiencing tensions with the EU in this period. Since its EU accession in 2007, Romania has consistently sided with the 'Euro-enthusiasts' (Troncotă and Loy 2018). But already, when it celebrated its first decade in the EU at the beginning of 2017, Romania started to experience increasing domestic political turmoil, which gave rise to the contestation of EU legitimacy in the field of anti-corruption. Following the general elections of December 2016 that marked the victory of the Social Democratic Party (PSD), Romania was marked by successive governmental crises and further political turmoil when it amended the justice laws adopted upon Romania's EU accession in 2007. Faced with a series of controversial decisions of the PSD Government in the field of the rule of law, citizens and opposition parties reacted in massive street protests and unprecedented civic mobilisation since the 1989 Revolution. These actions had antagonized relations between Romania's government and the EU Commission in a period when all eyes were on Romania, as it was preparing and then took over for the first time the Presidency of the Council of the EU (between January-July 2019).

We observed in the analysed data that beyond these problems that affected EU-Romania relations, after 2017, the Romanian-Turkish bilateral relations experienced a revival, especially in the economic field, with the leaders of the two states' emphasis. However, situations such as Ankara's aggressive posturing in the Eastern Mediterranean, the acquisition of the Russian missile defence systems, and the offensive against organizations linked to Fethullah Gulen led to tensions between Bucharest and Ankara. All these events occurred after the AKP had seized yet another electoral victory with its coalition partner in July 2018, leading to a period marked by intense 'De-Europeanisation' in terms of EU-Turkey relations. Between 2017 and 2020, Ankara continued its offensive against Lumina Educational Institutions and requested the Romanian authorities to extradite several persons affiliated with the aforementioned institution, among them Fatih Gursoy, the president of the institution (Mososianu 2018). Romania not only refused to accept the request of the Turkish side but also decided to grant political asylum to some Turkish citizens affiliated with Lumina Educational Institutions. However, the situation has not escalated tensions between the two countries, with both sides aiming to limit the damage.

In 2019, during the Romanian Presidency of the Council of the European Union, Bucharest reiterated the constant support for Turkey's European path (Romanian MFA 2020). Support for the EU's enlargement to the Western Balkans and Turkey's relations with the EU were among the priorities of the Romanian EU Presidency. In this context, Bucharest made efforts to give a pragmatic and constructive dynamic to EU-Turkey relations. In order to foster cooperation in the region together with Turkey, the Romanian officials organized a working lunch during which they brought together officials from the Western Balkans and Turkey (Sevinç 2019). The main achievement of the Romanian officials during the rotating presidency was to facilitate and strengthen the Turkey-EU dialogue in a pragmatic manner. These efforts allowed the EU-Turkey Association Council to take place in 2019 after a four-year break.

Despite the positive developments, in the context of Turkey's assertive stance in the Eastern Mediterranean from 2020, Romania expressed solidarity with Greece and Cyprus and its support for ongoing EU-level efforts to de-escalate the tensions. Moreover, the Romanian officials reiterated the need to maintain a comprehensive EU-Turkey dialogue, given the wide range of issues of common interest, such as migration, trade and the fight against terrorism. Turkey's aggressive stance against Greece and Cyprus and the threat of opening the borders with the EU for the Syrian refugees strained the relationship between Brussels and Ankara. Furthermore, during the Summit in December 2020, the EU officials agreed to impose new sanctions on an unspecified number of Turkish officials and entities involved in gas drilling in Cypriot-claimed waters (Wintour 2020), marking a peak in the deterioration of relations between EU and Turkey.

In April 2021, on the 10th anniversary of the signing of the strategic partnership, the Romanian and Turkish authorities organized a conference in Bucharest to celebrate the signing of the agreement, during which the Turkish Foreign Minister, Mevlut Cavusoglu, has had meetings in Bucharest with Romanian diplomats and with Romanian President Klaus Werner Iohannis. The conclusions reached by the Romanian and Turkish officials during the discussions highlight that in the last ten years there has been an intensification of Romanian-Turkish cooperation, especially in the economic and military fields. Regarding the economic area, during the meetings, the officials of the two sides committed to increasing trade exchanges up to 10 billion US dollars.

It is interesting to note that Turkey has manifested a particular interest in becoming one of the leading foreign investors in Romania and aimed to increase the number of Turkish companies operating on the Romanian market, which currently stands at 16,200 (Huza 2021). To mark the importance given by the Turkish government to the investment sector in Romania, Turkish Foreign Minister Mevlut Cavusoglu pointed out that Romania is Turkey's largest trading partner in the Balkans. He also added Turkey is among the top foreign investors in Romania (Bayar 2021).(Figure 1)

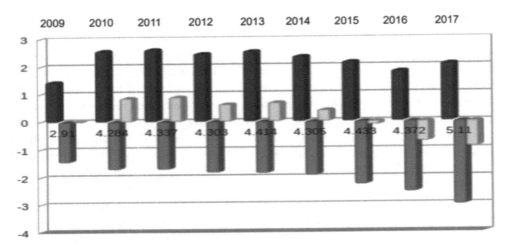

Figure 1. Romania-Turkey trade balance 2009–2017 (billion euros). Source: http://www.imm.gov.ro/adaugare_fisiere_imm/2018/11/TURCIA_Indrumar-de-afaceri-sept.2018-1.pdf

In the last ten years of bilateral relations, cooperation has not only been limited to the bilateral framework but has also extended to the multilateral one. Turkey supported Romania's candidacy for the Secretary-General of the BSEC. Moreover, during the joint conference in Bucharest in April 2021, the Foreign Minister of Turkey stated that Turkey would support the activities of the new Secretary-General of the BSEC, Lazăr Comănescu, former Romanian Minister of Foreign Affairs (Romanian MFA 2021).

As far as security cooperation between Romania and Turkey is concerned, developments in recent years show that Bucharest and Ankara are aware of the importance of mutual support in this field. Existing or potential crises in the Balkans and the Black Sea region constitute some of the most critical security threats for Romania and Turkey, which is why coordination between the two countries is vital. Turkish Foreign Minister Mevlut Cavusoglu reaffirmed this during his visit to Bucharest in April 2021, when he stated that 'Turkey and Romania share a common understanding of regional security' and that 'Romania and Turkey are the main providers of peace in south-eastern Europe and the Black Sea region' (Bayar 2021). Romanian and Turkish officials also committed to strengthening their coordination within the NATO framework and discussed the prospect of intensifying Romanian-Turkish cooperation in the military field. It is worth noting that in the last ten years, Romania and Turkey have attached great importance to the collaboration in the field of defence and security, with discussions and strategies in these areas being conducted mainly in the trilateral Romania-Turkey-Poland format. According to Mevlut Cavusoglu, the trilateral consultation mechanism between Poland, Romania, and Turkey has become a solid platform to discuss various aspects of Trans-Atlantic security. Romania's President called for the continuation and diversification of multidimensional political consultations within the framework of the Romania-Poland-Turkey security trilateral. Discussions focused on the main ways of cooperation in this format, with emphasis on the security situation in the Eastern Neighbourhood of the North-Atlantic Alliance, the advancement of the regional security agenda and preparations for the NATO Summit in 2021 (Lupitu 2021).

Even though the number of meetings between Romanian and Turkish officials has followed a downward trend in the last ten years, the bilateral relationship has intensified, especially in the economic field. Also, as far as the strategic dimension is concerned, the two countries have expressed their openness to strengthen cooperation to manage regional issues jointly. The importance given to the bilateral relationship by both sides is one of the reasons why in recent years, none of the opposing views managed to endanger the close ties between Romania and Turkey.

Conclusions

Since 2011, Turkey's foreign policy shifted towards more regional activism in the Balkans and an accentuated 'De-Europeanisation' and anti-Western stances. In terms of the RSCT, this shift implied the end of the 'insulator' status, and the often-close relation between religion and culture was exploited by the Turkish government in relation to its Balkan neighbours in order to achieve foreign policy goals and it was designed to improve both the country's national status and its outside perception as a strong regional power. In this context, the article scrutinized Romania-Turkey's last decade bilateral relations in the regional context of Turkey's relations with its Balkan neighbours and its new regional identity marked by 'De-Europeanization'. We argue that despite different foreign policy strategies, especially with regard to the EU and NATO, cooperation between Turkey and Romania in both multilateral and bilateral formats has a unique character. The findings show that Turkey used only to a lesser extent its new foreign policy practices in relation with Romania, and the 'De-Europeanisation' approach can explain only a part of this complex regional picture. Following the main milestones identified in the literature, we proposed a 3-stages periodization in Romania-Turkey relations, each marked by domestic and regional changing dynamics.

Looking closely at the frequency and content of bilateral diplomatic contacts between the two countries, our analysis confirms that Turkey's foreign policy became more assertive after the 15 July 2016 coup attempt. This was visible particularly in the context of its search for autonomous action in its neighbourhood, where Turkey affirmed the ability to conduct cross border and overseas military operations without the support of its traditional Western allies. We also observed that, considering Turkey's influence in the Black Sea Region and the fact that there are no problematic issues on the agenda of the Romanian-Turkish bilateral relations, Bucharest was cautious in formulating any open criticism against the Turkish officials' actions that could lead to a destabilization of the Euro-Atlantic relationship. However, policies including Turkey's decision to block certain NATO initiatives, the intensification of cooperation with the Russian Federation, the increase of Turkish activism in the Black Sea and the Balkans, together with the acceleration of 'De-Europeanisation' remained important obstacles between the two countries cooperation at the security level. Economic relations, however, Romania and Turkey had been unprecedentedly positive. In terms of soft power, the analysis showed that Turkey attempted to use foreign policy tools with religious overtones, similar to the ones it has utilized in Western Balkans, in Romania (most visibly during the 2015 incident with building a Mosque in central Bucharest), but such initiatives was in time abandoned. Romania also has a Turkish minority, but its small size and the strong influence of the Orthodox Church did not allow Turkey to instrumentalize it as it happened in the case of Bulgaria or in other Western Balkans countries.

Overall, we have seen that between 2008 and 2020 the bilateral ties intensified and the acceleration of 'De-Europeanisation' in Turkey did not visibly impact the relationship with Romania. However, the strained relations between Ankara and its Euro-Atlantic partners, concomitant with the rapprochement with the Russian Federation, had a negative impact on Romania's strategic interests in the Black Sea, but this was not visible in the bilateral contacts. During 2017–2020, the AKP government's pressure on Gulenist organizations overseas intensified and led to new challenges in the relations between Ankara and Bucharest. Though, during its mandate at the Presidency of the EU Council, Bucharest made efforts to give a pragmatic and constructive dynamic to EU-Turkey relations, in the face of Turkey's aggressive stance in the Eastern Mediterranean in 2020, Romania expressed its solidarity with Greece and Cyprus and its support for ongoing efforts at EU level to de-escalate tensions, showing a clear rift in their strategic perspectives. By 2020 the bilateral contacts were reduced to a minimum, due to not only the COVID-19 pandemic, but also to the increasing tensions between Turkey and the Transatlantic partners and its accentuated 'De-Europeanisation'. This changed in 2021, when the two countries marked the anniversary of their strategic partnership and at the diplomatic level the contacts were re-energized.

In conclusion, while there are consistent contributions highlighting Turkey's foreign policy in the Western Balkans, over the last 15 years Romania-Turkey relations were under-researched, which is the primary contribution of this analysis. We showed that given the special status of their bilateral relations, mainly based on economic and security cooperation, Ankbara's activism in Romania has been much more moderate compared to the one in the Western Balkans. However, the rift between the EU and Turkey has begun to change the way Romanian officials look at Turkey's foreign policy, even if the reactions were limited to the discursive level and had a rather conciliatory tone. In line with Turkey's overall re-energized activism in the Balkans that includes the use of soft power, the bilateral relationship with Romania has maintained an ambivalent character moving from more intensified contacts or, by contrast, to opposing positions on certain topics – such as the AKP government's actions against the organizations allegedly coordinated by Fethullah Gulen, which Romania condemned by refusing to follow Ankara's requests to block the activities of the aforementioned Gulenist entities. To complement our findings, future research needs to explore in greater detail the perceptions and discourses that have shaped Romania-Turkey relations and their future evolution.

Acknowledgments

The first draft of this article was presented in the expert workshop "Turkey and the Balkans: Perspectives on the processes of Europeanisation and De-Europeanisation" organised by London Metropolitan University on 18th of December 2020 (online). The authors would like to thank the workshop participants and to the Journal's anonymous reviewers for their helpful comments, but also to Ahmet Ozturk and Basak Alpan for their overall guidance and patience while working on this article. For this research, Miruna Butnaru Troncotă benefited from funding offered by the project "Linking the Europe at Periphery (LEAP) number-612019-EPP-1-2019-1-TR-EPPJMO-NETWORK".

Disclosure statement

No potential conflict of interest was reported by the author(s).

References

Alpan, B. 2014. Europe-as-hegemony and discourses in Turkey after 1999: What has Europeanization got to do with it? *Journal of Balkan and near Eastern Studies* 16, no. 1: 2014. doi:10.1080/19448953.2013.864184.

Alpan, B., and A.E. Ozturk. 2022. Turkey and the Balkans: Bringing the Europeanisation/De-Europeanisation nexus into question. *Southeast European and Black Sea Studies* 22, no. 1: 26–32.

Alpan, B., and T. Diez. 2014. The devil is in the 'domestic'? European integration studies and the limits of Europeanization in Turkey. *Journal of Balkan and near Eastern Studies* 16, no. 1: 1–10. January 2. doi:10.1080/19448953.2013.864180.

Amour, P.O. 2020. *The regional order in the gulf Region and the Middle East: Regional rivalries and security alliances.* Cham: Springer International Publishing.

Aydın-Düzgit, S. 2012. *Constructions of European identity: Debates and discourses on Turkey and the EU.* Houndmills, Basingstoke, Hampshire, UK, and New York, NY: Palgrave Macmillan.

Aydın-Düzgit, S., and A. Kaliber. 2016. Encounters with Europe in an era of domestic and international turmoil: Is Turkey a De-Europeanising candidate country? *South European Society and Politics* 21: 1. doi:10.1080/13608746.2016.1155282.

Bahgat, F., 2021. EU-Turkey relations at 'historic' low point: European Parliament. Deutsche Welle, May 19. https://www.dw.com/en/eu-turkey-relations-at-historic-low-point-european-parliament/a-57589752 (accessed October 31, 2021).

Bami, X., 2020. Turkish-financed mosque sparks rival protests in Kosovo. *Balkan Insight*, July 22, https://balkaninsight.com/2020/07/22/turkish-financed-mosque-sparks-rival-protests-in-kosovo/ (accessedOctober 30, 2021).

Barrinha, A. 2014. The ambitious insulator: Revisiting Turkey's position in regional security complex theory. *Mediterranean Politics* 19, no. 2: 165–82. doi:10.1080/13629395.2013.799353.

Bayar, G., 2021. Turkey hails strategic partnership with Romania. *Anadolu Agency*, April 22. https://www.aa.com.tr/en/europe/turkey-hails-strategic-partnership-with-romania/2217180# (accessed October 30, 2021).

Biçer, Y., 2019. Turkish Cooperation and Coordination Agency (TİKA), Bucharest program coordination office. *Nineoclock*, October 29. https://www.nineoclock.ro/2019/10/29/turkish-cooperation-and-coordination-agency-tika-bucharest-program-coordination-office-3 (accessed January 08, 2021).

Börzel, T.A., and D. Soyaltin 2012. Europeanization in Turkey: Stretching a concept to its limits? (KFG Working Paper Series, 36). Berlin: Freie Universität Berlin, FB Politik- und Sozialwissenschaften, Otto-Suhr-Institut für Politikwissenschaft Kolleg-Forschergruppe "The Transformative Power of Europe". https://nbn-resolving.org/urn:nbn:de:0168-ssoar-371731 (accessed February 15, 2021).

Buzan, B., and O. Wæver. 2003. *Regions and powers: The structure of international security*. Cambridge: Cambridge University Press.

Cebeci, M. 2016. De-Europeanisation or counter-conduct? Turkey's Democratisation and the EU. *South European Society and Politics* 21, no. 1: 119–32. doi:10.1080/13608746.2016.1153996.

Chiriac, M. 2015. Turkey aids financing of Bucharest's first mosque. *Balkan Insight*, June 30, https://balkaninsight.com/2015/06/30/bucharest-to-have-its-first-genuine-mosque/. (accessed November 09, 2021).

Dąborowski, T., 2011. Romania is intensifying relations with Turkey. *Centre for Eastern Studies*, December, https://www.osw.waw.pl/en/publikacje/analyses/2011-12-21/romania-intensifying-relations-turkey (accessed January 03, 2021).

Dalacoura, K., 2017). A new phase in Turkish foreign policy: Expediency and AKP survival. Istituto Affari Internazionali, Future Notes 4, February, Roma, Italy: MENERA papers. https://www.iai.it/en/pubblicazioni/new-phase-turkish-foreign-policy-expediency-and-akp-survival (accessed September 03, 2021).

Damian, A., and R. Dinu 2017. FEUTURE EU 28 country report, Romania. *Center for European Policies*, March. https://feuture.uni-koeln.de/en/eu-28-country-reports/romania (accessedSeptember 01, 2021).

Devranoglu, N., and C. Caglayan 2014. Turkish exporters see profit from Russian ban on Western foods. *Reuters*, August, https://www.reuters.com/article/ukraine-crisis-sanctions-turkey-idCNL6N0QI2QU20140812 (accessed January 07, 2021).

Diez, T. 2005. Turkey, the European Union and security complexes revisited. *Mediterranean Politics* 10, no. 2: 167–80. doi:10.1080/13629390500141600.

Dursun-Özkanca, O. (2019). Turkey–West Relations: The Politics of Intra-alliance Opposition. Cambridge: Cambridge University Press. doi:10.1017/9781316998960

Gürzel, A. 2014. Turkey's role as a regional and global player and its power capacity: Turkey engagement with other emerging states. *Revista de Sociologia E Politica* 22, no. 50: 95–105. doi:10.1590/1678-987314225007.

Huza, A., 2021. Minister Aurescu: Turkey continues to remain a key-partner of Romania. *Stiri pe Surse*, April 22, https://www.stiripesurse.ro/minister-aurescu-turkey-continues-to-remain-a-key-partner-of-romania_1753278.html (accessed November 05, 2021).

Kaliber, A. 2009. Re-imagining cyprus: The rise of regionalism in Turkey's security Lexicon. In *Cyprus: A conflict at the crossroads*, ed. T. Diez and N. Tocci, 111–22. Manchester: Manchester University Press.

Kaliber, A. 2013. Contextual and contested: Reassessing Europeanization in the case of Turkey. *International Relations* 27, no. 1: 52–73. doi:10.1177/0047117812455352.

Kaliber, A. 2014. Europeanization in Turkey: In search of a new paradigm of modernization. *Journal of Balkan and near Eastern Studies* 16, no. 1: 30–46. doi:10.1080/19448953.2013.864182.

Kaliber, A., and E. Kaliber. 2019. From De-Europeanisation to Anti-Western populism: Turkish foreign policy in Flux. *The International Spectator* 54, no. 4: 1–16. doi:10.1080/03932729.2019.1668640.

Lupitu, R., 2021. Klaus Iohannis, la întâlnirea cu miniştrii de externe polonez şi turc: România, Polonia şi Turcia, îngrijorate de "desfăşurarea neobişnuită de forţe militare în Crimeea ilegal ocupată şi la frontiera de est a Ucrainei". *Calea Europeana*, April 22. https://www.caleaeuro

peana.ro/klaus-iohannis-la-intalnirea-cu-ministrii-de-externe-polonez-si-turc-romania-polonia-si-turcia-ingrijorate-de-desfasurarea-neobisnuita-de-forte-militare-in-crimeea-ilegal-ocupata-si-la-frontiera/ (accessed October 31, 2021).

Mososianu, A., 2018. România respinge extrădarea și acordă azil persoanelor acuzate de Turcia de apartenență la gruparea clericului Gülen, declarată teroristă de regimul Erdogan. *Profit*, December 06. https://www.profit.ro/stiri/politic/documente-precedente-romania-respinge-extradarea-si-acorda-azil-persoanelor-acuzate-de-turcia-de-apartenenta-la-gruparea-clericului-g-len-declarata-terorista-de-regimul-erdogan-18689361 (accessed May 08, 2021).

Müller, P., K. Pomorska, and B. Tonra. 2021. The domestic challenge to EU foreign policy-making: From Europeanisation to de-Europeanisation? *Journal of European Integration* 43, no. 5: 519–34. doi:10.1080/07036337.2021.1927015.

Öztürk, A.E. 2021. *Religion, identity and power: Turkey and the Balkans in the twenty-first century.* Edinburgh: Edinburgh University Press.

Romanian Ministry of Foreign Affairs. 2011–2020. Press releases. https://www.mae.ro/en/taxonomy/term/952 (accessed May 12, 2021).

Romanian Ministry of Foreign Affairs. 2020. Cea de-a doua zi a participării ministrului Bogdan Aurescu la reuniunea informală a miniștrilor de externe din statele membre ale UE de la Berlin. https://www.mae.ro/node/53454 (accessed November 03, 2021).

Romanian Ministry of Foreign Affairs. 2021. Participarea ministrului afacerilor externe Bogdan Aurescu și a ministrului afacerilor externe din Republica Turcia, Mevlüt Çavuşoğlu, la evenimentul de marcare a unui deceniu de Parteneriat Strategic România-Turcia. https://www.mae.ro/node/55460 (accessed November 03, 2021).

Romanian National Institute of Statistics. 2011. Population and housing census 2011. http://www.recensamantromania.ro/noutati/volumul-ii-populatia-stabila-rezidenta-structura-etnica-si-confesionala/ (accessed October 30, 2021).

Schmidt, S. 2020. The middle east regional security complex and the Syrian civil war. In *The war for Syria: Regional and international dimensions of the Syrian uprising*, eds. R.A. Hinnebusch and A. Saouli, 17–36. New York, USA: Routledge.

Sevinç, Ö., 2019. Romanian envoy: Enhancing Turkey-EU ties priority during Romania's term presidency. *Daily Sabah*, February 15, https://www.dailysabah.com/eu-affairs/2019/02/15/romanian-envoy-enhancing-turkey-eu-ties-priority-during-romanias-term-presidency (accessed November 05, 2021).

Siclitaru, L. 2016. Consulul Ali Bozçalışkan - "Statul turc a solicitat închiderea instituțiilor și a fundațiilor Gülen!" *Ziuaconstanta*, July 19. https://www.ziuaconstanta.ro/stiri/deschidere-editie/scolile-lumina-in-pericol-consulul-ali-boz-al-skan-statul-turc-a-solicitat-inchiderea-institutiilor-si-a-fundatiilor-g-len-600665.html (accessed November 05, 2021).

Tonra, B. 2018. Legitimacy and EU security and defence policy: The chimera of a simulacrum (part of the collection "Understanding legitimacy in EU foreign policy"). *Global Affairs* 4: 2–3, 265–275. doi:10.1080/23340460.2018.1532306.

Torbakov, I., 2008. The Georgia crisis and Russia-Turkey relations. *The Jamestown Foundation*. https://jamestown.org/wp-content/uploads/2008/11/GeorgiaCrisisTorbakov.pdf (accessed November 05, 2021).

Troncotă, M., and A. Loy. 2018. EU crises as 'Catalysts of Europeanization'? Insights from Eurobarometer data in Romania on the impact of the refugee crisis and Brexit. *Europolity* 12, no. 1: 171–232. http://europolity.eu/wp-content/uploads/2018/06/VOL-12-NO1_Troncota_Loy_Europolity_12_1_2018.pdf accessed November 05, 2021.

Wintour, P., 2020. EU leaders approve sanctions on Turkish officials over gas drilling. *The Guardian*, December 11. https://www.theguardian.com/world/2020/dec/11/eu-leaders-sanctions-turkey-gas-drilling (accessed November 05, 2021).

Yilmaz, G. 2016. From Europeanization to De-Europeanization: The Europeanization process of Turkey in 1999–2014. *Journal of Contemporary European Studies* 24, no. 1: 86–100. doi:10.1080/14782804.2015.1038226.

Table A1. Regional organizations/formats that include Romania and Turkey.

Organization/format and the year of establishment	Aims
(1) Commission on the Protection of the Black Sea Against Pollution – **1992**	Combating Pollution from land-based sources and maritime transport, achieving sustainable management of marine living resources, pursuing sustainable human development.
(1) Black Sea Economic Cooperation – **1992**	Fostering the economic cooperation among the Member States
(1) South-East Europe Cooperative Initiative – **1996**	Fostering regional peace and stability among the countries of south-eastern Europe through cooperative activities, and helping the countries integrate into the rest of Europe
(1) South-East European Cooperation Process – **1996**	Transforming this region into an area of peace, security, stability and cooperation
(1) Black Sea Trade and Development Bank – **1999**	Supporting economic development and regional cooperation in the Black Sea Region through trade and project finance lending
(1) BLACKSEAFOR – **2001**	Enhancing peace and stability in the Black Sea area
(1) Black Sea Forum for Partnership and Dialogue – **2006**	Meant to create new regional institutions, but rather to turn into a regular consultative process among countries of the extended Black Sea region
(1) Black Sea Synergy – **2008**	Strengthening cooperation in the area, with EU's involvement in a constructive agenda of dialogue and cooperation with the region

Table compiled by the authors on the basis of data provided by the official websites of the mentioned organizations

Table A2. Main developments in Turkey's domestic and foreign policy, including relations with the EU.

1999	- The candidacy status was recognized for Turkey in European Council Summit Meeting in Helsinki;
2002	- Islamist-based Justice and Development Party (AKP) wins landslide election victory;
2003	AKP leader Recep Tayyip Erdogan wins a seat in the Parliament. Within days Abdullah Gul resigns as prime minister and Erdogan takes over;
2005	European Union's start accession negotiations with Turkey;
2006	EU partially freezes Turkey's membership talks because of Ankara's failure to open its ports and airports to Cypriot traffic;
2007	AKP wins parliamentary elections;
2011	- Turkish general election resulting in a third consecutive victory for the incumbent Justice and Development Party (AKP), with its leader Recep Tayyip Erdoğan being re-elected as Prime Minister for a third term; - 'The downturn in EU-Turkey relations and the growing disenchantment by both sides';
2013	Nationwide protests and corruption allegations increase domestic and Western criticism of Erdogan and his government; the Gezi park protests
2014	Prime Minister Erdogan wins the first direct popular election for president;
2015	- Governing AK party regains parliamentary majority in snap elections; - European Union strikes a deal whereby Turkey restricts flow of migrants into Europe, in return for €3bn ($3.17bn) and concessions on stalled EU accession talks;
2016	- AKP government condemns EU and NATO partners for not intervening in the context of the coup attempt outbreak; - Ankara intensifies relations with Russian Federation;
2017	President Erdogan narrowly wins referendum to extend his powers;
2018	President Erdogan wins re-election as Turkey transitions to its new presidential system;
2020	- accession talks had 'effectively come to a standstill', due to Ankara's strained relations with Cyprus and human rights concerns; - Regional tensions rise in the Eastern Mediterranean and Middle East between Turkey and various NATO allies and U.S. partners;
2021	- EU Parliament calls for the suspension of Turkey's EU talks.

Table compiled by the authors.

Table A3. Total number of Bilateral consultations between Romanian and Turkish officials (2011–2020) and their topics.

Year	The frequency of the consultations	Meeting type/topics discussed
2011	6	General (9), business (1), experience exchange (1), **European matters (1)**, Romania-Turkey-Poland trilateral – RO-TR-PL – (1)
2012	13	General (5), energy (1)
2013	10	General (7), **European matters (1)**, RO-TR-PL (1), security (1)
2014	11	General (5), RO-TR-PL (3), **European matters (1)**, economic matters (1), security (1)
2015	5	General (4), **European matters (1)**
2016	7	**European matters (2)**, general (2), RO-TR-PL (3)
2017	7	General (2), RO-TR-PL (2), **NATO and EU matters (1), European matters (1)**, general (1)
2018	5	General (2), RO-TR-PL (2), military (1)
2019	7	General (3), **European matters (2)**, RO-TR-PL (2)
2020	3	Security (1), general (1), RO-TR-PL (1)

Table compiled by the authors on the basis of data provided by foreign ministries of Turkey and Romania.

Index

Page numbers in **bold** refer to tables and those with "n" refer to notes in the text.

accession phase 5
Adalet ve Kalkinma Partisi (AKP) 11
Adar, S. 88
Akgönül, S. 81
Aktas, Alinur 38
Albanian ethno-national identity 150
Albanian National Awakening movement 150
Albayrak Holding organization 55
Alliance of Liberal and Democrats for Europe (ALDE) 67
Amour, P. O. 164
Anadolu Agency (2020) 129, 130
Anadolu Youth Association (AGD) 133
Anavatan Partisi-ANAP governments 29
anti-Western populism concept 48
Aras, B. 84
arbitration and conciliation 167
authoritarianism 18
authoritarian rule 12, 101–5
Aydin-Düzgit, S. 84

Balkans: countries 2; enlargement 3; and Kosovo 152–4; Turkey's impact in 2–3
Bechev, D. 65
BiH 118–21, 130–1
bilateral consultations, Romanian and Turkish officials **181**
bilateral relations 63–4
Blue Homeland doctrine 81
boomerang effect 53
Borrell, Josep 49
Bosnian power fragmentation 125–30
'build-operate-transfer' *(yap-islet-devret)* model 33
Bulgarian Communist Party (BCP) 66
Buzan, B. 163

Campbell, D. 28
capitalist rationality 104
'capitulation' concept 4
Çelik, Ömer 37
Cengiz Construction organization 55

Central Bank of Bosnia And Herzegovina (CBBiH) *122, 123, 127, 128*
Central European Free Trade Area (CEFTA) 123
Central European (CE) states 121
Çiller, Tansu 83
citizenship policy 48
civil society 48
Civil Society Organizations (CSOs) 134
climax of cooperation (2008–2013) 168–70
The Cold War 29
communist regimes 66
consolidated authoritarian power 105
consolidated statehood 5
constructivism 28
Cooperation Verification Mechanism 4
Copenhagen criteria 83
coronavirus diplomacy 35
Council of Europe Parliamentary Assemby (CoE PA) 124
country's political deadlock 30
CoViD-19 diplomacy 35
Covid Performance Index 2021 26
'credible enlargement perspective' 5
cultural attraction 47
cultural diplomacy, Ankara's new foreign policy tool 148–9
culture and education 131–5

Davos Peace Process 82
Davutoglu, Ahmet 3, 12, 14, 27, 49, 80
de-Europeanisation 2–6, 12, 83–8, 165–6, 172–5
delicate balancing act: Bulgarian authorities 69; domestic politics 69–74; 'Erdogan's henchman' 68–9; trade and tourism 68
Democratic Union for Integration (DUI) 20
democratization 15, 104
desecuritization process 84
Diez, T. 164
Dimitrov, P. 64
The Directorate of Religious Affairs 19–20
divergence concept 48

INDEX

domestic governance 50
domestic politics 48

EastMed Gas Forum 91
economic hybridity 104
economic relations 126–30
education policy 48
Erdogan, Tayyip 1, 11, 14, 25–6, 44
ethnic Turks during communism 64
ethno-nationalist religion-oriented foreign
  policy 2, 164
Europeanisation 2–6, 46, 83–8
European Policy Centre 101
European Union (EU) accession process 118
EU-Turkey Customs Union 12
Exclusive Economic Zone (EEZ) 87
'exemplary country' concept 26
external identity 28
'external players' category 12
external powers 18

face-to-face interviews 45
Fazal, T. 35
Fethullahist Terrorist Organization (FETÖ) 17–
  18, 131
fight information regions (FIR) 92
Foreign Direct Investments (FDIs) 120
foreign meddling 18
foreign policy decision-makers 28, 166
'foreign protection' concept 4
Freedom House Index 33
Free Trade Agreement (2009) 107

Ganev, V. 64
gender equality policy 48
Gezi Park protests (2013) 86
Governor of Lebanon 150
Grabher, K. 104
'great excursion' 67
Greek-Turkish relations 82–3, 89–92
Gülen Movement 48–9, 124

health diplomacy 35
Hellman, J. S. 103
human connectivity 13
'hybrid regime' 102
hydrocarbons in Cyprus basin 87

identity 27; through foreign policy 27–8
ideology 47
images vs. realities 32–5
institutional weaknesses and instabilities 32
internal identity 28
Internal Macedonian Revolutionary Organization
  (IMRO) 70
international environment 28
international institutions 47
international relations (IR) theory 27–8
International Republican Institute (IRI) 133

International University of Sarajevo (IUS) 133
Izetbegovi, Alija 126

Jeanci factory 100, **108–10**
Justice and Development Party 26, 44, 161

Kaliber, A. 164
Keskin slawyers 125
Kirişçi, K. 86
Koca, Fahrettin 33
Köksal, Y. 64
Kosovo Electricity Distribution Supply
  (KEDS) 148
Kosovo Liberation Army (KLA) 144
The Kosovo problem 143–5
The Kurdistan Workers' Party 46

Ledeneva, A. 104
Liberal International 67
Libyan Government of National Accord
  (GNA) 90–1
limited statehood 5
literature as de-Europeanization 45
'logic of interdependence' 80
'logic of strategic autonomy' 80

Macshane, Denis 121
The Madrid Declaration (1997) 83
marketization 103
mask diplomacy 35
material soft power 45, 54–6
The Mavi Vatan Doctrine 88–9
media freedom 48
medical aid to Balkans, Turkey 37
Memorandum of Understanding (MoU) 91
Merkel, Angela 84
Mexico, Indonesia, Republic of Korea, Turkey and
  Australia (MIKTA) 29
migration crisis 3
migration policy 48
Miloševic, Slobodan 18
Ministry of Foreign Affairs 123–4, 150
Movement for Rights and Freedoms (MRF)
  20, 63, 64
multilateral cooperation 15

National Anti-Corruption Directorate 4
national balances re-arrangement 146–7
National Front for Salvation of Bulgaria
  (NFSB) 70
nationalism 14
Nationalist Action Party (MHP) 17
Nation Alliance (Millet Ittifaki) 33
National Statistics Agency of the Republic of
  Serbia (2018) **107**
nation-state-formation 103
NATO membership 12
neo-imperialist and neo-colonial projects 1
neo-Ottomanism framework 15, 18, 81

Neuberger, M. 64
New Democracy (ND) party 87
newspaper sources 27
non-aggression 167
non-governmental organizations (NGOs) 82, 133
normative soft power 45; religion synthesized
    with nationalism 53–4
North Atlantic Treaty Organisation (NATO) 118
Nye, J. S. 149

Offe, C. 111
Öktem, K. 81
Olsen, J. P. 85
Önis-Kutlay, 2017 27
Önis, Z. 49, 82
open borders 15
Operation Olive Branch 47
opposition-led municipalities 26
Ottoman multi-sided legacy 1
Özal, Turgut 29
Öztürk, A. E. 81

pandemic diplomacy 35
Pan-Hellenic Socialist Movement (PASOK) 83
parallel state 143
Parla, A. 64
Parlar Dal 2016 27
Party of Democratic Action (SDA) 124
Peace Implementation Council (PIC) 14
Peevski, Delyan 68
personalization and informalisation of power 105
personalized soft power 45, 56–7
personal relations 124–5
Petkova, L. 64
Polat, R. K. 84
politicians and commentators 17
politicization of the EU enlargement 6
post-accession phase 5
post-socialist societies 100
'powerful state' concept 26
The Presidency of Religious Affairs (Diyanet) 31
privatization, Western Balkan 103
pro-AKP groups 31
process-tracing: causal mechanisms 106;
    collecting a plethora of information 106
'putinization' 17

Radio Free Europe (2020) 148, 151
're-feudalisation of power' 105
regional identity 163–5
regional organizations/formats, romania and
    turkey **180**
regional powers 27; and identity
    construction 35–9
regional role 163
Regional Security Complex Theory (RSCT) 162,
    163, 166
religious relations 135–7
re-nationalisation 168
Republican People Party (CHP) 120

revival process 66–7
the rule of law 48
Rumi, Mevlana Jalaluddin 36–7

Sarkozy, Nicolas 84
Schmidt, S. 164
secondary academic sources 27
security policy views 168
Serb factor 125
Serbia-Bosnia-Turkey trilateral summits 19
Serbian Business Registers Agency 107
Serbian parliament condemnation 19
Serbian–Turkish economic relations (2009 to
    2018) 107–8
Serb party, Alliance of Independent Social
    Democrats (SNSD) 124
simultaneous democratization 103
social hybridity 105, 111
social structure 28
Solana, Javier 47
Soner Cagaptay's book (2019) 15
Southeast European Cooperation Process
    (SEECP) 14, 15
Southern Gas Corridor developments 168
Spirova, M. 64
stabilitocracy concept 102
stability dilemma 102
state capture 15
state-driven transformation 14
state formation 14
'state identity' concept 28
state-initiated efforts 35
Strategic Depth 27, 80
Strategic Partnership (2011) 166–7

The Turkish Cooperation and Coordination
    Agency (TIKA) 30
Tonra, B. 47
Toygür, I. 88
'transformative power' 16
Treaty of Friendship 167
Tudjman, Franjo 18
Turkey graduates 133–5, 134
Turkey-Romania relations (2008–2020) 167
Turkey's embeddedness, the Balkans 15
Turkey's political influence, non-Western
    actors 121
Turkey's relations with Kosovo (since 2008) 145–6
Turkey's soft power actions 170–2
Turkish activism, Balkans 20
Turkish-Bulgarian relations 119–20; domestic
    politics 64; EU-Turkish 64; Ottoman
    Empire 63; refugees, human rights and
    energy 64; in scholarly literature 64–5; see also
    delicate balancing act
Turkish Cooperation and Coordination Agency
    (TIKA) 51–2, 126, 149
Turkish Cypriot community 86
Turkish decision-makers 27
Turkish Foreign Ministry 145

INDEX

Turkish foreign policy (TFP) 28–32, 45;
   europeanization/de-europeanization 47–50;
   security-oriented perspective 46–7
Turkish governmental institutions 27
Turkish Medical Association (TMA) 26, 34
'Turkish model' 11
Turkish National Liberation Movement of
   Bulgaria 67
Turkish Premier Ecevit 144–5
Turkish Radio Television (TRT) 130
Turkish sovereignty 86–8
Tusk, Donald 92
Tziarras, Z. 90

unbalanced bilateral economic cooperation 148
Union of International Democrats (UID) 133
United Nations Interim Administration Mission
   in Kosovo (UNMIK) 145
United Nations Security Council (UNSC) 46–7
University of Sofia's Political Science
   Department 50

UN Security Council 67
U.S. Bosna Sema Schools 124

violent extremism and foreign influence *134*
Vucic, Aleksandar 12, 98

Wæver, O. 163
Website of Turkish Health Ministry 26
Western and Eastern powers 50
Western Balkan (WB) 15, 121
Writing Security: United States Foreign Policy and
   the Politics of Identity 28

Yugoslav Constitution (1974) 143
Yugoslav succession 26
Yunus Emre Institute (YEI) 106, 129, 131

Zankina, E. 63, 65
'zero problems with neighbours' policy 30, 44
Zetra Olympic Centre 21
Zhivkov, Todor 66

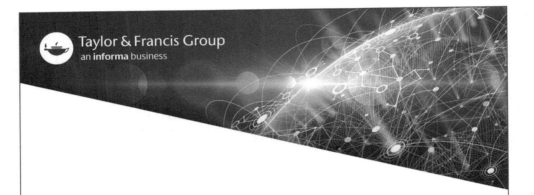

Taylor & Francis eBooks

www.taylorfrancis.com

A single destination for eBooks from Taylor & Francis with increased functionality and an improved user experience to meet the needs of our customers.

90,000+ eBooks of award-winning academic content in Humanities, Social Science, Science, Technology, Engineering, and Medical written by a global network of editors and authors.

TAYLOR & FRANCIS EBOOKS OFFERS:

- A streamlined experience for our library customers
- A single point of discovery for all of our eBook content
- Improved search and discovery of content at both book and chapter level

REQUEST A FREE TRIAL
support@taylorfrancis.com